Springer Proceedings in Business and Economics

More information about this series at http://www.springer.com/series/11960

Gandolfo Dominici • Manlio Del Giudice •
Rosa Lombardi
Editors

Governing Business Systems

Theories and Challenges for Systems Thinking in Practice

Editors
Gandolfo Dominici
Professor of Management
University of Palermo and Business Systems Laboratory
Palermo and Avellino, Italy

Manlio Del Giudice
Professor of Management
University of Rome "Link Campus"
Naples, Italy

Rosa Lombardi
Law and Economics of Productive Activities
Sapienza University of Rome
Rome, Italy

ISSN 2198-7246 ISSN 2198-7254 (electronic)
Springer Proceedings in Business and Economics
ISBN 978-3-319-88159-1 ISBN 978-3-319-66036-3 (eBook)
DOI 10.1007/978-3-319-66036-3

Printed on acid-free paper

This Springer imprint is published by Springer Nature
The registered company is Springer International Publishing AG
The registered company address is: Gewerbestrasse 11, 6330 Cham, Switzerland

Preface

Introducing the Business Systems Laboratory Fourth International Symposium

The Business Systems Laboratory Symposia is a set of conferences aiming to address the global economic and social challenges of our time from a systemic perspective and to shed light on several interactions between natural social and economic systems. This multidisciplinary perspective includes management, psychology, economics, engineering, and sociology.

Triggered by economic evolution dynamics, management approaches have been reconsidered including a systemic perspective for the study of business systems. The new systemic approaches for the study of business systems are then characterized by the inclusion of the several interactions between natural social and economic actors in a multidisciplinary perspective that includes management, economics, engineering, and sociology.

The criticalities and opportunities of these interactions are faced according to cutting-edge research and practice in social science, aimed at providing a set of principles and facilities that can particularly have catalytic effects on today's most pressing social and economic issues, thus enhancing influence in global business.

These proceedings are based on research papers gathered from the 4th Business Systems Laboratory International Symposium 2016—"Governing Business Systems. Theories and Challenges for Systems Thinking in Practice"—held in Vilnius (Lithuania) on August 24–26, 2016. The 4th BSLab Symposium focused on the epistemological, theoretical, methodological, technical, and practical advancements in the theory and practice of governing business systems, which can be useful to address present and future challenges in global business scenarios.

Participants from more than 25 countries attended this conference, and 56 presented their research in seven tracks covering a wide range of topics in the business systems domain—Social and Organisational Systemic Theories (chair: Raul Espejo); Systems Thinking Applications for Markets and Firms (chairs: Maurice Yolles and Mike C. Jackson); System Dynamics (chair: Stefano Armenia); ICT and Knowledge Management (chairs: Francesco Caputo and Leonard Walletzký); Financial Systems (chair: Maurice Yolles); Sustainability, Business Ethics, and CSR (chair: Mauro Sciarelli); and the Interactions Revolution (chair: Gandolfo Dominici)—and a poster session.

The Articles in This Volume

This volume aims to contribute to the business management and innovation literature by providing transverse insights into the antecedents of the adoption of systems thinking in the business systems domain. The contributions explore the theory and practice of business systems in any kind of organization, addressing the benefits and criticalities of business management in today's global economic and social scenarios. Governing business systems according to systems thinking encompasses the introduction of new administrative, organizational, and managerial activities aimed at organizational innovation and control.

It was intended that the book would be kept wide in its scope, by including the application of systemic theories and models to almost every aspect of the business systems domain, and deep in its contributions, by focusing on epistemological, theoretical, methodological, technical, and practical topics that can represent advancements in the theory and practice of governing business systems.

The aim of the book is to catch the attention of scholars and management thinkers interested in exploring the antecedents of a firm's adoption of systemic models and practices.

Ten articles, in this volume, have been provided with a rich design–domain diversity in their enquiries on the theme. From viewpoints to cross-country analyses to empirical research, the articles follow various methodologies to reach their respective conclusions. The coverage of different domain areas such as financial management, strategic networks, smart grids, IoT, and conflict management across contexts such as public government, the culture industry, and automotive manufacturing may generate wider interest in the contents among those who are keen to discover system dynamics and management.

Eleonora Kontuš—in the first article titled "Financing Management of Companies"—explores the short- and long-term sources of financing available to companies on the basis of lowest cost criteria and taking into account the importance of scientifically based financial management.

The research idea considers a company taking into account the cost of all available sources along with their impact on its profitability and solvency and then deciding on the optimal amounts of short- and long-term sources of financing and their optimal composition from the cost-effectiveness point of view. The findings show that in determining which sources of financing to employ, it is important to take into consideration the cost of all sources available to companies and choose those most appropriate in terms of effective after-tax interest rates, because this is what represents the real cost of financing. Through systematic management literature and rigorous empirical analysis, this work provides equations for calculating an effective interest rate for different short- and long-term financing sources available to companies.

In the second article—"A New Approach to the Management of Cash in a Company"—Eleonora Kontuš tries to analyze the cash balances of companies by exploring the costs and benefits of cash management in order to determine the variables that impact net savings as a result of establishing a lockbox system and delaying cash payments, and to model the relationships between these variables. The purpose of the empirical part of the study is to demonstrate a correlation between the cash level and liquidity and to explore the dependence between companies' level of liquidity and profitability. The results of the work include mathematical models for calculating net savings from establishing or changing a lockbox system, as well as delaying cash payments. These results lead to the conclusion that the management of cash becomes easier, as calculations regarding net savings from establishing or changing a lockbox system and delaying cash payments are simplified by using the mathematical models provided. Concluding with these models, a company can consider net profitability in undertaking these activities in order to improve its cash position for investments and to improve profitability.

The third article, by Gabriella Levanti—titled "Governing Complex Strategic Networks: Emergence Versus Enabling Effects"—aims to shed light on the ways in which the processes of network coordination and governance take place. Particularly, according to the author, the sources of today's competitive advantage increasingly lie in webs of relationships between a variety of firms and organizations, which over time lead to the emergence of strategic networks. The performances of both the network actors and the whole network are strictly linked with the coordination and governance of network actors and their activities. In this regard, strategic networks should be considered as complex adaptive systems. Thus, this viewpoint article provides, on one hand, insights into the emergent nature of network interactions stemming from the self-organizing behaviors that spontaneously arise inside the strategic network. On the other hand, the author is able to show that the leadership action of network-central firms sparks enabling effects that join the self-organizing network behaviors. As a result, the expansion of two-tier network interaction potential permits both network actors in the strategic network to reach a level of performance that would not otherwise be accomplished.

The fourth article—"Challenges of the Priority Sectors of Entrepreneurship in Georgia" by Leila Kadagishvili—provides deeper insights into a major topic of entrepreneurship by evoking a viewpoint on program documents adopted in the economic and social fields in Georgia in recent years. Special attention is paid to the further development of a real sector of entrepreneurship where manufacturing industry, agriculture, and tourism are the priorities. The author emphasizes how development of these fields is an important precondition for economic growth in general and growth in gross domestic product and national income in particular. These sectors ensure the creation of new jobs, guarantee employment, and increase the middle class in the country. Unemployment and poverty remain serious problems in Georgia. The findings and opinions are certainly insightful to explore the current situation in the above priority fields of entrepreneurship with academic literature, reports, and statistical data provided by governmental and nongovernmental organizations, as well as by national and international organizations. Furthermore, measures for improving the situation are suggested, the strengths and weaknesses of the reforms of recent years are revealed, and the importance of entrepreneurship in the development of the economy is demonstrated to gain new insights and/or test established theories.

"Towards Discovering the Limits of Smart Grid Communication Infrastructure"—authored by Miroslav Kadlec, Jan Rosecky, Filip Prochazka, Barbora Buhnova, and Tomas Pitner—represents the fifth contribution in the book, focused on the negative impact of power generators on environment issues. The research design investigates the ways to incorporate power sources in spite of the negative impact of production variability by highlighting the smart city approach as a way to build an eco-sustainable community through energy optimization within the particular area, while preserving comfort for the inhabitants. In this sense, the article provides the concept of effective electricity management and a smart grid distribution network enhanced by information and communication technologies (ICT). In particular, the data collected show that energy distribution companies are motivated to deploy smart grids in order to minimize energy losses in the power grid. Indeed, smart grid research has become a subject of investment from both electricity distributors and governments. Since no extensive review on simulations of communications in smart grids has been conducted, this paper aims to describe particular approaches and simulation tools for general modeling and simulation of smart grids, such as GridMind.

Preparatory to the previous work, the sixth article, by Tindara Abbate—titled "Exploiting Internet-of-Things: Platforms and Business Models"—proposes an investigation of IoT business model applications, which are expected to play a key role in the near future due to the possibility to spur processes of economic growth by fostering differentiated business applications. To exploit several possibilities, firms need to define and adopt appropriate business models. By analyzing the case of FIWARE, the findings indicate that IoT business model solutions (such as cloud-based platforms) could be adopted by different actors. More importantly, such platforms are likely to represent a general-purpose technology, which allows innovative forms of division of labor among technology suppliers and technology users, with positive revenues for the involved actors, providing a rich context for future research development for managers and scholars across the world.

The seventh contribution—"The Leadership Competencies and Intuitive Decision-Making of Top and Middle Level Managers in the Automotive Industry" by Ivan Erenda, Aleksej Metelko, Vasja Roblek, and Maja Meško—sheds light on intuitive decision making by top and middle managers in the Slovenian automotive industry, in order to meet a threefold research objective: (1) to identify the influence of their behavioral competencies and emotional intelligence on intuitive decision making; (2) to identify their level of intuitiveness; and (3) on the basis of theoretical and empirical research, to establish competencies and factors of the model of leadership competencies based on intuitive decision making.

Supported by a strong quantitative research method (descriptive statistics, factor analysis, regression analysis, and variance analysis), a statistical data analysis was carried out using SPSS software, while the model was created using the program Pajek 3.

The results are robust and reliable in showing that respondents are often directed by intuition when making important decisions (79.3% make decisions based on intuition). Afterward, the research findings indicate that behavioral competencies do not have any significant impact on intuitive decision making, and the same is true for emotional intelligence. Furthermore, a more significant research finding shows a relatively high level of intuitiveness, which is boosted by years of leadership experience and a higher level of education.

In the eighth manuscript—"Government Performance, Ethics and Corruption in the Global Competitiveness Index"—Davide Di Fatta, Roberto Musotto, and Walter Vesperi try to show how public sector performance is affected by ethics and corruption issues, which apparently represent the crucial point for public management, by noting that managerial conduct is not always supported by ethical principles, and this results in disruptive phenomena such as corruption. In order to explain such a relationship, the author runs a cross-country analysis, where indices of public sector performance are juxtaposed with corruption levels. By using the Global Competitiveness Index (GCI) from the World Economic Forum, with a strong empirical assessment through regression analysis, on a dataset made up of 140 countries in 2014–2015, the results provide a convincing correlation between government efficiency and ethics. These findings could be an inspiration for government workers and managers to establish an ethical culture that can increase public performance.

Alternatively, providing an anchor to the issue of public management, the ninth article—titled "Innovation in Cultural Districts: The Cases of Naples and Washington" by Valentina Della Corte, Giovanna Del Gaudio, Chiara D'Andrea, and Fabiana Sepe—aims to draw attention to the role played by cultural heritage and arts in revitalizing and regenerating central and peripheral areas of contemporary cities. Chiefly, in the era of global markets and knowledge sharing, the production of culture represents an increasingly complex activity showing an unspoken need for managerialism. On one hand, culture should adapt to goods and services that are different in content and technology; on the other hand, it should try to satisfy a very heterogeneous demand. With these premises in mind, it seems to be clear that culture represents an essential resource for several geographical areas to relaunch themselves and to be competitive in the global arena.

The scholars' purpose is to analyze evolved cultural districts in order to understand what role innovation plays at both the systemic and firm levels, and furthermore to capture the way innovation can support cultural districts in their promotional activities, both in the organic phase and during service provision.

In order to proceed with this analysis, the research provides discussion and implications of innovation in cultural districts from a managerial systems perspective by presenting empirical developments taking into account two cultural districts—D.A.T.A.B.E.N.C. in Naples (Italy) and the District of Washington—which successfully implemented innovation in their activities.

The last paper—titled "Only Pricing Policy Matters: Discount Is the Only Determinant of Conversion Rate on Apparel e-Commerce Websites" by Davide Di Fatta and Ivan Nania—has important implications for the business systems audience to determine which factors affect the e-commerce conversion rate, which is the relationship between website visitors and purchasers.

Focusing on apparel e-commerce websites, this paper uses a fixed-effect estimator on a perfectly balanced panel, finding that pricing policy is the only relevant factor and, specifically, that a discount has a positive effect on the conversion rate.

This finding contributes to advancing the theory of conversion rate management, shedding light on its determinants and providing better understanding of online consumer behavior. This research is also extremely relevant for practitioners, providing managerial implications for retailers addressing their e-commerce strategy.

Retailing is shifting more and more toward retail firms focusing on digital distribution and sales channels, analyzing the online market and its customer needs.

This empirical paper aims to focus on apparel e-commerce websites to determine which factor most affects the conversion rate once users have arrived at the website. Moreover, the authors discuss how users arrive at the website, focusing on purchasing behavior on the site. In this regard, the paper contributes, on one hand, to advancing the theory of conversion rate management and, on the other hand, to the practical implications, providing concrete guidelines for retailers wishing to decrease their cost per conversion by understanding online consumer behavior while browsing an e-commerce website.

We wish to thank all of the authors, who have greatly contributed to the production of this book. Without their efforts and intriguing research, it would never have seen the light of day!

Palermo and Avellino, Italy — Gandolfo Dominici
Naples, Italy — Manlio Del Giudice
Rome, Italy — Rosa Lombardi

Contents

Chapter 1
Financing Management of Companies

Eleonora Kontuš

Abstract The aim of this paper is, firstly, to explore the short- and long-term sources of financing available to companies, and secondly, to determine the sources of short- and long-term financing to be employed on the basis of lowest cost criteria and taking into account the importance of scientifically-based financial management. A company should consider the cost of all available sources along with their impact on its profitability and solvency, and decide on the optimal amount of short- and long-term sources of financing and their optimal composition from the cost-effective point of view. In determining which sources of short- and long-term financing to employ, it is important to take into consideration the cost of all sources available to companies and choose those most appropriate in terms of effective after-tax interest rate because this is what represents the real cost of financing. The result of the work will provide equations for calculating an effective interest rate for different short- and long-term financing sources available to companies.

Keywords Short-term financing sources • Long-term financing sources • Cost of financing • Effective interest rate after tax

1.1 Introduction

Financing management of companies requires decision making based on both an appropriate balance between short- and long-term financing sources and their optimal composition. Given that costs are the most important factor in making such decisions, financial managers have to find ways to minimize them. The Effective Interest Rate After Tax (EIRAT) is a true measure of the effective cost of sources of financing and it is therefore important to calculate it for each type of short- and long-term sources before deciding which one to use.

The finance manager should opt for the least expensive alternative and for the financing source with the lowest EIRAT. We hypothesize that by applying scientifically-based short- and long-term financing management and with an optimal

E. Kontuš (✉)
University of Rijeka, Rijeka, Croatia
e-mail: eleonora.kontus@ri.t-com.hr

G. Dominici et al. (eds.), *Governing Business Systems*, Springer Proceedings in Business and Economics, DOI 10.1007/978-3-319-66036-3_1

choice of the company's financing sources from the cost-effective point of view, companies can earn a satisfactory profit and return on investments.

The purpose of this study is to determine how to make optimum use of available short- and long-term financing sources from a cost perspective. Short- and long-term debts have been studied in many papers, but there are still gaps relating to their real cost expressed as EIRAT in the existing literature. In striving to fill the gaps relating to EIRAT as the real cost of financing, the study makes its own contribution to research and, thereby, to managers.

The study will investigate various sources of short- and long-term financing available to companies and introduce new equations for calculating the EIRAT for various short- and long-term sources of financing available to companies. The purpose of this study is not only to define the variables important for determining the EIRAT and establish the functional relations between them in order to achieve this, but also to give general recommendations for financial managers.

1.2 Literature Review

1.2.1 Essentials of Financial Management of Companies

Financial management of companies involves managing total assets, total liabilities and equity. Effective financial management requires decisions on the amount and composition of assets and on how these assets are to be funded. Financing choices begin with the amount of money needed and a decision about the proportions of debt and equity.

Managers look at specific characteristics of financing, such as maturity and priority of claims, and the particular investors to be approached. The company seeks the lowest possible cost of funds, which requires meeting investor needs, consideration of taxes and dealing with agency costs as effectively as possible (Seitz and Ellison 1995).

Once the management of a company has determined the appropriate amount of current and fixed assets coupled with the amount of permanent and temporary current assets, it must decide how to finance these assets. The demarcation line separating permanent from temporary assets becomes the relevant determinant of whether the assets should be financed from short- or long-term sources.

Walker and Petty (1986) suggested that all permanent assets should be financed either with long-term debt or equity financing, while the remaining current assets should be financed by short-term sources. Temporary current assets should be financed with short-term liabilities, and fixed and permanent current assets should be funded by long-term financing sources. However, such a policy assumes that management is able to predict asset requirements with a great deal of certainty.

The foregoing principle often represents a serious problem for the financial manager of a company due to limited funds, which is why many companies place themselves in a financial difficulty by violating this principle. If the financial manager attempts to finance permanent growth with short-term financing, the company may face serious cash flow problems.

1.2.2 Short-Term Financing Management

Short-term assets and liabilities are especially important for small and medium-sized companies because such companies often carry a higher percentage of both than do larger companies. Pinches (1994) found that, in comparison with larger companies, the survival of small and medium-sized companies has been much more dependent on effective short-term financial management since they do not have the same degree of accessibility to as many sources of capital and thus have to rely more heavily on short-term sources. Consequently, short-term liabilities play a more substantive role in the financing of small and medium-sized companies.

Short-term credit is defined as any liability originally scheduled for payment within 1 year. The major sources of short-term credit available to companies are accruals, accounts payable and bank loans. Accruals, which are continually recurring short-term liabilities, represent free, spontaneous credit. Accounts payable, or trade credit, is the largest category of short-term debt (Brigham and Gapenski 1994). The percentage cost of trade credit is given by following equation (Kolb 1987):

$$Cost\ of\ Trade\ Credit = \frac{Discount\ (percent)}{100 - Discount\ (percent)} \times \frac{365}{Net\ Period - Discount\ Period}$$

Bank financing may take any of the following forms: lines of credit, unsecured loans and secured loans. Under a line of credit, the bank agrees to lend money to the borrower on a recurring basis up to a specified amount. The advantages of a line of credit for a company are the easy and immediate access to funds during tight money market conditions and the ability to borrow only as much as needed, and repay immediately when cash is available. The bank charges a commitment fee on the amount of the unused credit line and an interest on the amount of the used credit line.

Unsecured loans are recommended for use by companies with excellent credit ratings for financing projects that have quick cash flows. The disadvantages of this kind of loan are that, given that it is made for a short term, it carries a higher interest rate than a secured loan and payment in a lump sum is required. A secured loan is a loan on a secured basis, with some form of collateral behind the loan. Collateral may take many forms including inventory, accounts receivable or securities.

Commercial paper is unsecured short-term debt issued by a large, financially strong corporation. Its interest rate is lower than that of a bank loan and it can be issued only by companies possessing the highest credit ratings. The yields on commercial paper are generally lower than the effective cost of bank lines of credit, which explains why banks have lost a portion of their short-term lending to those companies that can access the commercial paper market (Maness and Zietlow 2005).

Factoring receivables involves the purchase of accounts receivable by the lender. The receivables may be sold «without recourse». In such a case the factor makes the credit-granting decision and incurs any losses from nonpayment by the company's customers. Under recourse factoring, the granting company typically makes the credit-granting decision and, therefore, bears the consequences of any nonpayment by the customers. Factoring operates in two basic ways. The first is maturity factoring, in which the factor purchases all receivables and once a month pays the seller for the receivables. The second factoring method is advance factoring, in which the factor provides a loan against the receivables (Pinches 1994). According to Shim and Siegel (2007), the effective interest rate associated with factoring accounts receivable is:

$$\textit{Effective interest rate} = \textit{interest rate}/\textit{proceeds}, \%$$

Inventory financing is an extremely important component of the total financial plan of most corporations. This is because inventory has generally represented a significant portion of the corporation's total working capital, and inventory represents a resource commitment which has yet to release cash and will not do so until the item is sold and cash collected (Maness and Zietlow 2005). A substantial amount of credit is secured by business inventories.

Short-term financing arrangements have several features that cause the stated interest rate on the financing to be different from the effective interest rate (Maness and Zietlow 2005). Bank loans are an important source of short-term credit. Interest on bank loans may be quoted as simple interest, discount interest and add-on interest (Brigham and Gapenski 1994). In the simple interest loan, the borrower receives the face value of the loan and repays the principal and interest at maturity. According to Brigham and Gapenski (1994), the effective rate for a simple interest loan could be calculated as follows:

$$\textit{Effective rate}_{\textit{Simple}} = \frac{\textit{Interest}}{\textit{Amount received}}$$

In a discount interest loan, the bank deducts the interest in advance and the borrower receives less than the face value of the loan. The effective rate for a discount interest loan could be calculated as follows (Brigham and Gapenski 1994):

$$\textit{Effective rate}_{\textit{Discount}} = \frac{\textit{Naminal rate}\ (\%)}{1.0 - \textit{Naminal rate}\ (\textit{fraction})}$$

According to Shim and Siegel (2007), the effective interest rate for short-term bank loans with discount interest rates can be computed as follows:

$$\textit{Effective interest rate}_{\textit{Discount}} = \frac{\textit{interest rate} \times \textit{principal}}{(\textit{proceeds}, \% \times \textit{principal}) - \textit{interest}}$$

Banks sometimes need to maintain compensating balances, which are deposit requirements set at between 10% and 20% of the loan amount. When a loan has a compensating balance requirement associated with it, the proceeds received by the borrower are decreased by the amount of the compensating balance. Compensating balances and discount interest raise the effective interest rate on bank loans. The effective interest rate for a simple interest loan with compensating balances could be expressed as follows (Kolb 1987):

$$\mathit{Effective\ interest\ rate}_{\mathit{compensating\ balances}} = \frac{\mathit{interest\ rate}}{1 - \mathit{compensating\ balances}\ (\%)}$$

According to Brigham and Gapenski (1994), the effective rate for a simple interest loan with compensating balances could be calculated as follows:

$$\mathit{Effective\ rate}_{\mathit{simple/CB}} = \frac{\mathit{Nominal\ rate}\ (\%)}{1.0 - \mathit{CB}\ (\mathit{fraction})}$$

The effective rate for a discount interest loan with compensating balances could be calculated as follows (Brigham and Gapenski 1994):

$$\mathit{Effective\ rate}_{\mathit{Discount/CB}} = \frac{\mathit{Nominal\ rate}\ (\%)}{1.0 - \mathit{Nominal\ rate}\ (\mathit{fraction}) - \mathit{CB}\ (\mathit{fraction})}$$

A line of credit is a short-term source of funds in that it represents a sum of funds that a bank stands ready to lend a corporate client upon demand at any time during a given period. According to Maness and Zietlow (2005), the annual effective rate of interest for a credit line can be computed as follows:

$$I = \frac{\Sigma i_t \times TLOAN_t + f \times CRLN}{\Sigma TCCN_t/12}$$

where

i_t = *the monthly interest rate for each month t*
$TLOAN_t$ = *the total loan borrowed during month t*
f = *the annual commitment fee rate based on the size of the credit line*
$CRLN$ = *the dollar amount of the credit line*
$TCCN_t$ = *total cumulative cash needs*

Childs et al. (2005) find that financial flexibility stimulates taking on short-term debt resulting in a reduction in the agency costs. Dangl and Zechner (2016) as well as Miltersen and Torous (2007) investigate the joint choice of debt maturity and leverage in a dynamic capital structure model and find that short-term debt motivates the reduction of debt levels in response to poor firm performance.

Jiraporn and Tong (2007) focus on the role of short-term debts in reducing agency costs of equity. The agency theory seems to suggest that companies whose agency costs are more severe should find short-term debt more beneficial to the extent that these costs are mitigated by short-term debt. Employing the amount of available free cash flow to represent the extent of likely agency conflicts, they document that the beneficial effect of short-term debt is concentrated only in companies where agency problems are severe.

They investigate changes in company's value with respect to changes in the debt maturity structure and find consistent evidence that short-term debt enhances a company's value. Jiraporn and Tong (2007) find robust empirical evidence in favour of the beneficial effect of short-term debt usage when they investigate both the levels and the changes of debt maturity and a company's value.

Custodio et al. (2013) discover that companies with higher information asymmetry as well as new companies issue more short-term debts. Harford and Maxwell (2014) find that higher cash holdings mitigate the refinancing risks of companies and that short-term debt can be substituted for cash. Park (2015) finds a company with high volatility of earnings optimally issues debts of shorter maturity and highlights the flexibility benefits of short-term financing during volatile earning periods.

1.2.3 Long-Term Financing and Agency Problems

Once the need for long-term financing has been acknowledged, a number of factors must be recognized in ascertaining which source of financing to employ. The three basic instruments of long-term financing in all market economies are common stock, preferred stock and long-term debt.

According to the pecking-order theory, companies prefer to finance investments with retained earnings. If external finance is required, companies use long-term debt, then hybrid securities and equity as a last resort (Brealey et al. 2011). In the static trade-off theory, companies balance the tax benefits of debt against the deadweight costs of financial distress and bankruptcy. Companies favour debt over equity because they are allowed to deduct interest paid on debt from their tax liability (Bessler et al. 2011).

An agency problem arises whenever one person hires another person to do something. Shareholders face an agency problem in that their agents, the managers, may not act diligently on their behalf and may thus consume excessive wages or excessive perquisites. Managers can be too conservative or too aggressive in their investment strategy. The creditors of a company entrust their money to the managers, who can increase the wealth of the shareholders at the expense of the creditors by moving to a more risky asset structure. Creditors will demand an interest rate that provides an equilibrium return after agency costs (Seitz and Ellison 1995).

Jensen and Meckling (1976) find that managers of levered companies have an incentive to engage in asset substitution and underinvestment. They suggest that decreases in one type of agency conflicts, underinvestment or asset substitution are offset by increases in bankruptcy costs when companies use short-term debt. Using financial leverage can help overcome the agency problems and agency costs inherent in the relationship between managers and outside investors as well as creditors. Jensen and Meckling (1976) point out that using debt helps overcome the agency costs of outside equity. Myers (1977) suggests that short-term debt helps mitigate the agency costs of debt by resolving the underinvestment and asset substitution problems.

Shareholders may use the increase in debt as a means of controlling managers. Managers have an incentive to generate the financial resources needed to service the debt. Financial leverage is used to restructure ownership claims and change the managers' aim to fully maximise the value of the company's assets at their disposal (Jensen 1986).

Shleifer and Vishny (1997) investigate the role of debt in reducing the conflict of interests between managers and shareholders. Companies should trade off between the agency costs of debt and the agency costs of equity in choosing their debt-equity level. Capital structure can balance the conflicts between shareholders and management, as well as that between management and creditors. Increased leverage also has costs and as leverage increases, the agency costs of debt rise, including bankruptcy costs (Jensen 1986).

Ericsson (2000) develops a capital structure model in which companies consider the bankruptcy costs, tax benefits and the agency costs associated with debt financing in order to determine the maturity date and the leverage ratio. He predicts that the leverage ratio will be reduced and the debt maturity shorter when managers aim to minimize the agency costs of asset substitution. The agency costs of outside equity derive mainly from informational asymmetries and excessive perquisite consumption, while the agency costs of debt, though deriving from the same phenomena, are mainly related to risk incentives, investment incentives and bankruptcy costs (Moschandreas 2000).

The problem with a short-term debt is that the company has to raise funds to pay back the debt more often than when it finances itself with a long-term debt. As long as the value of the company exceeds the face value of the debt, the company can refinance the debt. In the presence of agency costs and information asymmetries, it is perfectly possible for the true value of the company to exceed the value of the debt and yet for the company to be unable to find funds to refinance the debt (Auernheimer 2003).

Harvey et al. (2004) provide new evidence that debt creates shareholder value for companies that face potentially high managerial agency costs. Their results indicate that shareholders benefit from intensively monitored debt in circumstances in which information asymmetry is severe enough for the shareholders to be able to reasonably infer what managers are doing with a company's funds.

Using debt means a company can sell less external equity and still finance its operations. The second and a more important benefit of using debt is that it reduces managerial perquisite consumption or lack of effort (Graham et al. 2010).

According to Bessler et al. (2011), agency costs represent the type of costs that should be weighed against the tax advantage of debt. Managers of debt-financed companies tend to engage in risk-shifting strategies when they have free cash flow available. They favour risky projects that benefit shareholders in the case of success but burden losses on bondholders in the case of failure. Bondholders demand a risk premium as well as a higher interest payment, and these increased costs reduce the attractiveness for companies to issue debt.

The modern trade-off model of corporate leverage predicts that a company's optimal debt level is set by trading off the tax benefits of increasing leverage against the increasingly severe bankruptcy costs and agency costs of heavy debt usage (Graham et al. 2010). The optimal debt ratio occurs when the debt's marginal benefits equal its costs. In order to arrive at optimal financing decisions, managers need to evaluate the agency costs of debt risk shifting and underinvestment against the agency costs of equity – free cash flow problem (Bessler et al. 2011).

According to the trade-off theory, bankruptcy costs, taxes and agency costs push more profitable companies towards higher leverage because:

- Expected bankruptcy costs decline when profitability increases,
- The deductibility of interest payments for tax purposes induces more profitable companies to finance with debt,
- Higher leverage helps to control agency problems by forcing managers to pay out more of the company's excess cash (Bessler et al. 2011).

Bankruptcy costs associated with debt can help explain why debt finance does not predominate over a company's capital structure. Since the probability of bankruptcy affects the net present value of the debt holders returns, bankruptcy costs affect the cost of debt.

The cost of debt increases with the debt ratio since managerial incentives to transfer wealth from the bondholders increase with the size of debt, the monitoring costs which these managerial incentive effects create also increase with debt and financial risk and managerial incentives to undertake risks increase with debt enhancing the probability of bankruptcy as debt finance increases (Moschandreas 2000).

The management of a company should consider a number of key elements in finally deciding on the choice between debt and equity. The cost and availability of long-term funds would have to be considered of prime importance. The component cost of debt is the effective interest rate on new debt, adjusted for taxes (Seitz and Ellison 1995).

Long-term arrangements have several features that cause the stated interest rate on the financing to be different from the effective interest rate. Bank loans are an important source of long-term debt for companies, and the interest on bank loans may be quoted as simple interest and discount interest. In comparison with short-term debt, long-term debt usually has a higher explicit cost but lower risk, in which the risk refers to that of insolvency or default.

Consequently, the merits of the different sources of financing should be considered carefully before a company borrows money. The most important factor in this is the cost of financing sources, the effective interest rate being the real rate of interest on a loan expressed as an annual percentage applicable for the life of the loan. Naturally, the management of a company should aim to minimize its cost of financing.

1.3 Research

1.3.1 Sample and Methods

The empirical research was based on a sample of randomly selected small and medium–sized companies in the Republic of Croatia. Although the Small and Medium-sized Enterprises (SME) definition is subject to considerable differences in prior studies, there is an increasing tendency to rely on the European Commission SME definition. In line with this definition, we selected companies that met the following criteria: (1) fewer than 250 employees; (2) sales below 50,000,000 EUR; and (3) total assets below 43,000,000 EUR.

Based on these criterias, we randomly selected an initial sample of 200 small and medium-sized companies that operated in the year 2013. We excluded companies that belong to the financial or governmental sectors because of additional requirements that apply to these sectors. We also discarded observations with missing values. In so doing, we ended up with our final sample of 158 small and medium-sized companies.

We analyzed the structure of short- and long-term financing sources used by Croatian small and medium-sized companies in 2013 along with a dependence between short-term debt and profitability as well as long-term debt and profitability. For each company we calculated the ratio of short-term debt to total assets, the ratio of long-term debt to total assets, and the return on assets. Using methods from statistics, we investigated whether there was a relation between short-term debt and profitability as well as long-term debt and profitability expressed in terms of return on assets.

We also analyzed various short- and long-term financing sources available to companies from a cost-effective point of view and EIRAT as a true measure of the effective cost of sources of financing. The Effective Interest Rate After Tax (EIRAT) can be calculated by applying procedures for computing this. In this research, it is essential to determine independent variables which impact on EIRAT as a dependent variable and to establish their relation to these independent variables.

Models have been designed on the basis of the results of analysis. We have specified the independent variables in the modeling process and determined the relationship between the selected independent variables so that EIRAT can be computed. For precise formulation of the relationship between a set of independent variables, mathematical methods have been adapted in order to yield EIRAT as a dependent variable.

Table 1.1 Financial structure of companies in the Republic of Croatia in 2013 (in thousands of Euros)

Asset/Source	Amount	Percent	Arithmetic mean
Fixed assets	164,809.45	61.62	1043.10
Current assets	102,655.75	38.38	649.72
Total assets	**267,465.20**	**100.00**	**1692.82**
Equity capital	137,052.87	**51.24**	867.42
Total long-term liabilities	38,990.41	14.58	246.78
Bank loans	38,990.41	14.58	246.78
Total short-term liabilities	91,421.92	34.18	578.62
Accruals	7316.99	2.74	46.31
Accounts payable	48,454.25	18.12	306.67
Bank loans	21,171.23	7.91	134.00
Other short-term liabilities	14,479.45	5.41	91.64
Total capital	**267,465.20**	**100.00**	**1692.82**

Source: Author's calculations

1.3.2 Results of Analysis

We analyzed the structure of financing sources used by small and medium-sized companies in the Republic of Croatia in 2013 along with a dependence between short-term debt and profitability as well as long-term debt and profitability. We also analyzed various financing sources available to companies.

The structure of assets, current and long-term liabilities in small and medium-sized companies in the Republic of Croatia in 2013 has been analyzed and presented in Table 1.1.

Small and medium-sized companies finance fixed assets and 4.20 percent of current assets with long-term financing sources, through either equity financing or long-term debt. The remaining current assets are financed by short-term sources. Equity financing constitutes 51.24 percent of the total capital, while debt constitutes 48.76 percent. Long-term debt accounts for only 14.58 percent of the total capital, while short-term liabilities account for 34.18 percent. It should be noted that small and medium-sized companies have to rely more heavily on short-term liabilities than long-term debt because they do not have the degree of accessibility to long-term loans as large companies.

Small and medium-sized companies mainly use accounts payable or trade credit for financing their current assets. Short-term bank loans represent only 7.91 percent of the companies' total capital. Small and medium-sized companies with liquidity problems may stretch their accounts payable. All forms of bank loans in 2013 accounted for 22.49 percent of the capital structure of small and medium-sized companies under consideration.

We investigated whether there was a relation between short- and long-term debt level and profitability and analyzed the dependence between short-term debt and profitability as well as long-term debt and profitability. The level of short- and

Table 1.2 Descriptive statistics for debt ratios and return on assets in surveyed companies

	Short-Term Debt Ratio (STDR)	Long-Term Debt Ratio (LTDR)	Return On Assets (ROA)
Arithmetic mean	34.18	14.58	0.06
Standard deviation	28.86	21.01	0.17
Coefficient of variation	84.43	144.10	283.33
Correlation coefficient – STDR – ROA			−0.71
Correlation coefficient – LTDR – ROA			−0.67

Sources: Author's calculations

long-term debt and return on assets in small and medium-sized companies in the Republic of Croatia in 2013 have been analyzed in Table 1.2. Using methods from statistics, we analyzed the level of short-term debt expressed as a ratio of short-term debt to total assets, the level of long-term debt expressed as a ratio of long-term debt to total assets, and profitability expressed as a return on assets, as well as a possible dependence between short- and long-term debt and profitability.

The average value of short-term debt for small and medium-sized companies during the examined period was 34.18, while the average value of Return On Assets (ROA) was 0.06. We have found a moderately strong negative dependence between short-term debt and return on assets, showing that an adverse correlation between variables short-term debt and ROA may be an indication that an increase in the level of short-term debt triggers a decrease in the value of the return on assets.

Repeating our analysis for long-term debt, we have found similar relations between long-term debt and return on assets. We have found a moderately strong negative dependence between long-term debt and return on assets, indicating that as values of long-term debt increase, the values on the return on assets tend to decrease. We confirm that during the examined period the correlation between variables short-term debt and return on assets as well as long-term debt and return on assets for surveyed small and medium-sized companies is negative and an increase of short- and long-term debt triggers a fall in profitability expressed in terms of return on assets.

1.3.3 Effective Cost of Sources of Financing

We have analyzed various short- and long-term financing sources available to companies from a cost-effective point of view and Effective Interest Rate After Tax (EIRAT) as a true measure of the effective cost of financing. The independent variables which impact EIRAT for various short- and long-term financing sources are selected and the relations between them are defined. To enable us to model the relations between independent variables, which determine EIRAT as a dependent variable for various short- and long-term financing sources, new equations have been introduced. Consequently, the main findings are new equations for calculating EIRAT for different short- and long-term financing sources available to companies.

1.3.3.1 Models

Short-Term Financing Sources

We have analyzed the following short-term financing sources available to companies: simple interest bank loans, bank loans with discount interest, bank loans with compensating balances and bank loans with discount interest and compensating balances, line of credit, factoring accounts receivable, inventory financing and commercial papers.

The effective interest rate before tax for different short-term financing sources available to companies can be defined as follows:

$$\textit{Effective interest rate} = \frac{\textit{Costs}}{\textit{Net amount of financing}}$$

The ultimate cost to the company is influenced by the tax rate of the company. The after-tax cost to the company can be expressed as follows:

$$\textit{Effective interest rate after-tax} = \textit{effective interest rate before tax} \times (100\text{–}\textit{profit tax rate})$$

where

profit tax rate is expressed as percentage.

The effective interest rate after tax for simple interest bank loans can be expressed as follows:

$$EIRAT = \frac{\frac{i \times P}{100}}{P} \times (100 - t)$$

After rearrangement, we evidently obtain

$$EIRAT = i \times (1 - t)$$

The independent variables which have an impact on EIRAT for simple interest bank loans are nominal interest rate and profit tax rate. The principal is labeled as not relevant variable for EIRAT and is excluded (Kontuš 2012). EIRAT can be expressed in terms of these independent variables as follows:

$$EIRAT = i \times (1 - t)$$

where

i – nominal interest rate expressed as percentage
t – profit tax rate expressed as decimals.

The effective interest rate after tax for bank loans with discount interest can be defined as follows:

$$EIRAT = \frac{\frac{i \times P}{100}}{P - \frac{i \times P}{100}} \times (100 - t)$$

After rearrangement, we obtain

$$EIRAT = \frac{i}{100 - i} \times (100 - t)$$

The independent variables which have an impact on EIRAT for bank loans with discount interest are nominal interest rate and profit tax rate (Kontuš 2012). EIRAT can be expressed in terms of these independent variables as follows:

$$EIRAT = \frac{i}{100 - i} \times (100 - t)$$

where

i – nominal interest rate expressed as percentage
t – profit tax rate expressed as percentage.

The effective interest rate after tax for simple interest bank loan with compensating balances can be defined as follows:

$$EIRAT = \frac{\frac{i \times P}{100}}{P - \frac{cb \times P}{100}} \times (100 - t)$$

After rearrangement, we obtain

$$EIRAT = \frac{i}{100 - cb} \times (100 - t)$$

The independent variables which have an impact on EIRAT for simple interest bank loan with compensating balances are nominal interest rate, compensating balances and profit tax rate (Kontuš 2012). EIRAT can be expressed in terms of these independent variables as follows:

$$EIRAT = \frac{i}{100 - cb} \times (100 - t)$$

where

i – nominal interest rate expressed as percentage
cb – compensating balances expressed as percentage
t – profit tax rate expressed as percentage.

The effective interest rate after tax for bank loan with discount interest and compensating balances can be expressed as follows:

$$EIRAT = \frac{\frac{i \times P}{100}}{P - \frac{i \times P}{100} - \frac{cb \times P}{100}} \times (100 - t)$$

After rearrangement, we obtain

$$EIRAT = \frac{i}{100 - i - cb} \times (100 - t)$$

The independent variables which have an impact on EIRAT for a bank loan with discount interest and compensating balances are nominal interest rate, compensating balances and profit tax rate (Kontuš 2012). EIRAT can be expressed in terms of these independent variables as follows:

$$EIRAT = \frac{i}{100 - i - cb} \times (100 - t)$$

where

i – nominal interest rate expressed as percentage
cb – compensating balances expressed as percentage
t – profit tax rate expressed as percentage.

The effective interest rate after tax for line of credit can be defined as follows:

$$EIRAT = \frac{\frac{P \times i \times n}{12 \times 100} + \frac{P \times cf \times (12 - n)}{12 \times 100}}{P} \times (100 - t)$$

After rearrangement, we obtain

$$EIRAT = \frac{i \times n + cf \times (12 - n)}{12} \times (1 - t)$$

The independent variables which have an impact on EIRAT for line of credit are nominal interest rate, commitment fee (%), used period and profit tax rate (Kontuš 2012). EIRAT can be expressed in terms of these independent variables as follows:

$$EIRAT = \frac{i \times n + cf \times (12 - n)}{12} \times (1 - t)$$

where

i – nominal interest rate expressed as percentage
cf – commitment fee expressed as percentage
t – profit tax rate expressed as decimals
n – used period expressed in months.

The effective interest rate after tax for factoring accounts receivable can be defined as follows:

$$EIRAT = \frac{\frac{R\times i}{100}}{R - \frac{R\times i}{100} - \frac{R\times ff}{100}} \times (100 - t)$$

where

R – the amount of receivables purchased
i – nominal interest rate
ff – factor fee
t – profit tax rate

After rearrangement, we obtain

$$EIRAT = \frac{i}{100 - i - ff} \times (100 - t)$$

The independent variables which have an impact on EIRAT for factoring accounts receivable are nominal interest rate, factor fee and profit tax rate (Kontuš 2012). EIRAT can be expressed in terms of these independent variables as follows:

$$EIRAT = \frac{i}{100 - i - ff} \times (100 - t)$$

where

i – nominal interest rate expressed as percentage
ff – factor fee expressed as percentage
t – profit tax rate expressed as percentage.

The effective interest rate after tax for inventory financing can be defined as follows:

$$EIRAT = \frac{\frac{P\times i}{100} + Wc}{P} \times (100 - t)$$

After rearrangement, we obtain

$$EIRAT = \left(i + \frac{100 \times Wc}{P}\right) \times (1 - t)$$

The independent variables which have impact on EIRAT for inventory financing are nominal interest rate, warehousing cost, principal and profit tax rate (Kontuš 2012). EIRAT can be expressed in terms of these independent variables as follows:

$$EIRAT = \left(\mathrm{i} + \frac{100 \times \mathrm{Wc}}{\mathrm{P}} \right) \times (1 - \mathrm{t})$$

where

i – nominal interest rate expressed as percentage
Wc– warehousing costs
P – principal
t– profit tax rate expressed as decimals.

The effective interest rate after tax for commercial papers can be defined as follows:

$$EIRAT = \frac{\frac{P \times i}{100} + Ci}{P} \times (100 - t)$$

After rearrangement, we obtain

$$EIRAT = \left(i + \frac{100 \times Ci}{P} \right) \times (1 - t)$$

The independent variables which have impact on EIRAT for commercial papers are nominal interest rate, cost of issuance, principal and profit tax rate (Kontuš 2012). EIRAT can be expressed in terms of these independent variables as follows:

$$EIRAT = \left(\mathrm{i} + \frac{100 \times Ci}{\mathrm{P}} \right) \times (1 - \mathrm{t})$$

where

i – nominal interest rate expressed as percentage
Ci – cost of issuance
P– principal
t – profit tax rate expressed as decimals.

To determine what sources of short-term financing to employ, the financial manager of company should take into consideration the cost of all available sources expressed as a comparable EIRAT and choose the source in accordance with EIRAT because that represents the real cost of financing. Finally, the source that has the lowest EIRAT should be chosen.

Long-Term Financing Sources

We have analyzed the following long-term financing sources available to companies: long-term bank loans with simple interest, long-term bank loans with discount interest, long-term bank loans with compensating balances and long-term bank loans with discount interest and compensating balances.

The effective interest rate before tax for any long-term bank loan available to companies can be defined as follows:

$$\textit{Effective interest rate} = \frac{\textit{Nominal interest on face of long} - \textit{term loan}}{\textit{Net proceeds of long} - \textit{term loan}}$$

The after tax cost to the company can be expressed as follows:

$$\textit{Effective interest rate after-tax} = \textit{effective interest rate before tax} \times (100\text{–}\textit{profit tax rate})$$

where

profit tax rate is expressed as percentage.

In our research we have found that the independent variables which have an impact on EIRAT for long-term bank loans with simple interest are nominal interest rate (i), nominal amount of debt (N_j) and profit tax rate (t).

The effective interest rate after tax for long-term bank loans with simple interest can be expressed in terms of these independent variables as follows:

$$EIRAT = \frac{\frac{\sum_{j=1}^{n} Nj \times i/100}{n}}{\frac{\sum_{j=1}^{n} Nj}{n}} \times (100 - t)$$

After rearrangement, we obtain

$$EIRAT = \frac{\sum_{j=1}^{n} Nj \times i/100}{\sum_{j=1}^{n} Nj} \times (100 - t),$$

The effective interest rate after tax for long-term bank loans with simple interest can be expressed as follows:

$$EIRAT = \frac{\sum_{j=1}^{n} Nj \times i/100}{\sum_{j=1}^{n} Nj} \times (100 - t) \quad \textit{for}\, j = 1, \ldots, n$$

where

i – interest rate expressed as percentage
N_j – nominal amount of debt
t – profit tax rate expressed as percentage.

The effective interest rate after tax for long-term bank loans with discount interest can be defined as follows:

$$EIRAT = \frac{\frac{\sum_{j=1}^{n} Nj \times i/100}{n}}{\frac{\sum_{j=1}^{n} Nj - Nj \times i/100}{n}} \times (100 - t)$$

After rearrangement, we obtain

$$EIRAT = \frac{\sum_{j=1}^{n} Nj \times \mathrm{i}/100}{\sum_{j=1}^{n} Nj - Nj \times i/100} \times (100 - t)$$

The independent variables which have an impact on EIRAT for long-term bank loans with discount interest are nominal interest rate (i), nominal amount of debt (Nj) and profit tax rate (t). EIRAT can be expressed in terms of these independent variables as follows:

$$EIRAT = \frac{\sum_{j=1}^{n} Nj \times i/100}{\sum_{j=1}^{n} Nj - Nj \times i/100} \times (100 - t), \quad for\, j = 1, \ldots, n,$$

where

i – interest rate expressed as percentage
N_j – nominal amount of debt
t – profit tax rate expressed as percentage.

In our research we have found that the independent variables which have an impact on EIRAT for long-term bank loans with compensating balances are nominal interest rate (i), nominal amount of debt (Nj), the amount of compensating balances (CB) and profit tax rate (t).

The effective interest rate after tax for long-term bank loans with compensating balances can be expressed in terms of these independent variables as follows:

$$EIRAT = \frac{\frac{\sum_{j=1}^{n} Nj \times i/100}{n}}{\frac{\sum_{j=1}^{n} Nj - CB}{n}} \times (100 - t)$$

After rearrangement, we obtain

$$EIRAT = \frac{\sum_{j=1}^{n} Nj \times i/100}{\sum_{j=1}^{n} Nj - CB} \times (100 - t)$$

The effective interest rate after tax for long-term bank loans with compensating balances can be expressed as follows:

$$EIRAT = \frac{\sum_{j=1}^{n} Nj \times i/100}{\sum_{j=1}^{n} Nj - CB} \times (100 - t), \quad for\, j = 1, \ldots, n,$$

where

i – interest rate expressed as percentage
N_j – nominal amount of debt

CB – the amount of compensating balances
t – profit tax rate expressed as percentage.

In our research we have found that the independent variables which have an impact on EIRAT for long-term bank loans with discount interest and compensating balances are nominal interest rate (i), nominal amount of debt (Nj), the amount of compensating balances (CB) and profit tax rate (t).

The effective interest rate after tax for long-term bank loans with discount interest and compensating balances can be expressed in terms of these independent variables as follows:

$$EIRAT = \frac{\frac{\sum_{j=1}^{n} Nj \times i/100}{n}}{\frac{\sum_{j=1}^{n} Nj - Nj \times i/100 - CB}{n}} \times (100 - t)$$

After rearrangement, we obtain

$$EIRAT = \frac{\sum_{j=1}^{n} Nj \times i/100}{\sum_{j=1}^{n} Nj - Nj \times i/100 - CB} \times (100 - t)$$

The effective interest rate after tax for long-term bank loans with discount interest and compensating balances can be expressed as follows

$$EIRAT = \frac{\sum_{j=1}^{n} Nj \times i/100}{\sum_{j=1}^{n} Nj - Nj \times i/100 - CB} \times (100 - t), \quad for\, j = 1, \ldots, n,$$

where

i – interest rate expressed as percentage
N_j *– nominal amount of debt*
CB – the amount of compensating balances
t – profit tax rate expressed as percentage.

The real rate of interest as real cost for these long–term bank loans can be calculated on the basis of a loan amortization schedule by using these equations. To determine what sources of long-term financing to employ, the financial manager of company should take into consideration the cost of all available sources expressed as a comparable EIRAT and choose the long-term source in accordance with EIRAT because that represents the real cost of financing. Finally, the source that has the lowest EIRAT should be chosen.

The equation models for calculating EIRAT for different short- and long-term financing sources can be tested and used in practical calculations by using different financing sources available to companies. Numerical results obtained by using these equations should be considered and compared so that the financing sources that result in the lowest EIRAT should be chosen.

1.3.3.2 Discussion

This research shows that a wide range of factors affect the Effective Interest Rate After Tax (EIRAT) for short-term financing sources. For all these sources, EIRAT is a function of a nominal interest rate and a profit tax rate. An upsurge in the nominal interest rate produces an increase in terms of EIRAT, while a rise in the profit tax rate triggers a decrease of EIRAT.

Other factors that influence EIRAT are: compensating balance, cost of issuing commercial papers, warehousing costs, factor fee, commitment fee as well as a method of calculating interest. A compensating balance increases EIRAT. The methods for computing interest costs, such as the discount and installment method, also increase EIRAT. This subsequently rises, as the cost of issuing commercial papers or warehousing costs escalate accordingly. A hike in the factor or commitment fee also produces an upsurge in terms of EIRAT (Kontuš 2012).

The independent variables over which management can exert some degree of control for short-term financing sources are a nominal interest rate, compensating balance, cost of issuing commercial papers, warehousing costs, factor fee and commitment fee, while profit tax rate is the variable which manager should take as given. A manager can also impact on the method of calculating interest which will be used.

The independent variables over which management can exert some degree of control for long-term bank loans are nominal interest rate and compensating balance, while profit tax rate is the variable which manager should take as given. A manager can also impact on the method of calculating interest for long-term bank loans.

The findings of this research show that the following general recommendations for financial managers can be made. Financial managers should impact on the independent variables over which they have some degree of control in order to reduce them. They should obtain bank loans without compensating balance and arrange payment of interest costs on the real used amount of a bank loan, because compensating balance and discount interest raise EIRAT on bank loans.

On the basis of the new equation models offered for calculating EIRAT for various financing sources available to companies, the following benefits can be derived:

- Easier consideration and comparison of available short- and long-term sources regarding the costs, as calculation of EIRAT is simplified by using the given equations.
- An optimal selection of short- and long-term financing sources.
- Significant cost savings can be achieved by taking into consideration the cost of all sources available to companies.

This research indicates that the following factors exert an adverse impact on profitability, which is an important measure of the efficiency with which the management has used its available resources to generate income and solvency: lack of scientifically-based financial management of companies, a relatively large amount of long-term sources used for financing current assets as well as a non-optimal composition of the company's short- and long-term sources from a cost-financing aspect.

Companies should adopt a more advanced financial policy, taking into account the importance of scientifically-based financial management. The financial manager of a company should formulate a financing strategy, define the optimal ratio of short- and long- term financing sources, choose the appropriate financing sources from the short- and long-term financing sources available, and compute the effective cost of financing alternatives prior to making a decision.

1.3.3.3 An Illustrative Example

These models for calculating EIRAT can be tested and used for business practice. In order to validate results from the models for calculating EIRAT for various short-term financing sources, we offer the following example. We assume that company needs 500,000 EUR and is weighting the alternatives of arranging a short-term bank loan, going to factor or issuing commercial papers. The bank loan terms are 12 percent interest, discounted, with a compensating balance of 20 percent required. The factor will charge a four percent commission on invoices purchased monthly and the interest rate on the purchased invoices is 12 percent, deducted in advance. The company can issue 500,000 EUR of commercial papers at 11 percent. The costs of issuance amount 5000 EUR. Profit tax rate is assumed to be 20 percent.

The finance manager should compute EIRAT associated with the alternatives and select the least expensive alternative.

1. The EIRAT associated with the bank loan is:

$$EIRAT = \frac{i}{100 - i - cb} \times (100 - t)$$

$$EIRAT = \frac{12}{100 - 12 - 20}(100 - 20) = 14.12\%$$

2. The EIRAT associated with factoring accounts receivable is:

$$EIRAT = \frac{i}{100 - i - ff} \times (100 - t)$$

$$EIRAT = \frac{12}{100 - 12 - 20}(100 - 20) = 11.43\%$$

3. The EIRAT associated with issue of commercial papers

$$EIRAT = \left(i + \frac{100 \times ci}{p}\right) \times (1 - t)$$

$$EIRAT = \left(11 + \frac{100 \times 5,000}{500,000}\right) \times (1 - 0.2) = 9.6\%$$

The least expensive method of financing is the issue 500,000 EUR of commercial papers.

1.4 Conclusion

The financial manager of a company must lay out two financial determinants: the desired percentage of short- and long-term financing and the composition of short- and long-term sources. The Effective Interest Rate After Tax (EIRAT) represents the real cost of financing, and in determining which sources of short- and long-term financing a company ought to employ, it is important to take into consideration the cost of all available sources and choose the best one in accordance with EIRAT.

We have analyzed various short- and long-term financing sources in order to define independent variables which determine EIRAT and investigate if there is a possible relation between them, and have proposed models designed on the basis of the results of this analysis.

The major findings are the new equation models for calculating EIRAT for the following long-term financing sources: bank loans with simple interest, bank loans with discount interest, bank loans with simple interest and compensating balances, and bank loans with discount interest and compensating balances as well as for short-term financing sources. The equation models can be used by companies as a tool to help minimize their costs and develop an optimal composition of both the company's short-term liabilities and its long-term bank loans with regard to the economy.

References

Auernheimer, L. (2003). *International financial markets: The challenge of globalization*. Chicago: The Bush School.

Bessler, W., Drobetz, W., & Kazemieh, R. (2011). *Factors affecting capital structure decisions, Capital structure and corporate financing decisions*. New Jersy: Wiley.

Brealey, R., Myers, S., & Allen, F. (2011). *Principles of corporate finance* (10th ed.). New York: Mc Graw-Hill Irvin.

Brigham, E. F., & Gapenski, L. C. (1994). *Financial management* (7th ed.). Fort Worth: The Dryden Press.

Childs, P., Mauer, D., & Ott, S. (2005). Interactions of corporate financing and investment decisions: The effects of agency conflicts. *Journal of Financial Economics, 76*(3), 667–690.
Custodio, C., Ferreira, M., & Laureano, L. (2013). Why are US firms using more short-term debt. *Journal of Financial Economics, 108*(1), 182–212.
Dangl, T., & Zechner, J. (2016). Debt maturity and the dynamics of leverage, CFS WP No. 547.
Ericsson, J. (2000). Asset substitution, debt Pricing, optimal leverage and maturity. *Finance, 21*(2), 39–70.
Graham, J., Smart, S., & Megginson, W. (2010). *Corporate finance linking theory to what companies do* (3rd ed.). Mason: South-Western Cengage Learning.
Harford, J., & Maxwell, W. (2014). Refinancing risk and cash holdings. *Journal of Finance, 69*(3), 975–1012.
Harvey, C., Lins, K., & Roper, A. (2004). The effect of capital structure when expected agency costs are extreme. *Journal of Financial Economics, 74*, 3–30.
Jensen, M. C. (1986). The agency cost of free cash flow: Corporate finance and takeovers. *American Economic Review, 76*(2), 323–329.
Jensen, M. C., & Meckling, W. H. (1976). Theory of the firm, mangerial behavior, agency costs and ownership structure. *Journal of Financial Economics, 3*, 305–360.
Jiraporn, P., & Tong, S. (2007). Debt maturity structure, agency costs and firm value: Evidence from 1973–2004. Working Paper.
Kolb, R. W. (1987). *Financial management*. Glenview: Scott, Foresman and Company.
Kontuš, E. (2012). Sources of short-term financing. *International Journal of Management Cases, 14*(2), 178–197.
Maness, T. S., & Zietlow, J. T. (2005). *Short-term financial management*. South Western: Thomson.
Miltersen, K., & Torous, W. (2007). Risky corporate debt with finite maturity, Working paper.
Moschandreas, M. (2000). *Business economics* (2nd ed.). London: Thomson.
Myers, S. (1977). Determinants of corporate borrowing. *Journal of Financial Economics, 5*(2), 147–175.
Park, K. S. (2015). Capital structure redux: Maturity, leverage and flexibility, Working paper, Copenhagen Business school.
Pinches, G. E. (1994). *Financial management*. New York: Harper Collins College Publishers.
Seitz, N., & Ellison, M. (1995). *Capital budgeting and long-term financing decisions* (2nd ed.). Orlando: Dryden Press.
Shim, J. K., & Siegel, J. G. (2007). *Financial management* (3rd ed.). New York: McGraw Hill.
Shleifer, A., & Vishny, R. (1997). A survey of corporate governance. *Journal of Finance, 52*, 737–783.
Walker, E. W., & Petty, J. W. (1986). *Financial management of the small firm*. Englewood Cliffs: Prentice-Hall.

Chapter 2
A New Approach to the Management of Cash in a Company

Eleonora Kontuš

Abstract The aim of the study is, firstly, to analyze the cash balances of companies; secondly, to explore the costs and benefits of cash management; and thirdly, to determine the variables that impact on net savings as a result of establishing a lockbox system and delaying cash payments, and to model the relationships between these variables. The purpose of the empirical part of the study is to demonstrate a correlation between the cash level and liquidity and to explore the dependence between companies' level of liquidity and profitability. The results of the work include mathematical models for calculating net savings from establishing or changing a lockbox system, as well as delaying cash payments. These results lead to the conclusion that the management of cash becomes easier, as calculations regarding net savings from establishing or changing a lockbox system and delaying cash payments are simplified by using the mathematical models provided. With these, models a company can consider net profitability in undertaking these activities in order to improve its cash position for investments and to improve profitability.

Keywords Cash balance • Liquidity • Net savings • Lockbox system

2.1 Introduction

Cash management involves having the optimum amount of cash at the right time, and also requires knowing the amount of funds available for investment, as well as the length of time for which they can be invested. The purpose of cash management is to invest surplus cash for a return while at the same time ensuring there is adequate liquidity to meet future needs; the goal of cash management is to minimize the cost of providing cash liquidity to the company. A company can maximize its rate of return and minimize its liquidity and business risk by optimally managing cash.

E. Kontuš (✉)
University of Rijeka, Rijeka, Croatia
e-mail: eleonora.kontus@ri.t-com.hr

G. Dominici et al. (eds.), *Governing Business Systems*, Springer Proceedings in Business and Economics, DOI 10.1007/978-3-319-66036-3_2

The aim of this paper is, to contribute to the debate by modeling the relationships between the variables that determine net savings from accelerating cash receipts and delaying cash payments, in order to develop new mathematical models and by empirically investigating the relationship between cash balance and companies' level of liquidity, as well as the relationship between level of liquidity and profitability.

This new approach is based on mathematical models. Modern scientific knowledge is best constructed by carefully developing mathematical models and testing their ability to explain behavior. Using the principles of mathematical modeling, as well as those of economics, we have developed mathematical models to explain some aspects of the management of cash which have not been explored entirely in previous studies.

The purpose of this study is to describe and explore ways of improving the cash position of a company in order to invest surplus cash and achieve the maximum return at an acceptable level of risk. By accelerating cash receipts and delaying cash payments, as well as by conserving cash, management increases its flexibility, thus improving its ability to invest surplus cash in profitable projects. This paper addresses how a company's cash and liquidity position affects profitability and how the cash balance will be influenced by the profitability of a company.

The net profitability from accelerating cash receipts and delaying cash payments, which have important implications for efficient management of cash, have not been entirely explored in previous studies. With the aim of filling in the gaps relating to net savings gained by accelerating cash receipts and delaying cash payments, this study will explore the costs and benefits of performing these activities and the net profitability of these important activities in managing cash balances.

The outcome represents a new mathematical model for calculating net savings from establishing or changing a lockbox system, while delaying cash payments; with these models, a company can consider the net profitability from performing these activities in order to improve cash balance for investment and to improve profitability. It also gives general recommendations to financial managers on how cash management decisions should be made.

The contribution of this paper to the literature is a new mathematical model for calculating the net savings from establishing or changing the lockbox system, as well as a new mathematical model for calculating net savings from delaying cash payments. These models can help to ensure that setting up a lockbox arrangement and delaying cash payments will result in net savings and help managers to managing cash optimally. The models allow the rapid evaluation of alternatives, leading to optimal solutions that are not otherwise obvious. This paper has strong implications for management, as these models can be used in business practice. A financial manager should accelerate cash inflows and delay cash payments in order to earn a greater return on money.

2.2 Literature Review

2.2.1 Determinants of Cash Holdings

The management of cash and other liquid assets focuses on cash inflows and outflows, the trade-off between holding cash versus investing in marketable securities, and how to structure the marketable security portfolio. The goal of the financial manager is to minimize the amount of cash the company must hold to conduct its activities while, at the same time, to have sufficient cash to take trade discounts, to maintain its credit rating, and to meet unexpected cash needs (Brigham and Daves 2004).

According to Ferreira and Vilela (2004), the benefits of holding cash are: a reduction in the likelihood of financial distress, the ability to pursue investment policies when financial constraints are met, and the minimal costs of raising external funds. Myers and Majluf (1984), as well as Almeida et al. (2004), argue that costly external finance makes it important for companies to maintain a cash reserve that provides sufficient liquidity, so that positive net present value projects can continue to be funded, even when internal cash flows decline.

Kusnadi and Wei (2011) examined the determinants of corporate cash management policies and found that firms in countries with strong legal protection of minority investors are more likely to decrease their cash holdings in response to an increase in cash flow than are companies in countries with weak legal protection. Ramirez and Tadesse (2009) found that cultural factors, as well as firm multinationality, influence corporate cash holdings. Firms in countries with high levels of uncertainty avoidance tend to hold more cash. Against the commonly held views on cash management, the degree of multinationality of the firm is positively correlated with cash holdings.

Agency problems between shareholders and debt holders may also affect a company's cash holdings. Myers (1977) argues that agency conflicts increase the cost of issuing additional debt and may cause a company to forego profitable investment opportunities. Managers can choose low levels of debt and hold excess cash in order to avoid the agency costs of debt. Jensen (1986) develops a free cash flow argument, in which managers hold excess cash for their own self- interest, allowing them the flexibility to spend cash to pursue their own objectives.

Easterbrook (1984) and Jensen (1986) argue that the agency costs of managerial entrenchment will cause shareholders to prefer that a company not hold meaningful cash balances, because these could potentially lead to overinvestment in negative net present value projects that serve managers better than they do shareholders. Shareholders of companies that are likely to have managerial agency problems should therefore benefit if these companies use their cash to make dividend and interest payments.

Dittmar et al. (2003) explain that agency problems are important determinants of cash holdings. Schwetzler and Reimund (2003) find operating underperformance in a sample of companies that hold persistent large excess cash holdings, and they attribute this underperformance to agency problems. Harford (1999) and Mikkelson and Partch (2003) show that managerial agency cost proxies are unrelated to the levels of cash holdings by companies. Wang (2010) finds that free cash flows have a significant impact on agency costs and that the effects are contrary. Free cash flows could increase the management's incentive for perquisite consumption and shirking, thus leading to an increase in agency costs. On the other hand, free cash flows are generated due to management's operating efficiency, such that there may exist a negative relationship between free cash flows and agency costs.

Duchin (2010) points out that companies with higher degrees of diversification tend to hold less cash as a fraction of their assets, and that it is optimal for such companies to hold less cash because of the costs that accompany cash holdings, namely agency costs and tax costs. Tong (2011) finds that the value of cash is lower in diversified firms than in single-segment firms, and these findings are consistent with the interpretation that firm diversification reduces the value of corporate cash holdings through agency problems. Khan et al. (2012) find that a firm's leverage plays an important role in reducing the agency costs of free cash flow.

Opler et al. (1999) argue that companies with greater likelihood of financial distress should hold more cash. Guney et al. (2007) find that companies with strong creditor protection have a greater probability of bankruptcy in financial distress and should carry excess cash to avoid financial distress. Their results show that companies with strong investor protection and high ownership concentration hold less cash.

Ferreira and Vilela (2004) investigated the determinants of cash holdings; their findings suggest that cash holdings are positively affected by the investment opportunities set, as well as cash flows, and are negatively affected by asset liquidity, leverage and size. Nguyen (2005) finds that cash holdings are positively associated with firm level risk, but negatively related to industry risk. Cash holdings decrease with the firm's size and debt ratio and increase with its profitability, growth prospects, and dividend payout ratio.

Drobetz and Gruninger (2007) confirm that asset tangibility and company size are both negatively related to cash holdings while dividend payments and operating cash flows are positively related to cash reserves.

Guney et al. (2007) found a nonmonotonic relation between cash holdings and leverage. Using a large sample of companies, they obtained a negative relationship between cash holdings and leverage at low levels of leverage. Hardin et al. (2009) found that cash holdings are inversely related to funds from operations, leverage, and internal advisement, and are directly related to the cost of external finance and growth opportunities. Cash holdings are negatively associated with credit line access and use. Debt and net working capital are negatively related to cash holdings. Megginson and Wei (2010) suggest that smaller, more profitable, higher growth companies hold more cash. Cash holdings fluctuate with the cash flow of a company, and hence one would expect a positive relationship between profitability and cash holdings.

Cash management should be a central function of any business, since cash must be available in the correct amounts and with the proper timing to ensure that company functions are not impeded (Bragg 2012).

Determining the amount to hold in a company's demand deposit account, versus the amount to invest in marketable securities, depends on forecasting and the incremental interest that can be earned from marketable securities. The Miller-Orr and EOQ models provide insight into how companies control their cash balances and suggest that cash balances should be as low as possible so that funds can be channeled to profitable investment opportunities (Chambers and Lacey 2011). Newer models have been developed to attempt to build on the Miller-Orr model by incorporating the predictability of some cash flows. All cash management models share the objective of finding the least-cost approach to providing a company with an adequate cash balance to meet its liquidity needs.

A company's profitability, as an indication of its ability to earn a satisfactory profit and return on investment, affects its cash level. Companies with higher profitability, whose operations are managed from both a profit perspective and a cash flow perspective, can ensure an optimal or appropriate cash balance. These companies have more internally-generated funds, which are preferred over debt and equity financing.

A company's level of liquidity depends upon the amount of the company's cash, the amount of other assets that can be quickly converted to cash, the amount of liabilities that require repayment in the near future, and the ability of the company to raise more cash by issuing securities or borrowing money.

Despite the generally accepted idea that cash positively affects a company's liquidity, we have examined the dependence between cash level and liquidity of surveyed companies; we expect that companies with high cash levels will have a higher liquidity position.

Literature reports demonstrated that there is a trade-off between liquidity and profitability which discourages companies from having excessive liquidity. Holding working capital is costly and reduces a company's return on invested capital and free cash flow. In contrast to previous findings, Banos-Caballero et al. (2011) found that there is an inverted U-shaped relationship between working capital level and profitability, which in turn indicates that both high and low working capital levels are associated with a lower profitability. Their results confirm that companies have an optimal level of working capital that balances costs and benefits and maximizes their profitability; companies' profitability thus decreases as they move away from this optimal level.

Our study examines the relationship between liquidity as measured by net working capital ratio and profitability, as well as the cash to current liabilities ratio and profitability. We expect company's liquidity level and profitability to relate negatively, leading to our hypotheses:

Liquidity as measured by the cash to current liabilities ratio, as well as by the net working capital, is negatively correlated with profitability.

2.2.2 Concepts Underlying Cash Management

The main concepts underlying cash management and investment are: accelerating receipts of cash, delaying payments of cash, and investing surplus cash. Implicit in each of these three concepts is the corporate objective of maximizing shareholder wealth.

The financial manager should manage the cash flow timeline related to collection, concentration, and disbursement of the company's funds; any delay in timing on either the collection or disbursement side is referred to as float. Float is important in the cash conversion cycle, because its application increases both the company's average collection period and its average payment period (Maness and Zietlow 2005).

Float can be viewed from the perspective of either the receiving party or the paying party. Mail float and processing float are viewed the same from both perspectives. The third float component is availability float to the receiving party; the fourth is clearing float to the paying party. The receiving party's goal is to minimize collection float, whereas the paying party's goal is to maximize disbursement float. In managing collections, the cash manager attempts to reduce collection float using various collection systems, which include field banking systems, mail- based systems, and electronic systems (Graham et al. 2010).

The primary function of the cash manager in the collection process is to accelerate the collection of cash receipts; the cash manager must transform credit sales into cash, so that these funds can be used to pay for the company's liabilities. Among the methods used to accelerate collection of cash receipts are the following (Franklin et al. 1995):

- Use of automated clearinghouses (ACHs) and wire transfers to speed collections
- Use of lockboxes
- Billing as soon as possible
- Creativity in setting credit terms
- Monitoring the handling of checks
- Auditing the system of cash processing.

The use of automated clearinghouses (ACHs) and wire transfers allows funds to be available faster because they are automatically transferred and credited to a company's account from its customer's account on the same day. Collection problems are also reduced through the use of EFT and charges for returned checks and check-clearing float are decreased. Accelerating invoice data is a critical starting point in the cash manager's focus on accelerating cash receipts (Franklin et al. 1995).

The primary means for accelerating cash receipts are lockboxes and an efficient banking arrangement. A lockbox system is a popular technique for speeding up collections, because it affects three components of float. If lockboxes are employed, they are generally set up at the regional concentration banks, which maintain the lockbox and forward the funds to the company's central concentration bank.

A lockbox arrangement is a means to place the optimum collection point near customers and is used both to speed collections and to direct funds where they are needed.

The primary advantage of a lockbox is that the cash is collected and made available for use more quickly, because the record keeping associated with accounts receivable is done after the cash is deposited rather than before (Franklin et al. 1995). Wholesale lockboxes are used for checks received from other companies, and are most useful for companies that have gross revenues and that receive large checks from distant customers.

The delays in check collection and presentment have spurred the development of faster means of moving funds or electronic-based payments. These electronic funds transfer techniques transfer value in an electronic form. As electronic corporate payments become more common, wholesale lockboxes are phased out and electronic lockboxes are increasingly used. Such collection systems are offered by banks for companies to receive payments via wire transfer, rather than by paper checks. Companies find wire transfers economical for moving balances from several banks to a concentration bank, where the total amount can be used to pay down borrowings or invested in a higher-interest, large-denomination investment (Maness and Zietlow 2005).

Wire transfers can eliminate mail float and clearing float, and may provide processing float reductions as well. For cash concentration, the company moves funds using a wire transfer from each deposit account to the concentration account. Wire transfers are a substitute for automated clearinghouse debit transfers, but they are much more expensive: both the sending and receiving banks charge significant fees for the transaction. Wire transfers are usually used only for high-dollar transfers, where the investment value of the funds outweighs the cost of the transfer. As a result of being near the company's customers, lockboxes reduce mail time and clearing time. They reduce processing time to nearly zero, as the bank deposits the payments before the company processes them. A lockbox system reduces collection float, but is not without a cost (Graham et al. 2010).

Before a lockbox system is implemented, the company should make a cost-benefit analysis that considers the average amount of payments or checks received, the costs saved by having lockboxes, the reduction in time delay per payment or check, and the processing cost. The cost-benefit analysis must be undertaken to ensure that the lockbox arrangement will result in net savings and that the return earned on freed cash must be compared to the cost of the lockbox arrangement.

The company must therefore perform a cost-benefit analysis to determine whether a lockbox system should be implemented, and the following equation presents a simple formula for cost-benefit analysis of a lockbox system (Graham et al. 2010):

$$\textit{Net benefit or cost} = (FVR \times r_a) - LC$$

where

FVR = *float value reduction in dollars*
r_a = *cost of capital*
LC = *lockbox cost (annual operating cost of the system).*

According to McKinney (2015), the following formula aids in assessing the costs and benefits of the lockbox system:

$$\boldsymbol{BAL = (NUM) \times (AVG) \times (TIM)}$$

where

BAL = *usable balances generated due to the lockbox system*
NUM = *number of checks per day*
AVG = *average value per check*
TIM = *reduced number of transit days.*

Based on the increase in usable balances (BAL) and annual interest rate (INT), the annual dollar returns related to the additional funds (ADR) generated from the lockbox system can be determined, and are represented by the following expression:

$$\boldsymbol{ADR = (BAL) \times (INT)}$$

To determine the annual total cost (ATC) of the lockbox system, we need to identify the bank processing cost per check (UC) and the number of checks processed during the year (ANU), generating the following:

$$\boldsymbol{ATC = (UC) \times (ANU)}$$

Finally, the determination of the break-even point, where the benefit generated is equal to the costs incurred for the system, is calculated as follows:

$$\boldsymbol{ADR = ATC}$$

Whenever the benefit of the lockbox system exceeds the costs, the system should be implemented; if the reverse is true, it should be rejected (McKinney 2015).

As financial manager attempts to reduce collection float through development of a lockbox collection system, a cash concentration system becomes essential in moving the collected deposit balances into banks where the balances can be better managed. An effective cash concentration system provides deposit information to the corporate cash manager that is critical if the cash manager is to effectively manage the company's daily liquidity. The improved deposit information allows the cash manager to move the accumulating balances from the original banks of deposit to fewer deposit accounts of greater balances so that the funds can be managed more efficiently (Maness and Zietlow 2005).

The payment methods, disbursement banks, and locations chosen constitute the company's disbursement system. A company's decision regarding the payment methods and systems that will be used in various situations is a major financial decision (Maness et al. 2005). Disbursements can be managed by using controlled disbursing, zero balance accounts, and similar arrangements. Delaying cash payments can help a company earn a greater return and have more cash available.

Disbursing cash efficiently is critical to effective cash management and the cash manager's primary objectives are to have the correct amount of cash available at the company's bank when it is needed, and to time the company's payments so that cash balances earn the maximum additional funds. There are a number of ways a company can conserve cash through its payment program:

- Centralization of accounts payable
- Slowing the bill-paying function
- Paying through drafts
- Remote disbursements
- Zero- balance accounts (Franklin et al. 1995).

As most business is conducted by large companies that collect cash from many sources and make payments from different places, a cash management system must be in place to transfer funds from where they come in to where they are needed, to arrange loans to cover net corporate shortfalls, and to invest net corporate surpluses without delay.

Companies often have surplus cash balances that could be invested to generate additional income. When a company has surplus cash, it should invest the maximum amount of this cash for the longest possible time and at the best rate of return in keeping with the company's policies regarding risk. Efficient cash management means more than preventing bankruptcy, as it improves the profitability and reduces the risk to which the company is exposed.

Net profitability from accelerating cash receipts and delaying cash payments, as well as investing surplus cash, has not been thoroughly explored in previous studies. Our study will explore the costs and benefits that arise from performing these activities, as well as the net profitability of these activities in managing cash balances so as to improve cash balance for investment and to improve profitability.

2.3 Research

2.3.1 Methodology

This paper presents results from empirical research undertaken on a representative sample of Croatian companies with the aim of exploring their cash balances along with the dependence between profitability and cash level, the dependence between cash balance and liquidity, as well as the dependence between the companies' level of liquidity and profitability. The dataset was provided by the Financial Agency (FINA) for Croatian companies on a yearly basis.

We construct our initial sample from 250 companies included in the Financial Agency (FINA) database. The companies in the sample meet the European Commission's definition of SMEs. Although the precise definition of an SME has varied greatly in prior studies, there is an increasing tendency to rely on the European Commission's. In line with this definition, we selected companies that met the following criteria: (1) fewer than 250 employees; (2) sales below 50,000,000 EUR; and (3) total assets below 43,000,000 EUR. We also selected large companies that met the following criteria: (1) more than 250 employees; (2) sales over 50,000,000 EUR; and (3) total assets over 43,000,000 EUR.

This sample is reasonably representative of Croatian companies, as they cover all sectors, other than finance and insurance, due to their distinct financial behavior and specificity. We also excluded companies that belong to the financial and governmental sectors because of additional requirements that apply to these sectors. Companies showing extreme or inconsistent figures in any of the variables were excluded from the sample. In addition, we discarded observations with missing values. In so doing, we ended with a final sample of 168 companies. The empirical research was based on a sample of 51 randomly-selected large companies and 117 small and medium-sized companies. A larger proportion of micro-sized firms were excluded due to their accounting reports being of low quality.

In this section, we provide an overview of the variables that were used in our empirical analysis:

(1) Cash level is measured as the ratio of cash to current assets.
(2) Liquidity is measured as

- Cash ratio: the ratio of cash to current liabilities
- Quick ratio: the ratio of cash and accounts receivable to current liabilities
- Current ratio: the ratio of current assets to current liabilities
- Net working capital.

(3) Profitability is defined as return on total assets.

All the dependent and independent variables used in our study are based on book values, since the large and small and medium-sized companies are listed and unlisted companies.

Using methods from statistics, we investigated whether there was a relation between profitability and cash level, a relation between cash level and liquidity expressed in terms of liquidity ratios, and a relation between liquidity and profitability. To improve the quality of the analysis, we used financial ratios.

In this study, we also analyzed the costs and benefits arising from establishing or changing the lockbox system and delaying cash payments, as well as the net earnings from performing these activities. The independent variables that determine net earnings have been selected and the relations between them have been defined. For a precise formulation of the relationship between a set of independent variables, mathematical methods have been adapted to yield net savings as a dependent variable. On the basis of our research results, we have introduced a new generalized model for calculating the net savings from establishing or changing a lockbox system and a model for calculating the net savings from delaying cash payments.

2.3.2 Results of Empirical Analysis

We separately analyzed the impact of profitability on the cash balance, the dependence between cash level and liquidity, and the dependence between the liquidity and profitability of the examined companies.

2.3.2.1 Relation Between Profitability and Cash Level

Based on a sample of companies in the Republic of Croatia in 2014, we tested the impact of profitability expressed in terms of return on assets on cash level. The value of the return on assets and cash level in surveyed companies, taking into consideration their size in the Republic of Croatia in 2014, have been analyzed, as shown in Table 2.1.

The average value of return on assets for small and medium-sized companies during the examined period was 0.07, with a standard deviation of 0.12; the average value of cash to current assets ratio was 11.68, with a standard deviation of 17.66. The correlation coefficient was 0.58, which indicates that the correlation between return on assets and cash level is positive and moderately strong. The positive correlation between the return on assets variable and the cash level may be an indication that a change in the value of the return on assets is associated with an equivalent change in the level of cash.

The correlation coefficient for large companies during the period was 0.09, which indicates that the correlation between return on assets and cash level is positive and weak.

Table 2.1 Descriptive statistics for return on assets and cash level in surveyed companies

Financial ratio	Small and medium-sized companies	Large companies
Return on assets		
Arithmetic mean	0.07	0.03
Standard deviation	0.12	0.08
Coefficient of variation	171.43	278.23
Cash/current assets ratio		
Arithmetic mean	11.68	11.86
Standard deviation	17.66	20.97
Coefficient of variation	151.19	176.79
Correlation coefficient	0.58	0.09

Source: Author's calculations

Table 2.2 Descriptive statistics for cash and liquidity ratios in surveyed companies

Financial ratio	Small and medium-sized companies	Large companies
Cash/current assets ratio		
Arithmetic mean	11.68	11.86
Standard deviation	17.66	20.97
Coefficient of variation	151.19	176.79
Cash/current liabilities ratio		
Arithmetic mean	0.61	0.23
Standard deviation	0.27	0.55
Coefficient of variation	44.26	239.13
Correlation coefficient	0.45	0.82
Quick ratio		
Arithmetic mean	1.41	0.77
Standard deviation	2.91	1.08
Coefficient of variation	206.38	140.89
Correlation coefficient	0.41	0.46
Current ratio		
Arithmetic mean	2.27	1.12
Standard deviation	4.00	1.16
Coefficient of variation	176.21	103.40
Correlation coefficient	0.37	0.41

Source: Author's calculations

2.3.2.2 Relation Between Cash Level and Liquidity of Surveyed Companies

As cash presents a certain standard of liquidity, we analyzed the liquidity position of the examined companies along with the dependence between cash level and liquidity, as measured by different liquidity ratios.

The level of cash expressed in terms of the ratio of cash to current assets and liquidity in the considered is shown in Table 2.2.

For small and medium-sized companies, the correlation coefficient between the cash-to-current-assets ratio and the liquidity expressed in terms of cash liquidity ratio is 0.45, which confirms that the correlation is positive and weak.

Repeating our analysis for the large companies, the correlation coefficient between the cash-to-current- assets ratio and the liquidity expressed in terms of the cash liquidity ratio was 0.82, which confirms that liquidity is correlated positively and strongly with the variable cash level. Linear regression analysis indicates that the value of the liquidity level dependent variable expressed in terms of cash liquidity ratio can be estimated on the basis of a predictor variable cash level expressed in terms of the cash-to-current- assets ratio for the large surveyed companies. The results of the linear regression analysis are presented in Table 2.3.

The linear regression equation used to determine the estimated value of the dependent variable cash liquidity level is:

Table 2.3 Linear regression results for large surveyed companies

Regression output
Dependent variable: cash liquidity ratio
Number of observations: 51

Variable	Coefficient	Std. error	t-Statistic	Prob .
Intercept	*5.972554*	*2.027121*	*2.946323228*	*0.004911*
Cash to current assets ratio	*32.67735*	*3.283515*	*9.951941226*	*2.36E-13*
R-squared	*0.669011*		*F-statistic*	*99.04113*
Adjusted R-squared	*0.662256*		*Significance F*	*2.36E-13*
Standard error of regression	*13.29473*			

$$y = 5.972554 + 32.67735x$$

where

y: liquidity level expressed in terms of cash liquidity ratio
x: cash level expressed in terms of cash- to-current- assets ratio

The coefficient of determination between cash level and liquidity level is 0.669011 indicating the proportion of variance in the dependent variable cash liquidity ratio that is statistically explained by the regression equation or by knowledge of the associated independent variable cash-to-current-assets ratio.

2.3.2.3 Relation Between Liquidity Level and Profitability

We next investigated whether there was a relationship between liquidity level, expressed in terms of net working capital, as well as the cash-to-current-liabilities ratio and profitability, and analyzed the dependence between them. Table 2.4 presents the descriptive statistics for liquidity level and profitability in the companies, taking into consideration their size.

The correlation coefficient between the variables cash-to-current-liabilities ratio and the return on assets for small and medium-sized companies during the observed period is –0.34, which indicates that the correlation between cash-to-current-liabilities ratio and ROA is negative and weak. The negative correlation between the variable cash-to-current-liabilities ratio and ROA may be an indication that a change in the level of cash-to-current-liabilities ratio is not associated with a consistent and equivalent change in the value of ROA. The correlation coefficient between the variables net working capital and ROA is –0.26, which indicates that the correlation between net working capital and ROA is negative and weak.

Repeating our analysis for large companies, we found that the correlation coefficient between the variables cash-to-current-liabilities ratio and ROA is –0.04, indicating that the correlation between cash- to-current-liabilities ratio and ROA is negative and weak. The correlation coefficient between the variables net working capital and ROA is 0.02, which indicates that the correlation between net working capital and ROA is positive and weak.

Table 2.4 Descriptive statistics for liquidity level and return on assets in surveyed companies

Financial ratio	Small and medium-sized companies	Large companies
Cash/current liabilities ratio		
Arithmetic mean	0.61	0.23
Standard deviation	0.27	0.55
Coefficient of variation	44.26	239.13
Net working capital		
Arithmetic mean	917,249	121,714,772
Standard deviation	2,965,720	566,856,749
Coefficient of variation	323.33	465.73
Return on assets		
Arithmetic mean	0.07	0.03
Standard deviation	0.12	0.08
Coefficient of variation	171.43	278.23
Correlation coefficient Cash/current liabilities ratio – ROA	−0.337	−0.042
Correlation coefficient Net working capital – ROA	−0.258	0.016

Source: Author's calculations

2.3.3 Models

As the main concepts underlying cash management are speeding up receipts of cash, delaying payments of cash, and investing surplus cash, we explored the very important activities of accelerating cash receipts and delaying cash payments. We explored the costs and benefits of establishing or changing a lockbox system and delaying cash payments as well as the net earnings from performing these activities.

Using economic and mathematical principles, we have developed new mathematical models to explain how decisions in cash management are to be made. We have defined independent variables which determine net savings from establishing or changing a lockbox arrangement and delaying cash payments and determined the relationships between independent variables in order to produce net savings from establishing or changing a lockbox arrangement and delaying cash payments.

2.3.3.1 Establishing or Changing a Lockbox Arrangement

In developing a new model for calculating net savings from establishing or changing the lockbox arrangement, we have used the basic analytical concept of comparing the incremental costs versus the incremental benefits.

Net annual savings from establishing a lockbox system can be defined as

$$net\ annual\ savings = incremental\ benefits - incremental\ costs \tag{2.1}$$

Benefits from establishing a lockbox system can be expressed as follows

$$\begin{aligned} \textit{incremental benefits} = {} & \textit{accelerated cash receipts} \times \textit{rate of return}/100 \\ & \times (1 - \textit{profit tax}) \end{aligned} \tag{2.2}$$

The costs of a lockbox system can be expressed as follows

$$\textit{incremental costs} = \textit{annual costs} \times (1 - \textit{profit tax}) \tag{2.3}$$

Net annual savings from establishing a lockbox system can be reexpressed as follows

$$\begin{aligned} \textit{net annual savings} = {} & (\textit{accelerated cash receipts} \times \textit{rate of return}/100) \\ & \times (1 - \textit{profit tax}) - \textit{annual costs} \times (1 - \textit{profit tax}) \end{aligned} \tag{2.4}$$

Rearranging this equation we arrive at the expression

$$\begin{aligned} \textit{net annual savings} = {} & (\textit{accelerated cash receipts} \times \textit{rate of return}/100 \\ & - \textit{annual costs}) \times (1 - \textit{profit tax}) \end{aligned} \tag{2.5}$$

If the existing lockbox operation does not increase sufficient efficiency and reduce float, we should consider alternative lockbox arrangements.

Net annual savings from changing the lockbox system can be defined as follows

$$\textit{net annual savings} = \textit{incremental benefits} - \textit{incremental costs} \tag{2.6}$$

Benefits from changing the lockbox system can be expressed as follows

$$\begin{aligned} \textit{incremental benefits} = {} & [(\textit{accelerated cash receipts} - \textit{increased compensating} \\ & \textit{balance}) \times \textit{rate of return}/100] \times (1 - \textit{profit tax}) \end{aligned} \tag{2.7}$$

The costs from changing the lockbox system can be expressed as follows

$$\textit{incremental costs} = \textit{changes in annual costs} \times (1 - \textit{profit tax}) \tag{2.8}$$

Net annual savings from changing the lockbox system can be reexpressed as follows

$$\begin{aligned} \textit{net annual savings} = {} & [(\textit{accelerated cash receipts} - \textit{increased compensating} \\ & \textit{balances}) \times \text{rate of return}/100] \times (1 - \textit{profit tax}) \\ & - \textit{changes in annual costs} \times (1 - \textit{profit tax}) \end{aligned} \tag{2.9}$$

Rearranging this equation we arrive at the expression

$$\textit{net annual savings} = \begin{bmatrix} (\textit{accelerated cash receipts} \\ -\textit{increased compensating balance}) \\ \times\, \textit{rate of return}/100 \\ -\,\textit{changes in annual costs} \end{bmatrix} \times (1 - \textit{profit tax}) \tag{2.10}$$

It will be convenient to define variables that determine net savings from establishing or changing the lockbox system.

The independent variables that determine net savings are:

- Accelerated cash receipts
- Daily average collections
- Reduction in float time
- Compensating balance before establishing or changing the lockbox system
- Compensating balance after establishing or changing the lockbox system
- Annual costs before establishing or changing the lockbox system
- Annual costs after establishing or changing the lockbox system
- Rate of return
- Profit tax rate (Kontuš 2012).

This leads us to formulate the corresponding generalized model for calculating net savings from establishing or changing the lockbox system which includes all components for calculating net savings.

The relations between independent variables that determine net savings can be established as follows

$$\textit{net annual savings} = \begin{bmatrix} (\textit{accelerated cash receipts} \\ -\textit{changes in compensating balances}) \\ \times\, \textit{rate of return}/100 \\ -\quad \textit{changes in annual costs} \end{bmatrix} \times (1 - \textit{profit tax}) \tag{2.11}$$

whereby

$$\begin{aligned} \textit{changes in compensating balances} = {} & \textit{compensating balance after establishing or} \\ & \textit{changing the lockbox system} - \textit{compensating balance before} \\ & \textit{establishing or changing the lockbox system} \end{aligned}$$

$$\begin{aligned} \textit{changes in annual costs} = {} & \textit{annual costs after establishing or changing} \\ & \textit{the lockbox annualsystem} - \textit{costs before establishing} \\ & \textit{or changing the lockbox system} \end{aligned}$$

profit tax rate expressed as decimals

The compensating balance before establishing a lockbox system as well as annual costs before establishing a lockbox are equal to zero.

If we use checks as a payment medium, the accelerated cash receipts can be expressed as follows

$$accelerated\ cash\ receipts = daily\ average\ collection \times reduction\ in\ float\ time$$

We must ensure that this condition is met in our decision to establish or change the lockbox system:

$$net\ annual\ savings\ from\ establishing\ or\ changing\ the\ lockbox\ system > 0.$$

If the net annual savings are greater than zero, then the company should set up or change the lockbox system, because the incremental benefits from establishing or changing the lockbox system are greater than the incremental costs.

2.3.3.2 Delaying Cash Payments

A company can delay cash payments in order to improve its cash position and earn a greater return on its money. Before delaying cash payments, a profitability analysis should be made to determine the optimal time to pay back debt or to determine the expected date for a check to be cleared and payments of cash should be delayed only if net profitability occurs.

We have analyzed delaying cash payments, defined the independent variables that determine costs and benefits of delaying cash payments, and determined relationships between these variables in order to develop a model for calculating net savings. Finally, this model can help to ensure that delaying cash payments will result in net savings. In developing a new model for calculating net savings from delaying cash payments, we have used the basic analytical concept of comparing the incremental costs versus the incremental benefits.

The independent variables that determine net annual savings from delaying cash payments are:

- Delayed amount of cash to be paid (A_i)
- Annual rate of return
- The time of delayed payment of cash in days
- Profit tax rate.

The relation between the independent variables can be established as follows:

$$net\ annual\ savings = \left[\sum_{i=1}^{n} (delayed\ amount\ of\ cash\ (Ai) \times\ annual\ rate\ of\ return \times\ number\ of\ days)\,/36500\right] \times (1 - profit\ tax) \tag{2.12}$$

where

i - number of delayed payments
profit tax rate expressed as decimals.

This simple model predicts that cash payments should be delayed as long as there is no associated financial charge or impairment in credit rating and if net annual savings is greater than zero.

In the event of delaying cash payments if associated financial charge occurs, the annual net savings can be expressed as follows:

$$\textit{net annual savings} = \left[\sum_{i=1}^{n} \begin{array}{c} (\textit{delayed amount of cash } (Ai) \times \textit{ annual} \\ \textit{rate of return} \times \textit{ number of days}) \\ /36500 - \textit{financial charge} \end{array} \right] \times \times (1 - \textit{profit tax}) \tag{2.13}$$

where

i - number of delayed payments
profit tax rate expressed as decimals.

A financial manager may decide to delay cash payments even when an associated financial charge occurs only if net profitability occurs and must ensure that in his decision to delay cash payments this condition is met:

$$\textit{net annual savings from delaying cash payments} > 0.$$

Finally, new models for calculating net savings from establishing or changing a lockbox arrangement as well as delaying cash payments can help to ensure that setting up a lockbox arrangement and delaying cash payments will result in net savings and can help menagers in managing cash optimally. With these models a company can consider net profitability from performing these activities in order to improve its cash position and invest surplus cash as well as to improve profitability. In measuring the effectiveness of these important activities in the management of cash, we believe our findings are also interesting for business practice.

2.3.3.3 An Illustrative Example

These models for calculating net savings can be tested and used for business practice. In order to illustrate our approach and validate the results from the model for calculating net savings from establishing or changing a lockbox system, we offer the following example. We assume that we presently have a lockbox arrangement with bank A in which it handles 5 million EUR a day in return for 800,000 compensating balances.

We are thinking of cancelling this arrangement and further dividing our western region by entering into contracts with two other banks. Bank B will handle 3 million EUR a day in collection with a compensating balance of 700,000 EUR and bank C will handle 2 million EUR a day with a compensating balance of 600,000 EUR. Collections will be half a day quicker than the current situation and the rate of return is 12 percent. Profit tax rate is assumed to be 20 percent.

$$net\ annual\ savings = \begin{bmatrix} (accelerated\ cash\ receipts \\ -changes\ in\ compensating\ balances) \\ \times\ rate\ of\ return/100 \\ -\quad changes\ in\ annual\ costs \end{bmatrix} \times (1 - profit\ tax)$$

whereby

$$changes\ in\ compensating\ balances = compensating\ balance\ after\ establishing\ or\ changing\ the\ lockbox\ system - compensating\ balance\ before\ establishing\ or\ changing\ the\ lockbox\ system$$

$$changes\ in\ annual\ costs = annual\ costs\ after\ establishing\ or\ changing\ the\ lockbox\ system - annual\ costs\ before\ establishing\ or\ changing\ the\ lockbox\ system$$

accelerated cash receipts = *5000,000x0.5*
changes in compensating balances = *700,000* + *600,000–800,000*
changes in annual costs = *0.00*
net annual savings = *((5000,000x0.5 – (700,000* + *600,000–800,000)) x 12/100 – 0.00) x (1–0.2)*
net annual savings = *192,000 EUR*

By using the model for calculating net savings from establishing or changing the lockbox system, we calculate the net savings and find that the net savings is 192,000 EUR. New lockbox arrangement should be implemented as net profitability occurs.

2.3.4 Discussion

Our research shows that, by establishing or changing a lockbox system and delaying cash payments, a financial manager can improve the cash position of a company in order to invest surplus cash and achieve a maximum return at an acceptable level of risk.

New mathematical models have been introduced and the benefits that can be derived from these models include the following:

- The ability to explore more alternatives is given by using these equation models.
- Consideration and comparison of the net profitability arising from establishing and changing a lockbox system, as well as delaying cash payments, are easier, as the calculation of net profitability is simplified by using the given equation models.
- The models can help management to better understand the business and its functional relationships and may help to improve the ability to make decisions in managing cash. Better quality and faster decisions can be made.
- More effective planning and more accurate forecasts can be made.

We have found a positive correlation between the return on assets variable and the cash level, which indicates that an increase in the value of the return on assets triggers an increase in the cash level. The moderately strong positive correlation between return on assets and cash level for small and medium-sized companies supports the view that an increase in the value of the return on assets triggers an equivalent increase in cash level. However, the small and medium-sized companies examined here need to invest surplus cash in order to manage their cash optimally, improve profitability, and maximize rate of return.

We add that the correlations between cash level and the liquidity as measured by different liquidity ratios all have the predicted sign. We confirm that, during the observed period, the correlation between the cash level and liquidity for the surveyed companies is positive, and an increase in the cash level triggers an increase in liquidity as expressed in terms of liquidity ratios. Our results are also consistent with an existing theory of liquidity, as we observe a positive relationship between cash level and liquidity.

The study has provided empirical evidence of a negative relationship between companies' level of liquidity, as expressed in terms of the cash-to-current-liabilities ratio and the return on assets. The relation appears to be stronger for small and medium-sized companies than for large companies. We confirm that, during the observed period, the correlation between liquidity expressed in terms of the cash-to-current- liabilities ratio and the return on assets for the examined companies is negative and weak, and an increase in the cash-to-current-liabilities ratio triggers a decrease in profitability. Contrary to expectations, the results also show that liquidity, as expressed in terms of net working capital for large companies, is positively related to profitability expressed in terms of return on assets.

We can summarize that these findings support the notions that liquidity position depends on cash. The study has not in any case provided empirical evidence that liquidity is negatively related to profitability, but the findings support the notion that there exists a trade-off between the liquidity position and profitability.

Our findings have potentially important implications for managers and in the literature on cash management. They indicate that managers should aim to keep as close to the optimal cash balance as possible, and try to avoid any deviation, either positive or negative, in order to maximize the company's profitability.

2.4 Conclusion

This paper highlights the importance of efficient cash management for companies. This implies establishing an appropriate credit policy, along with a policy concerning collection, speeding up receipts of cash, and delaying payments of cash in order to improve the cash position, and to ensure adequate liquidity, as well as invest surplus cash and maximize the rate of return while also improving profitability.

The major findings are new equation models for calculating the net savings from establishing or changing a lockbox arrangement, as well as from delaying cash payments. The contribution of this paper is to model all the relationships between the independent variables that determine the net savings arising from establishing or changing a lockbox arrangement and delaying cash payments.

The new model for calculating the net savings arising from establishing or changing a lockbox arrangement, as well as delaying cash payments, can help to ensure that setting up a lockbox arrangement and delaying cash payments will result in net savings and may help managers to manage cash optimally. The equation models can be used as a tool to help minimize costs and to make the optimum use of the available cash in order to achieve a maximum return at an acceptable level of risk. By properly managing cash, financial managers can increase the rate of return and should attempt to accelerate cash receipts and delay cash payments as much as is feasible.

This study has provided empirical evidence of a positive relationship between cash level and companies' level of liquidity, which is consistent with the theory of liquidity. We also found that profitability expressed in terms of return on assets is positively related to cash level. The study has not in any case provided empirical evidence that liquidity is negatively related to profitability.

As a limitation of our study, it should be noted that the study is based on secondary data taken from the published annual reports of the selected companies. In Croatia, small and medium-sized companies can prepare an abridged financial statement which is, therefore, less elaborate and presents less detailed information than the financial statements of large companies. Some of the information required for this study is, therefore, unavailable for such companies. The study is also based on ratio analysis, which has its own limitations.

A new approach to the management of cash based on mathematical modeling motivates future research in the area of cash management, and it would be interesting to extend the lockbox and disbursement models in the future.

References

Almeida, H., Campello, M., & Weisbach, M. S. (2004). The cash flow sensitivity of cash. *The Journal of Finance, LIX*(4), 1777–1804.

Banos-Caballero, S., Garcia-Teruel, P. J., & Martinez-Solano, P. (2011). How does working capital management affect the profitability of Spanish SMEs. *Small Business Economics*. doi:10.1007/s11187-011-9317-8.

Bragg, S. M. (2012). *Corporate cash management*. Colorado: Accounting Tools.
Brigham, E., & Daves, P. (2004). *Intermediate financial management*. Ohio: Thomson South-Western.
Chambers, D., & Lacey, N. (2011). *Modern corporate finance*. Michigan: Hayden McNeil Publishing.
Dittmar, A., Mahrt-Smith, J., & Servaes, H. (2003). International corporate governance and corporate cash holdings. *Journal of Financial and Quantitative Analysis, 38*(1), 111–133.
Drobetz, W., & Gruninger, M. C. (2007). Corporate cash holdings: Evidence from Switzerland. *Financial Markets Portfolio, 21*, 293–324.
Duchin, R. (2010). Cash holdings and corporate diversification. *The Journal of Finance, 65*(3), 955–992.
Easterbrook, F. (1984). Two agency-cost explanations of dividends. *The American Economic Review, 74*, 650–659.
Ferreira, M. A., & Vilela, A. S. (2004). Why do firms hold cash? Evidence from EMU countries. *European Financial Management, 10*(2), 295–319.
Franklin, J. P., Jr., & Friedlob, G. T. (1995). *Understanding cash flow*. New York: Wiley.
Graham, J. R., Smart, S. B., & Megginson, W. L. (2010). *Corporate finance*. Ohio: South Western.
Guney, Y., Ozkan, A., & Ozkan, N. (2007). International evidence on the non-linear impact of leverage on corporate cash holdings. *Journal of Multinational Financial Management, 17*(1), 45–60.
Hardin, W. G., III, Highfield, M. I., Hill, M. D., & Kelly, G. W. (2009). The determinants of REIT cash holdings. *Journal of Real Estate Finance and Economics, 39*(1), 39–57.
Harford, J. (1999). Corporate cash reserves and acquisitions. *The Journal of Finance, 54*, 1969–1997.
Jensen, M. C. (1986). Agency cost of free cash flow, corporate finance and takeovers. *The American Economic Review, 76*, 323–329.
Khan, A., Kaleem, A., & Nazir, M. S. (2012). Impact of financial leverage on agency cost of free cash flow: Evidence from the manufacturing sector in Pakistan. *Journal of Basic and Applied Scientific research, 2*, 6694–6700.
Kontuš, E. (2012). Management of current assets. *International Journal of Sales, Retailing and Marketing, 1*(3), 125–132.
Kusnadi, Y., & Wei, J. (2011). The determinants of corporate cash management policies: Evidence from around the world. *Journal of Corporate Finance, 17*(3), 725–740.
Maness, T. S., & Zietlow, J. T. (2005). *Short-term financial management*. Ohio: Thomson South-Western.
Mckinney, J. B. (2015). *Effective financial management in public and non profit agencies* (Fourth ed.). Santa Barbara: Praeger.
Megginson, W.I., & Wei, Z., (2010). Determinants and value of cash holdings: Evidence from China's privatized firms. SSRN Working Paper Series, 1–37.
Mikkelson, W. H., & Partch, M. M. (2003). Do persistent large cash reserves hinder performance? *Journal of Financial and Quantitative Analysis, 38*, 275–294.
Myers, S. C. (1977). Determinants of corporate borrowing. *Journal of Financial Economics, 5*(2), 147–175.
Myers, S. C., & Majluf, N. S. (1984). Corporate financing and investment decisions when firms have information the investors do not have. *Journal of Financial Economics, 13*, 187–221.
Nguyen, P. (2005). How sensitive are Japanese firms to earnings risk? Evidence from cash holdings. 1–41.
Opler, T., Pinkowitz, I., Stulz, R., & Williamson, R. (1999). The determinants and implications of corporate cash holdings. *Journal of Financial Economics, 52*(1), 3–46.
Ramirez, A., & Tadesse, S. (2009). Corporate cash holdings, uncertainty avoidance, and the multinationality of firms. *International Business Review, 18*(4), 387–403.
Schwetzler, B., & Reimund, C. (2003). Valuation effects of corporate cash holdings: Evidence from Germany. HHL Working paper.

Tong, Z. (2011). Firm diversification and the value of corporate cash holdings. *Journal of Corporate Finance, 17*(3), 741–758.

Wang, G. Y. (2010). The impact of free cash flows and agency costs on firm performance. *Journal of Service Science and Management, 3*(4), 408–418.

Chapter 3
Governing Complex Strategic Networks: Emergence Versus Enabling Effects

Gabriella Levanti

Abstract In today's knowledge-based economy, the sources of competitive advantage increasingly lie in webs of relationships between a variety of firms and organizations that, over time, lead to the emergence of strategic networks. As the performances of both the network actors and the whole network are strictly linked with the coordination and governance of network actors and their activities, this study aims to shed light on the ways in which the processes of network coordination and governance take place.

Strategic networks are here viewed as complex adaptive systems, and the twin nature of the processes of strategic network coordination and governance is examined. On one hand, I underscore the emergent nature of network interactions stemming from the self-organizing behaviors that spontaneously arise inside the strategic network. On the other hand, I show that the leadership action of network-central firms sparks enabling effects that join the self-organizing network behaviors. The result of these two forces is the expansion of the network's interaction potential to permit both the network actors and the strategic network as a whole to reach level of performance that would not otherwise be accomplished.

Keywords Strategic network • Complex adaptive system • Emergence • Leadership

3.1 Introduction

In today's knowledge-based economy, the sources of competitive advantage increasingly lie in strategic networks (Powell et al. 1996; Gulati et al. 2000; Ahuja et al. 2012; Phelps et al. 2012). Strategic networks are complex webs of linkages spanning and connecting an array of firms and organizations within and across industries. Each network actor is endowed with idiosyncratic and specialized sets of resources, knowledge, and capabilities. Strategic networks serve as conduits through which

---

G. Levanti (✉)
Department of Economics, Management and Statistics, University of Palermo, Viale delle Scienze, Ed. 13, 90128, Palermo, Italy
e-mail: gabriella.levanti@unipa.it

G. Dominici et al. (eds.), *Governing Business Systems*, Springer Proceedings in Business and Economics, DOI 10.1007/978-3-319-66036-3_3

information, knowledge, ideas, and other resources that are owned and controlled by network actors flow, and over which reputations are signaled (Poldony 2001; Owen-Smith and Powell 2004). As a result, those network actors that are able to exploit the opportunities associated with the diffusion and sharing of information, knowledge, and other resources throughout the strategic network may promote innovation (Dagnino et al. 2015) and achieve above-average rent.

The way in which strategic networks coordinate their actors and activities in order to increase the outcome of the network as a whole and of the individual participating actors is an underexplored topic (Müller-Seitz 2012; Müller-Seitz and Sydow 2012). With the aim of furthering the comprehension of the forces underlying network interactions, in this study strategic networks are viewed as complex adaptive systems (Stacey 1995; McKelvey 1997; Anderson 1999), and the logic of complex systems is used to delve into the processes of network coordination and governance.

On one hand, viewing strategic networks as complex adaptive systems, I underscore the emergent nature of network interactions. The evolutionary dynamics of network interactions stem from the self-organizing behaviors that spontaneously arise inside the strategic network. On the other hand, complexity (Marion and Uhl-Bien 2001; Lichtenstein et al. 2006; Hazy 2006; Uhl-Bien et al. 2007) and new-genre leadership theories (Burns 1978; Bass 1985; Conger and Kanungo 1998; Bryman 1992) allow me to scrutinize the leadership role played by network-central firms. These central firms exert an enabling leadership that fosters and speeds the surfacing of conditions that facilitate and enhance the emergence of fruitful network interactions. The leadership action of network-central firms joins with the evolutionary dynamic of interactions between actors, which spontaneously emerges in complex strategic network. As a result, leadership action expands the network interaction potential and permits levels of network performance to be reached that might not have been attainable otherwise.

The remainder of this study is organized as follows: The second section briefly depicts the streams of literature I use to sketch the analytical framework, as well as the reasons and logical and theoretical bases on which their integration rests. The third section leverages the contributions of complexity theory in order to explain the forces underlying network interactions and the role of enabling leadership in affecting network interactions. In the fourth and closing section, I discuss some significant network-related leadership considerations that stem from the conceptual underpinnings I have laid down in the previous parts, and I point out some limitations of the study.

3.2 Theoretical Background

3.2.1 Strategic Network Approach

The strategic network approach (SNA) underscores the need to extend the boundaries of strategic investigation from the single firm to the network of relationships in which firms are embedded (Powell et al. 1996; Gulati 1999; McEvily and Zaheer 1999; Gulati et al. 2000), given that relevant value-generating capabilities are increasingly found on the network level, rather than on level of the individual firms.

Strategic networks are complex webs of ties spanning and interconnecting an array of firms and other organizations within and across industries. They potentially provide participating actors with access to valuable resources, capabilities, information, and knowledge which is not fully owned or controlled by the organizations themselves (Lavie 2006), as well as advantages from economies of learning, scale, and scope. The ability of an individual firm to benefit from network opportunities arises from the interaction of two elements: its network position and the structure of the network itself (Gulati et al. 2000; Zaheer and Bell 2005). These elements determine, on one hand, which firm will have access to and control over the so-called 'network resources' (Gulati 1999) that flow through the network. On the other hand, they identify which firms are able to signal in an appropriate way that they are reliable and valuable partners (Poldony 2001; Owen-Smith and Powell 2004).

Additionally, studies conducted following SNA have drawn attention to firms that display critical roles inside the strategic network, as these are in network-central positions.[1] An individual actor's network position epitomizes the prominence that the actor plays within the strategic network and is mainly associated with the size and relevance of the firms' resources, capabilities, and knowledge. In fact, as a firm's attractiveness as a valuable partner and relational ability to manage network links rest on its unique resources, capabilities, and knowledge, the establishment of network relationships reflects and requires ownership and control of adequate resources and knowledge sets (Dagnino et al. 2016; Nosella and Petroni 2007). The position of specific actors within a network can be measured by means of distinct centrality indices, which take into consideration the number of relationships in which the network actor is involved as recipient (in-degree centrality) or source (out-degree centrality) of ties, and the extent to which the actor connects other pairs of actors that have no other direct relations (betweenness centrality) (Wasserman and Faust 1994).

[1]These firms are termed in a variety of manners, such as hub firms (Jarrillo 1988; Davis and Eisenhardt 2011), focal firms (Nohria and Garcia-Pont 1991; Gulati 1999; McEvily and Zaheer 1999; Gulati et al. 2000; Zaheer and Bell 2005), key actors (Knoke 1994), triggering entities (Browning et al. 1995; Doz et al. 2000), strategic centers (Lorenzoni and Baden-Fuller 1995), network orchestrators (Hinterhuber 2002; Dhanaraj and Parkhe 2006), and so on.

It is interesting to note that SNA has the tendency not only to adopt a perspective that has a static essence (Ahuja et al. 2012), but also to focus primarily on network structure (rather than on network processes) and on its influence on firm behavior and performance (McEvily and Zaheer 1999; Ahuja 2000; Rowley et al. 2000; Gulati 2007). As a result, it pays little attention to the role that individual actors play in shaping local network structures and in affecting network evolutionary dynamics and performance (Rowley and Baum 2008). In addition, by focusing on the effects that social contexts have on the firm, studies conducted within the SNA do not buttress a real shift from the individual firm level to the network level of analysis (Dagnino et al. 2008). As a consequence, they fail to capture the emergent properties and dynamic aspects that characterize the strategic network as an entire whole, fully capable of performing distinctive collective behaviors by itself. In this respect, the SNA underestimates the social advantages provided by strategic networks.

In order to overcome the limitations associated with the static essence and the firm-centered perspective that characterize the SNA, I re-elaborate this body of literature through the interpretative lens provided by complexity theory. As a result, I sketch on one hand an analytic framework capable of moving beyond a static view of the strategic network and propose a more dynamic conception of strategic networks and of network-based sources of competitive advantage. On the other hand, I represent the strategic network as a distinct conceptual macrocategory that, by embracing and interconnecting a variety of idiosyncratic firms and organizations, originates a complex adaptive system—that is, a system typified by distinct emergent properties and original aggregate behaviors that pave the way for the creation of superior economic opportunities, for both the strategic network as a whole and for the individual actors embedded in it.

The adoption of the complexity perspective calls into consideration complexity leadership theory so as to analyze leadership phenomenon inside complex strategic networks, as this theory is basically concerned with leadership in and of complex adaptive systems (Uhl-Bien and Marion 2009). In addition, due to the pervasive and broad-spectrum nature of the complexity perspective, adopting it allows us to better qualify leadership in complex networks through the suggestions of new-genre leadership theory (Burns, 1978; Bass 1985; Conger and Kanungo 1998; Bryman 1992). The framework thus developed can then enlighten the role played by the leadership of central firms in complex strategic networks.

From a methodological vantage point, the possibility of integrating the above perspectives so as to gain a more adequate view of strategic networks and their dynamics rests on the consideration that neither of them is deterministic.[2] The potential for integration is further sustained by the common emphasis accorded to the interactions among a variety of actors. In the following three subsections, I briefly depict the major traits of complexity theory and of complexity and new-genre leadership theories.

[2]In detail, neither SNA, complexity theory or complexity and new-genre leadership theories outline necessary and sufficient conditions for explaining strategic networks in all their relevant aspects.

3.2.2 Complexity Theory

A complex adaptive system (CAS) is an organization made up of many heterogeneous actors that interact locally (without the imposition of an overall plan by a central authority), in such a way as to produce original and fruitful emergent system behaviors.

Conceptualizing and analyzing strategic networks in the light of complexity theory (Morin 1977; Prigogine and Stengers 1984; Stacey 1995; McKelvey 1997; Anderson 1999), the explanatory capabilities of the framework elaborated in this study take advantage of the following properties of a CAS:

- **Emergence**. Some patterns and properties of the strategic network result from the spontaneous interactions of the actors participating in it, rather than being influenced by intentional managerially coordinated or controlled behaviors. As a consequence, the network's behaviors are new and not logically inferable from the behaviors of individual network components (Morin 1977);
- **Self-organization**. A CAS exhibits self-organizing behaviors accomplishing an endogenous dynamic process, thanks to which it spontaneously becomes increasingly organized. Thus, natural order evolves as a result of self-organization (Lewin 1999);
- **Adaptation**. Network behaviors stem from the continuous dynamic interactions and the synthesis of the various adjustments of individual actors' schemata[3] to feedback about other network actors' behaviors and to environmental stimuli, as well as systemic processes that seek the coherence of the whole network with the external environment(Anderson 1999; Volberda and Lewin 2003);
- **Nonlinear dynamics**. The relatively independent network actors base their behaviors on perceptions which lead to nonproportional overreactions or underreactions. That is, a small variation in one or more parameters of a single network actor's schema can produce unexpected small, medium, or large changes in the schemata of other network actors (the so-called butterfly effect) (Lorenz 1963). As a result, aggregate network behaviors can be very different from the sum of the behaviors of the individual network components, and network behaviors may be inherently unpredictable over the long term, while nevertheless having a recognizable pattern or structure (Stacey 1995);
- **Path dependence**. The way a strategic network behaves depends on the interaction between the stimuli it receives and the structural elements that define its nature and state at a given moment in time and space. As sufficiently known, the structural state of the network is the product of the accumulation of knowledge and capabilities that have occurred in the past. It therefore synthesizes the past behaviors of the network itself. This means that historical contingencies play a

[3]A network actors' schema is "a cognitive structure that determines what action the agent takes at time t, given its perception of the environment (at time t, or at time t – k if theoretical considerations suggest applying a lag structure)" (Anderson 1999, p. 219).

role in influencing the state and behaviors of the network. As a consequence, a strategic network "can be quite sensitive to small differences in initial conditions, so that two entities with very similar initial states can follow radically divergent paths over time" (Anderson 1999, p. 217).

In summary, complexity theory adopts a logic that is at the same time holistic and multilevel (Dominici and Levanti 2011). It entails simultaneously considering the network as a whole and the different complex subsystems of which it is composed (McKelvey 1997), as the order of each network level is considered an emergent property that depends on how lower-level behaviors are aggregated. As a result, the application of complexity theory to strategic networks draws attention to the synergies and the emerging properties that stem from interactions among heterogeneous actors.

3.2.3 Complexity Leadership Theory

Applying the concepts of complexity theory to the study of leadership has resulted in what is referred to as complexity leadership theory (Marion and Uhl-Bien 2001; Lichtenstein et al. 2006; Hazy 2006; Uhl-Bien et al. 2007). This is a theory that studies the relevant characteristics of leadership in a CAS. It begins from the consideration that "leadership is not merely the influential act of an individual or individuals but rather is embedded in a complex interplay of numerous interacting forces" (Uhl-Bien et al. 2007, p. 302); leadership is rather an emergent phenomenon that arises from interactions, tensions, and adjustments in perceptions and understanding taking place among the actors of the CAS (Lichtenstein et al. 2006).

Unlike traditional leadership approaches, which are largely deterministic and reductionist,[4] complexity leadership theory suggests a framework in which, on one hand, the leader *enables* rather than controls worthwhile future outcomes, and leaders' power rests in their ability to *allow* rather than to direct. On the other hand, as leadership emerges in the interactive space between people and ideas (Lichtenstein et al. 2006), it is a system phenomenon and its emergent properties cannot be locally inferred from the analysis of individual behaviors.

Effective complex leadership recognizes the importance of, and learns to capitalize on, complex dynamic attributes—such as interactions, correlation, and unpredictability among and within system actors and aggregates. It involves the creation of conditions that allow, foster, and accelerate intrasystemic interactions

[4]"Reductionism refers to research logic in which parts of a system are isolated and studied independently of the system from which they derive - the general idea is that, if one can understand the parts, one can draw conclusions about the whole. Determinism is the belief that all events are caused by preceding events and by knowing the preceding variables one can predict the future with certainty" (Marion and Uhl-Bien 2001, pp. 391).

and so it increases the likelihood of productive (though essentially unspecified) future outcomes and states emerging. Complex system interaction provides mechanisms by which conflicting constraints among the system actors can be addressed and changed in order to facilitate correlation—that is, the emergence of a common or shared understanding in the interacting system. Correlation leads to a degree of dynamic stability that entails a level of predictability on which leadership can operate, as it is possible to identify recognizable patterns in firms' behaviors.

In addition, complex leaders enable emergence by becoming catalysts for actions and functioning as "tags" (Holland 1995). Tags support or speed up specific behaviors and processes by directing attention to what is important and providing meaning to unfolding events. Accordingly, they permit or accelerate behaviors and processes that could plausibly happen without the tag (or catalyst), but which would take more time to do so, as well as behaviors and processes that might not have been accomplished otherwise. A leader becomes a tag when others recognize her as a symbolic reference for their system vision.

Finally, complex leadership drops seeds of emergence (Marion and Uhl-Bien 2001), encouraging novelty and destabilizing the system by disrupting existing patterns and behaviors (Plowman et al. 2007). In so doing, it injects tensions and perturbations into the CAS, pushing the system to the edge of chaos and creating opportunities for the development of adaptive, creative, and learning capacities (Regine and Lewin 2000).

It is noteworthy that, as complexity leadership theory focuses on leadership *in* and *of* a CAS (Uhl-Bien and Marion 2009), rather than on leaders, and conceptualizes leadership as an emergent and systemic phenomenon, it depersonalizes leadership processes. These processes occur in a variety of organizations that are described as CASs, including firms and bureaucratic organizations[5] (Regine and Lewin 2000; Uhl-Bien et al. 2007; Plowman et al. 2007; Uhl-Bien and Marion 2009); open source systems (O'Mahony and Ferraro 2007); network structures (Marion and Uhl-Bien 2003; Ritter et al. 2004); and so on. Consequently, in this study, viewing strategic networks as CASs allows us to use the findings of complexity leadership theory in order to scrutinize leadership phenomena occurring within complex strategic networks.

Thanks to its pervasive and broad-spectrum nature, complexity leadership theory provides an integrative theoretical framework for encompassing and connecting the interactive dynamics that have been recognized by a variety of leadership

[5]More in detail, complex leadership in a bureaucratic organization entails three interconnected functions: (a) *administrative* leadership refers to the actions of individuals and groups in formal managerial roles who plan and coordinate firm activities; (b) *adaptive* leadership is a generative dynamic that produces adaptive emergent change behaviors in a CAS; and, (c) *enabling* leadership catalyzes adaptive dynamics and supports the management of the interconnection between formal administrative subsystems and structures and informal adaptive subsystems and structures by nurturing enabling conditions and facilitating the dissemination and integration of innovative outcomes of adaptive leadership into the formal managerial subsystem (Uhl-Bien et al. 2007; Uhl-Bien and Marion 2009).

representations, such as new-genre leadership (Burns 1978; Bass 1985; Conger 1989; Conger and Kanungo 1998; Bryman 1992), shared (Pearce and Conger 2003), collective (Weick and Roberts 1993), and distributed (Gibb 1969; Brown and Gioia 2002; Gronn 2002) leadership, and considerations about followership and its impact on leadership (Howell and Shamir 2007). In particular, the complexity perspective does not replace other leadership studies; rather, it expands them (Lichtenstein et al. 2006; Uhl-Bien and Marion 2009). As Regine and Lewin (2000: 19) underscore "it's not about throwing away everything we know and do as leaders, but rather augmenting and encompassing different skills and placing those skills in a wider context of a new understanding of business".

Accordingly, in order to deeply qualify the ways through which network leadership can concretely take place, following the suggestions of the main scholars of complexity leadership theory (Marion and Uhl-Bien 2001; Uhl-Bien and Marion 2009), I make use of the suggestions of new-genre leadership theory. In more detail, new-genre leadership theory will help us to determine which characteristics of network strategic vision are able to attract and spur on incumbent and potential network actors.

3.2.4 New-Genre Leadership Theory

An interesting area of inquiry in leadership research focuses on leadership style and emphasizes symbolic leader behavior, visionary and inspirational messages, intellectual stimulation, and displays of confidence in followers (Burns 1978; Bass 1985; Conger 1989; Conger and Kanungo 1998; Bryman 1992). This area is referred to as charismatic or transformational leadership[6] (or new-genre leadership) and suggests that a leader using such a style provides a credible and persuasive strategic vision of the firms' future in order to influence followers. In so doing, he or she motivates subordinates to work for collective goals by going beyond simple transactions and base expectations and spurring followers to transcend their self-interest for the sake of the firm (Bass 1985; Conger and Kanungo 1998).

It is interesting to note that, in new-genre leadership theory, leadership is no longer simply described as an individual characteristic or difference, but is rather

[6]In essence, the formulation of charismatic and transformational leadership theories are highly complementary both portraying the leaders' strategic vision as playing a central role in motivating and empowering followers. Accordingly, it is a common practice in many studies to treat these two theories simultaneously and to term them new-genre leadership theories (Bryman 1992). Actually, they study the same phenomenon from different vantage points. Roughly, the *charismatic studies* have primarily seen leadership from the standpoint of perceived leader behavior (Weber 1947; Conger and Kanungo 1987, 1998), whereas the *transformational studies* have concerned themselves mainly with follower outcomes (Burn 1978; Bass 1985; Tichy and Devanna 1990). For further detail about similarities and differences between charismatic and transformational leadership see: Yukl (1999).

depicted as relational (Yukl 1999). Beginning from Weber's conceptualization of charismatic authority (Weber 1947), the results of studies maintain that leadership relationships find their legitimacy in the recognition of the leaders' role by the followers. As a result, leadership per se is not found solely in the leader and her individual attributes and behaviors, but is rather established in the interplay between the leaders' qualities and behaviors and her followers' perception, attributes, and goals (Conger and Kanungo 1998). Followers take an active role in leadership, as they truly become "followers" only when their values and goals are congruent with those of the leader. In summary, leadership involves a leader and a group of followers, and motivation and coordination through an articulated innovative *strategic vision* are the primary vehicles of leadership. The relationship between a leader and her followers is by nature interactive, as the leader wields power over the followers; however, the followers also have power over the leader (Takala 2005).

New-genre leadership studies are usually conceptualized at the dyadic level. Their primary interest is to explain leaders' direct influence over the individual followers, whilst the processes underlying leaders' influence over groups and organizations do not receive enough attention (Yukl 1999). Lately, an increasing number of scholars have pointed out the need to draw attention to the analysis of leadership processes at higher ontological levels (such as the group level, the organizational level, and the interorganizational level), on account of the critical role displayed by these processes in today's competitive environment. Accordingly, in this study I extend the notions provided by new-genre leadership theory so as to scrutinize the effectiveness of the leadership processes that take place on the interorganizational level of strategic networks. This extension is found in the relational and interactive nature of the leader–follower relationship which permits leadership to be depersonalized, switching the focus from the leader to leadership.

3.3 The Processes of Coordination and Governance in Complex Strategic Networks

Viewing a strategic network as a CAS means that the evolutionary dynamics of network interaction stems from the self-organizing behaviors that spontaneously arise inside the complex network. The self-organization and adaptation properties characterizing CAS behaviors drive the dynamics of the establishment, maintenance, transformation, and breakdown of network links and interactions, in order to support the survival and development of the complex strategic network over time. That is to say, complex networks are governed by the *metaguidance principle of network survival and development*.

The self-organizing and emergent nature of network dynamics turns network evolution into a relatively unplanned and spontaneous process, rather than something imposed by the overall plan of a central authority (Kauffman 1993; McKelvey 1999; Chiles et al. 2004). In detail, network scholars have found that the continuous process of complex network link association is not random (Axelrod and Cohen 2000), but it is guided by a combination of different logics, such as the tendency towards cumulative advantage, the inclination towards multiconnectivity, the preference for diversity, the propensity for homophily, and the inclination to follow trends (Powell et al. 2005; Kauffman 1993; McKelvey 1999; Chiles et al. 2004). Among these logics, the tendency towards cumulative advantage takes a relevant, and frequently prevailing, role. The phenomenon of cumulative advantage (that the "rich get richer") implies that the number of connections an actor obtains increases with the amount the actor already has[7] (Simon 1955, 1957; de Solla Price 1965). As complex strategic networks evolve, new links thus become preferentially attached to actors with a high number of prior connections (de Solla Price 1965; Barabási and Albert 1999). Accordingly, these actors have a higher probability to attract new actors and links.

The functioning of the cumulative advantage phenomenon is closely connected with the ability of high actor connectivity to signal the value of the actor as a partner. The attractiveness as a critical partner and the relational ability to manage network relationships rest on the firms' unique resources, knowledge, and capabilities. Thus, the establishment of network links requires and reflects ownership and control of adequate resources and knowledge sets (Dagnino et al. 2016; Nosella and Petroni 2007). As a result, a firm's degree of connectivity epitomizes its network position and identifies the prominence of the actor in the complex strategic network.

Thanks to the cumulative advantage mechanism, the process of network evolution is characterized by the rise of disparities and differences in the process of individual actor linking development and by the emergence of key roles played by central firms (the strongly connected nodes). Accordingly, numerous complex strategic networks display a core-periphery structure (Borgatti and Everett 1999; Holme 2005), typified by:

(i) one or more central firms—that is, network actors characterized by a high degree of connectivity and significant resources, knowledge, and capabilities that, at a given moment in time and space, are critical in the environment in which the strategic network operates. These nodes act as enabling leaders within the complex network; and
(ii) peripheral firms—that is, network actors characterized by a low degree of connectivity and few resources, knowledge, and capabilities that, at a given moment in time and space, are critical in the environment in which the strategic network operates. These nodes act as followers within the complex network.

In particular, network-central firms operate as network-enabling leaders since, on the basis of the resources and knowledge they possess, they have the ability

[7] Originally developed by Simon (1955, 1957), the "rich get richer" idea is referred to as the *Matthew effect* in sociology and as *cumulative advantage* by de Solla Price (1965), who applied it to network systems. Today, it is usually known under the label *preferential attachment*, coined by Barabási and Albert (1999).

and the power to affect the quality and quantity of the connections and interactions that arise in the complex strategic network. It is worth noting that, as affirmed by complexity leadership theory (Marion and Uhl-Bien 2001; Lichtenstein et al. 2006; Hazy 2006; Uhl-Bien et al. 2007), the role of network enabling leadership does not replace the evolutionary dynamics of actor interactions that spontaneously emerges in the complex strategic network—rather, it "grafts onto" these self-organizing and spontaneous dynamics with amplifying effects. As a result, leadership action expands the network interaction potential and permits high levels of strategic network performance that might otherwise be unobtainable to be reached.

Specifically, network leadership action is exerted through limited local actions that aim to directly activate interactions with other network actors, but above all through undirected actions striving to foster and speed up the emergence of conditions (such as an atmosphere of trust and commitment) and coordinating mechanisms (such as the network strategic vision and the network identity) that increase the odds that original and fruitful network interactions will surface. These conditions and mechanisms do not direct network evolution: rather, they allow network actors to spontaneously cocreate the path that will be taken in order to ensure the survival and development of the network over time (Keene 2000).

The primary vehicles of enabling leadership are *motivation* and *coordination* of network actors by means of an articulated and innovative *network strategic vision* that in broad terms delineates the (idealized) manner in which the leader sees the entire strategic network's future and provides simple rules and a "navigation system" for the network organization as a whole (Keene 2000). In order to attract potential network actors and spur on productive behaviors, the network's strategic vision is frequently discrepant with the status quo and the well-established strategies of the knowledge and technological domains in which the network operates (Dow 1969; Conger and Kanungo 1987). In addition, the network vision needs to be credible, a factor mainly associated with: (a) a realistic perception of future environmental evolution and a convincing assessment of opportunities and constraints associated with this evolution; (b) effective communication of the vision; and sometimes (c) the appropriate preparation of the "ground" in which the vision will be sown and waiting for the proper time, place, and the availability of resources, knowledge, and competencies (Conger and Kanungo 1987; Conger 1990).

A credible and persuasive network strategic vision directs network actors' attention to what is important and provides meaning to unfolding events. In so doing, network leadership becomes a catalyst for actions and fosters interfirm motivation to be involved in open-ended network cooperation. Specifically, follower actors are stimulated to openly share their valuable knowledge, on one hand, and to accomplish the network-specific investments needed in order to effectively and efficiently operate within the strategic network, on the other hand (Gulati 2007; Soda and Zaheer 2009). As a result, network leadership enables and accelerates the emergence of spontaneous interaction processes among network actors that could plausibly occur without the leaderships' catalyst action, but that would take more time to do so, as well as processes that might not have been accomplished otherwise.

At the same time, the surfacing of a common and shared understanding in the complex network due to the strategic vision plays a critical role in facilitating network correlation (or resonance). Network correlation enhances followers' awareness and acceptance of the metaguidance principle of network survival and development over time and spurs followers to transcend their self-interest for the sake of the network as a whole. In so doing, network order emerges from the interaction around constraints resulting in compromise and reconciliation among the different (and sometimes conflicting) network actors' goals and motivations (Uhl-Bien et al. 2007). In addition, it paves the way towards the formation of a strong shared network identity that engenders a sense of belonging, fosters mutual commitment, and curtails the risks of opportunistic behaviors (Dyer and Nobeoka 2000; Dyer and Hatch 2006) through the emergence of depersonalized trust among the network members (Ashforth and Mael 1996). In other terms, the shared identity allows the other actors to be perceived as reliable on the basis of their membership of the network independently of previous direct interactions (Sammarra and Biggiero 2001).

Finally, enabling leadership can inject tensions and perturbations into the network that push the strategic network to the edge of chaos and generate opportunities for the development of creative and learning capacities (Regine and Lewin 2000), leading network firms to activate adaptive and proactive behaviors (Lichtenstein et al. 2006; Uhl-Bien et al. 2007). Nevertheless, it is remarkable that central firms are usually deeply entrenched in the knowledge and technology platforms which, at a given moment in time and point in space, are dominant in the network competitive environment, as well as in the specific product and process technologies on which network competitive strategies are based. As a result, they exhibit the tendency to exploit the established key strategic sets of resources, knowledge, and capabilities (Levitt and March 1988; Levinthal and March 1993). The pressure to conform to the dominant knowledge platforms and technologies may limit their ability to explore more novel ideas and possibilities (Schilling 2005). Additionally, due to their adherence to previously successful strategies, central firms are likely to experience a drop in their economic and intrinsic motivation to experiment with new solutions and options. This state of affairs may cause temporarily central firms to experiences difficulty (or even inability) in sensing the emergence of opportunities or threats connected to changes in the external environment and in reacting to the changes perceived—especially when the changes entail radical and knowledge-competence destroying innovation effects (Gatignon et al. 2002).

As result, stimuli for change in the network status quo may arise in time due to the action of actors with peripheral or semiperipheral network positions, or those that are external (Cattani and Ferriani 2008; Uzzi and Spiro 2005). These less entrenched firms may sense the emergence of new valuable opportunities associated with network interactions and may activate in order to exploit these opportunities. This situation may over time rebalance the power distribution inside a complex strategic network (Davis and Eisenhardt 2011; Lichtenstein et al. 2006; Schreiber and Carley 2006).

3.4 Conclusion

In the previous section, I have illustrated how the enabling effects stemming from the leadership of network-central firms joins with the self-organizing behaviors that spontaneously arise inside a complex strategic network. The coupled effect of these two forces results in the expansion of network interaction potential and permits both the network actors and the strategic network as a whole to reach a high level of performance.

In conclusion, I underscore a few implications of the present study for both strategic network studies and practice, as well as a few limitations. Viewing strategic networks as CASs allows me to emphasize the dynamic and collective nature of these organizations. Their dynamic and collective nature means that behaviors and phenomena (i.e., network leadership) emerging in the complex strategic network are new and original in comparison with the behaviors that occur on the lower levels of the system. It is thus not appropriate to infer them through an additive and reductionist logic. The former consideration results in conceptual implications for strategic network studies. By adopting the complexity perspective, these studies have the opportunity to enhance their comprehension of network dynamics thanks to a real shift from the individual firm to the network level of analysis. Indeed, this perspective underlies a logic that is at the same time holistic and reductionist (Anderson 1999; Dominici and Levanti 2011), pushing scholars to avoid ignoring or compressing complexity, but rather to harness it (Axelrod and Cohen 2000), in order to fully appreciate the network organization, its evolutionary dynamics, and its effects upon network actors.

In addition, the study has managerial underpinnings, as it provides managers of network firms (independently of the specific position of their firm at a given space–time moment) with a framework that elucidates how operating inside a strategic network results in the emergence of interactions among the behaviors and goals of all the network actors. As a result, it becomes critical to consider these interactions in the process of individual firms' strategy definition and to focus on the issue of strategic intentionality and deliberation versus spontaneity and emergence in informing the evolutionary dynamics of complex strategic networks, as well as in structuring and managing the network link portfolio.

As regards the limitations of the present study, a question that inevitably arises in conceptual exploratory research such as ours is that of the overall explicative power of issues originating from the analytical scrutiny of strategic networks. In this regard, I contend that the use of a well-balanced blend of quantitative and qualitative empirical analysis instruments and methodologies could allow us to support the arguments I have suggested in this study. Specifically, I contend that a considerable support for and extension of the explicative power of this study could involve the longitudinal scrutiny of evolutionary dynamics of network structure and network actor positions and roles in existing (fully structured) complex strategic networks, as well as in networks in the embryonic stage.

References

Ahuja, G. (2000). Collaboration networks, structural holes and innovation: A longitudinal study. *Administrative Science Quarterly, 45*, 425–455.

Ahuja, G., Soda, G., & Zaheer, A. (2012). The genesis and dynamics of organizational networks. *Organization Science, 23*, 434–448.

Anderson, P. (1999). Complexity theory and organization science. *Organization Science, 10*(3), 216–232.

Ashforth, B. E., & Mael, F. A. (1996). Organization identity and the strategy as a context for the individual. In B. M. Staw & L. L. Cummings (Eds.), *Research in organizational behavior* (Vol. 13, pp. 17–62). Greenwich: Jai Press.

Axelrod, R., & Cohen, M. D. (2000). *Harnessing complexity. Organizational implications of a scientific frontier*. New York: Basic Books.

Barabási, A. L., & Albert, R. (1999). Emergence of scaling in random networks. *Science, 286*, 509–512.

Bass, B. M. (1985). *Leadership and performance beyond expectations*. New York: Free Press.

Borgatti, S. P., & Everett, M. G. (1999). Models of core/periphery structure. *Social Networks, 21*, 375–395.

Brown, M. E., & Gioia, D. A. (2002). Making things click. Distributive leadership in an online division of an offline organization. *The Leadership Quarterly, 13*, 397–419.

Browning, L. D., Beyer, J. M., & Shelter, J. C. (1995). Building cooperation in a competitive industry: SEMANTECH and the semiconductor industry. *Academy of Management Journal, 38*, 113–151.

Bryman, A. (1992). *Charisma and leadership in organizations*. London/Newbury Park: Sage.

Burns, J. M. (1978). *Leadership*. New York: Harper & Row.

Cattani, G., & Ferriani, S. (2008). A core/periphery perspective on individual creative performance: Social networks and cinematic achievements in the Hollywood film industry. *Organization Science, 19*(6), 824–844.

Chiles, T. H., Meyer, A. D., & Hench, T. J. (2004). Organizational emergence: The origin and transformation of Branson, Missouri's musical theatres. *Organization Science, 15*(5), 499–519.

Conger, J. A. (1989). *The charismatic leader: Beyond the mystique of exceptional leadership*. San Francisco: Jossey-Bass.

Conger, J. A. (1990). The dark side of leadership. *Organizational Dynamics, 19*(2), 44–55.

Conger, J. A., & Kanungo, R. N. (1987). Toward a behavioral theory of charismatic leadership in organizational settings. *Academy of Management Review, 12*(4), 637–647.

Conger, J. A., & Kanungo, R. N. (1998). *Charismatic leadership in organizations*. Thousand Oaks: Sage.

Dagnino, G. B., Levanti, G., & Mocciaro Li Destri, A. (2008). Evolutionary dynamics of interfirm networks: A complex system perspective. In J. A. C. Baum & T. J. Rowley (Eds.), *Network Strategy: Advances in Strategic Management, 25* (pp. 67–129). Oxford: JAI/Elsevier.

Dagnino, G. B., Levanti, G., Minà, A., & Picone, P. M. (2015). Interorganizational network and innovation: A bibliometric study and proposed research agenda. *The Journal of Business & Industrial Marketing, 30*(3/4), 354–377.

Dagnino, G. B., Levanti, G., & Mocciaro Li Destri, A. (2016). Structural dynamics and intentional governance in strategic interorganizational network evolution: A multilevel approach. *Organization Studies, 37*(3), 349–373.

Davis, J. P., & Eisenhardt, K. M. (2011). Rotating leadership and collaborative innovation: Recombination processes in symbiotic relationships. *Administrative Science Quarterly, 59*(2), 159–201.

de Solla Price, D. J. (1965). Network of scientific papers. *Science, 149*, 510–515.

Dhanaraj, C., & Parkhe, A. (2006). Orchestrating innovation networks. *Academy of Management Review, 31*(3), 659–669.

Dominici, G., & Levanti, G. (2011). The complex system theory for the analysis of interfirm networks: A literature overview and theoretic framework. *International Business Research, 4*(2), 31–37. doi:10.5539/ibr.v4n2p31.

Dow, T. E., Jr. (1969). The theory of charisma. *Sociological Quarterly, 10*, 306–318.

Doz, Y. L., Olk, P. M., & Ring, P. S. (2000). Formation processes of R&D consortia: Which path to take? Where does it lead? *Strategic Management Journal, 21*, 239–266.

Dyer, J. H., & Hatch, N. W. (2006). Relation-specific capabilities and barriers to knowledge transfers: Creating advantage through network relationships. *Strategic Management Journal, 27*, 701–719.

Dyer, J. H., & Nobeoka, K. (2000). Creating and managing a high-performance knowledge-sharing network: The Toyota case. *Strategic Management Journal, 21*, 345–367.

Gatignon, H., Tushman, M. L., Smith, W., & Anderson, P. (2002). A structural approach to assessing innovation: Construct development of innovation locus, types, and characteristics. *Management Science, 48*(9), 1103–1122.

Gibb, C. A. (1969). Leadership. In G. Lindzey & E. Aronson (Eds.), *Handbooks of social psychology* (pp. 205–282). Reading: Addison-Wesley.

Gronn, P. (2002). Distributed leadership as a unit of analysis. *The Leadership Quarterly, 13*, 423–451.

Gulati, R. (1999). Network location and learning: The influence of network resources and firm capabilities on alliance formation. *Strategic Management Journal, 20*(5), 397–420.

Gulati, R. (2007). *Managing network resources. Alliances, affiliations, and other relational assets.* Oxford: Oxford University Press.

Gulati, R., Nohria, N., & Zaheer, A. (2000). Strategic networks. *Strategic Management Journal, 21*(Special Issue), 203–215.

Hazy, J. K. (2006). Measuring leadership effectiveness in complex socio-technical systems. *Emergence: Complexity and Organization, 8*(3), 58–77.

Hinterhuber, A. (2002). Value chain orchestration in action and the case of the global agrochemical industry. *Long Range Planning, 35*, 615–635.

Holland, J. H. (1995). *Hidden order*. Reading: Addison-Wesley Publishing.

Holme, P. (2005). *Core-periphery organization of complex networks.* arXiv: physics/0506035v1 [physics.soc-ph] 6 Jun 2005.

Howell, J. M., & Shamir, B. (2007). The role of followers in the charismatic leadership process: Relationship and their consequences. *Academy of Management Review, 30*(1), 96–112.

Jarrillo, C. J. (1988). On strategic networks. *Strategic Management Journal, 9*, 31–41.

Kauffman, S. A. (1993). *The origins of order: Self-organization and selection in evolution.* New York: Oxford University Press.

Keene, A. (2000). Complexity theory: The changing role of leadership. *Industrial and Commercial Training, 32*(1), 15–18.

Knoke, D. (1994). Networks of elite structure and decision making. In S. Wasserman & J. Galaskiewicz (Eds.), *Advances in social network analysis* (pp. 274–294). Thousand Oaks: Sage.

Lavie, D. (2006). The competitive advantage of interconnected firms: An extension of the resource-based view. *Academy of Management Review, 31*(3), 638–658.

Levinthal, D. A., & March, J. G. (1993). The myopia of learning. *Strategic Management Journal, 14*, 95–112.

Levitt, B., & March, J. G. (1988). Organizational learning. *Annual Review of Sociology, 14*, 319–340.

Lewin, A. (1999). *Complexity: Life at the edge of chaos* (2nd ed.). Chicago: University of Chicago Press.

Lichtenstein, B. B., Uhl-Bien, M., Marion, R., Seers, A., Orton, J. D., & Schreiber, C. (2006). Complexity leadership theory: An interpretative perspective on leading in complex adaptive systems. *Emergence: Complexity and Organization, 8*(4), 2–12.

Lorenz, E. N. (1963). Deterministic nonperiodic flow. *Journal of the Atmospheric Sciences, 20*(2), 130–141. doi:10.1175/1520-0469(1963)020<0130:DNF>2.0.CO.

Lorenzoni, G., & Baden-Fuller, C. (1995). Creating a strategic center to manage a web of partners. *California Management Review, 37*(3), 146–163.

Marion, R., & Uhl-Bien, M. (2001). Leadership in complex organization. *The Leadership Quarterly, 12*, 389–418.

Marion, R., & Uhl-Bien, M. (2003). Complexity theory and al-Qaeda: Examining complex leadership. *Emergence, 5*(1), 54–76.

McEvily, B., & Zaheer, A. (1999). Bridging ties: A source of interfirm heterogeneity in competitive capabilities. *Strategic Management Journal, 20*(12), 1133–1156.

McKelvey, B. (1997). Quasi-natural organization science. *Organization Science, 8*(4), 352–380.

McKelvey, B. (1999). Avoiding complexity catastrophe in coevolutionary pockets: Strategies for rugged landscapes. *Organization Science, 10*(3), 294–321.

Morin, E. (1977). *La méthode I. La nature de la nature*. Paris: Editions du Seuil.

Müller-Seitz, G. (2012). Leadership in interorganizational networks: A literature review and suggestion for future research. *International Journal of Management Reviews, 14*, 428–443.

Müller-Seitz, G., & Sydow, J. (2012). Maneuvering between networks to lead – A longitudinal case study in the semiconductor industry. *Long Range Planning, 45*, 105–135.

Nohria, N., & Garcia-Pont, C. (1991). Global strategic linkages and industry structure. *Strategic Management Journal, 12*, 105–124.

Nosella, A., & Petroni, G. (2007). Multiple network leadership as a strategic asset: The Carlo Gavazzi space case. *Long Range Planning, 40*, 178–201.

O'Mahony, S., & Ferraro, F. (2007). The emergence of governance in an open source community. *Academy of Management Journal, 50*(5), 1079–1106.

Owen-Smith, J., & Powell, W. W. (2004). Knowledge networks as channels and conduits: The effects of spillover in the Boston biotechnology community. *Organization Science, 15*(1), 5–21.

Pearce, C. L., & Conger, J. A. (2003). *Shared leadership: Reframing the how and why of leadership*. Thousand Oaks: Sage.

Phelps, C., Heidl, R., & Wadhwa, A. (2012). Knowledge, networks, and knowledge networks: A review and research agenda. *Journal of Management, 38*(4), 1115–1166.

Plowman, D. A., Solansky, S., Beck, T. E., Baker, L., Kulkarni, M., & Travis, D. V. (2007). The role of leadership in emergent, self-organization. *The Leadership Quarterly, 18*(4), 341–356. doi:10.1016/j.leaqua.2007.04.004.

Poldony, J. M. (2001). Networks as pipes and prisms of the market. *American Journal of Sociology, 107*(1), 33–60.

Powell, W. W., Koput, K. W., & Smith-Doerr, L. (1996). Interorganizational collaboration and the locus of innovation: Networks of learning in biotechnology. *Administrative Science Quarterly, 41*, 116–145.

Powell, W. W., White, D. R., Koput, K. W., & Owen-Smith, J. (2005). Network dynamics and field evolution: The growth of international collaboration in the life sciences. *The American Journal of Sociology, 110*(4), 1132–1205.

Prigogine, I., & Stengers, I. (1984). *Order out of chaos: Man's new dialogue with nature*. Boulder: New Science Library.

Regine, B., & Lewin, R. (2000). Leading at the edge: How leaders influence complex systems. *Emergence, 2*(2), 5–23.

Ritter, T., Wilkinson, I. F., & Johnston, W. J. (2004). Managing in complex business networks. *Industrial Marketing Management, 33*, 175–183.

Rowley, T. J., & Baum, J. A. C. (2008). Introduction: Evolving webs in networks economics. In J. A. C. Baum & T. J. Rowley (Eds.), *Network strategy: Advances in strategic management* (Vol. 25, pp. xiii–xxxii). Oxford: JAI/Elsevier.

Rowley, T. J., Behrens, D., & Krackhardt, D. (2000). Redundant governance structures: An analysis of structural and relational embeddedness in the steel and semiconductor industries. *Strategic Management Journal, 21*, 369–386.

Sammarra, A., & Biggiero, L. (2001). Identity and identification in industrial districts. *Journal of Management and Governance, 5*, 61–82.

Schilling, M. A. (2005). A "small world" network model of cognitive insight. *Creativity Research Journal, 17*(2–3), 131–154.
Schreiber, C., & Carley, K. M. (2006). Leadership style as an enabler of organizational complex functioning. *Emergence: Complexity and Organization, 8*(4), 61–76.
Simon, H. A. (1955). On a class of skew distribution functions. *Biometrika, 42*, 425–440.
Simon, H. A. (1957). *Models of man*. New York: Wiley.
Soda, G., & Zaheer, A. (2009). Network evolution: The origins of structural holes. *Administrative Science Quarterly, 54*(1), 1–31.
Stacey, R. D. (1995). The science of complexity: An alternative perspective for strategic change processes. *Strategic Management Journal, 16*, 477–495.
Takala, T. (2005). Charismatic leadership and power. *Problems and Perspectives in Management, 3*, 45–57.
Tichy, N. M., & Devanna, M. A. (1990). *The transformational leader* (2nd ed.). New York: Wiley.
Uhl-Bien, M., & Marion, R. (2009). Complexity leadership in bureaucratic forms of organizing: A meso model. *The Leadership Quarterly, 20*(4), 631–650. doi:10.1016/j.leaqua.2009.04.007.
Uhl-Bien, M., Marion, R., & McKelvey, B. (2007). Complexity leadership theory: Shifting leadership from the industrial age to the knowledge era. *The Leadership Quarterly, 18*, 298–318. doi:10.1016/j.leaqua.2007.04.002.
Uzzi, B., & Spiro, J. (2005). Collaboration and creativity: The small world problem. *American Journal of Sociology, 111*(2), 447–504.
Volberda, H. W., & Lewin, A. Y. (2003). Co-evolutionary dynamics within and between firms: From evolution to co-evolution. *Journal of Management Studies, 40*(8), 2111–2136.
Wasserman, S., & Faust, K. (1994). *Social network analysis: Methods and applications*. New York: Cambridge University Press.
Weber, M. (1947). *The theory of social and economic organization* (Trans. A. M. Henderson & T. Parsons). New York: Oxford University Press.
Weick, K. E., & Roberts, K. (1993). Collective mind in organizations: Heedful interrelating on flight decks. *Administrative Science Quarterly, 38*, 357–381.
Yukl, G. (1999). An evaluation of conceptual weakness in transformational and charismatic leadership theories. *Leadership Quarterly, 10*(2), 285–305.
Zaheer, A., & Bell, G. G. (2005). Benefiting from network position: Firm capabilities, structural holes, and performance. *Strategic Management Journal, 26*, 809–825.

Chapter 4
Challenges of the Priority Sectors of Entrepreneurship in Georgia

Leila Kadagishvili

Abstract In the program documents adopted in the economic and social fields in Georgia in recent years, special attention is paid to the further development of the real sector of entrepreneurship. The manufacturing industry, agriculture, and tourism are the priorities. Development of these fields is a precondition for growth in the economy in general, and in gross domestic product and national income in particular. These sectors ensure the creation of new jobs, guarantee employment, and increase in the middle class in the country. Unemployment and poverty remain serious problems in Georgia. The current situation in the above priority fields of entrepreneurship is examined here on the basis of academic literature, reports, and statistical data provided by governmental and nongovernmental organizations, as well as by national and international organizations. Measures for improving the situation are suggested, strengths and weaknesses of the reforms of recent years are revealed, and the importance of entrepreneurship in the development of the economy is demonstrated. In the concluding part of the paper, recommendations are made based on the conclusions.

Keywords Entrepreneurship • Economic reform • Manufacturing • Agriculture • Tourism

4.1 Introduction

The concept of entrepreneurship was introduced to the academic literature by classical economists in the late eighteenth and early nineteenth centuries. There are a number of definitions of this concept, but from our point of view, the shortest and most comprehensive one is that provided by the American scholars Robert Hisrich and Michael Peters (Hisrich and Peters 1994). They consider entrepreneurship to be the process of creating something new of value by devoting the necessary time and effort, assuming the accompanying financial, mental, and social risks, and receiving

L. Kadagishvili (✉)
Ivane Javakhishvili Tbilisi State University, 17 Pekini Street, Tbilisi, Georgia 0160,
e-mail: leila.kadagishvili@tsu.ge

G. Dominici et al. (eds.), *Governing Business Systems*, Springer Proceedings in Business and Economics, DOI 10.1007/978-3-319-66036-3_4

the resulting monetary rewards, as well as those of personal satisfaction and independence. The entrepreneur, who operates the business and fully or partly owns its material assets, undertakes a risky activity and makes independent decisions about what, how, how much, and for whom to produce. The reward of the entrepreneur is the profit he or she received from these entrepreneurial activities, as well as the sense of satisfaction. According to the Georgian Entrepreneurs Law of October 28, 1994, which regulates the legal forms of entrepreneurial activity, *entrepreneurial activity shall be a legitimate and repeated activity carried out independently and in an organized manner to gain profit.* The concept of legitimacy implies the right of a citizen to perform all the activities not prohibited by the law at his or her own risk and expense. Thus, entrepreneurship is a special form of economic activity based on innovative and independent approaches to the production and delivery of goods to the market, which is profitable for entrepreneurs and which in addition helps him or her to realize himself or herself as a person. Along with the benefits the entrepreneur obtains, he or she also acts for the benefit of society (deliberately or otherwise); the development of entrepreneurship should thus always be supported.

Based on the Entrepreneurs Law and other legal and normative acts, several organizational and legal forms of entrepreneurial activities have gradually developed in Georgia. These are individual entrepreneur, general partnerships (GPs), limited partnerships (LPs), limited liability companies (LLCs), joint-stock companies, and cooperatives. "By creating these forms of entrepreneurship, a new type of entrepreneurship has actually developed in Georgia and prepared the basis for the formation of a mixed economy, which is characteristic of a market system" (Asatiani 2015). Yet the first few years based on the principles of the market economy proved especially difficult in post-Communist Georgia. The transition from a planned economy to a market economy was accompanied by social and political changes. Due to these changes, processes of development in the country became unpredictable. The collapse of the Soviet Union, followed by political disorder, ethnic conflicts, and irresponsible governance caused chaos and anarchy in the country. Unlike other post-Communist countries, the economic recovery and the introduction of social protection systems began from a very low level, and could not reach pre-crisis level, in spite of rapid progress (Social Protection and Social Inclusion in Georgia). With the help of the international community and the reforms carried out in the country over the following years, the situation gradually stabilized and entrepreneurial activities began to slowly increased.

4.2 Economic Reforms in Georgia

The period of transition to the market economy was characterized by a variety of reforms in Georgia. However, the social and economic outcomes of these reforms cannot be considered satisfactory. Some researchers believe that the process of transition to the market economy has finished, although, it is clear that the market economy in Georgia is unfortunately still far from western standards, and in particular from those of Europe (Papava et al. 2015). The reforms of the transition period in Georgia, unlike those in Poland, the Czech Republic, Slovakia, and the Baltic countries, were stalled and the expenditure of hundreds of millions of dollars of western aid proved fruitless (Kvaratskhelia 2013). Exit from the transition period—or even reaching the level of social and economic development of the previous noncrisis period in the Soviet Union in 1989 — proved impossible. Despite local economic successes at different times and to different extents, Georgia could not exceed the indicators of Communist period in any social field (Jibuti 2013). From independence till to the present day, three stages of economic reforms in Georgia can be identified: the beginning stage (1991–1994), which failed due to a lack of experience and knowledge, and many other negative factors; a comparatively more favorable political, economic, and legal environment was created for the development of business in the second stage of economic reforms (1995–2002), though this period was also characterized by some failures and slow-downs. In the third stage of reform (2003–2012), which involved some pseudo-reforms, significant economic advancement occurred, but this was accompanied by serious violations of property and human rights (Meskhia 2015). Although the economic reforms had serious drawbacks, one thing is indisputable: "Georgia, as a former Soviet republic and a transition economy country, has made substantial progress in strengthening economic and political freedom and reducing crime and corruption. Systemic changes have been implemented to eliminate corruption, reduce bureaucracy, improve the qualifications of public officers, and support economic growth" (Millennium Development Objectives in Georgia: National Report 2014).

As a result of the 2012 parliamentary elections, a new government came to power in Georgia. In 2014, the government approved a social-economic development strategy for the period until 2020. This is the first strategic document in the country to outline the basic goals of the country's economic development and approaches for ensuring sustainable economic development. The goal of economic development strategy is to improve the living standards of a considerable part of the population by achieving inclusive or comprehensive economic growth. The preconditions for the free development of the private sector have been determined in accordance with the guidelines of the economic development strategy of the country—in particular, effective and transparent governance and noninterference in business (Social and economic development strategy of Georgia). The key principle of the economic development strategy is that Georgia should become a country based on traditional and European values. One of the priorities of the government strategy needed to achieve inclusive economic growth is the improvement of business environment, which will contribute to the full realization of the country's economic potential and social and economic development. The introduction of an effective system to promote the development of entrepreneurship will contribute to overcoming a number of problems (weak innovation potential, low competitiveness, high unemployment, lack of new jobs, low standard of living) that the country is facing.

4.3 Entrepreneurship in the Real Sector

An increasing trend in the activity of the Georgian manufacturing sector has been seen in recent years. This is quite important for the country. In 2014, 553,359 enterprises were registered in Georgia, which is 18% more than the corresponding figure in 2012. In 2014, the turnover of the industrial sector amounted to 50,064.7 million GEL, which is 19% higher than the same indicator in 2012. In addition, the total value of the goods produced by the enterprises exceeded 26,068.8 million GEL, which is 12% higher than the corresponding figure in 2012. It is also worth noticing that the number employed in the industrial sector in 2014 was higher by 57.7 thousand people than in 2012 (10% growth was observed, with 592.1 thousand people employed in all) (http://www.geostat.ge/). Despite some achievements, the scale of poverty and low living standards remain serious problems. However, practical realization of the government's decisions related to improving the environment for entrepreneurship in the last 4 years should ensure the development of a private entrepreneurship sector and an improvement in living standards among the population.

Small and medium enterprises play a special role in creating jobs and in contributing to the economic development of the country. As is widely known, large businesses are involved with introducing up-to-date machinery and technologies, which in turn reduces jobs. On the other hand, small and medium enterprises create jobs and contribute to employment, which is particularly crucial for Georgia at present, as unemployment is one of the most pressing problems for the country (Kadagishvili 2016a). Small and medium enterprises represent a large share of all operating enterprises in developed countries (including European countries), accounting for over 50% of the total turnover of the manufacturing sector and creating two of every three jobs in the private sector. Over 99% of companies located in Organization for Economic Cooperation and Development (OECD) member countries are small or medium enterprises, and create two-thirds of the gross domestic product (GDP) of the country on average. Small and medium enterprises account for over 90% of all businesses in developing and transition economy countries, though their contribution to GDP is quite low—less than 20% in many cases (SME development strategy of Georgia 2016–2020).

With the support of the government and international organizations, as well as the entrepreneurial skills of the population of Georgia, small and medium business are operating despite impediments, and have begun to develop in the country—mainly in service industries, such as trade, hospitality, restaurants and catering, domestic services, transportation, and communication. According to official data on 2014, the total turnover of small and medium enterprises operating in Georgia amounted to 9038.6 million GEL, which is 26% higher than the corresponding figure for 2012. In addition, the overall output of products exceeded 5166.8 million GEL in value, also 26% higher than in 2012. Over the reporting period, the number of people employed in small and medium enterprises increased by 30.3 thousand (a 13% increase compared to 2012; 259.4 thousand people employed in all). Large part of small businesses operate in trade and repairing services, as these are the fields where starting a new business is relatively easy; such companies don't require large investments or highly skilled labor. In 2014, large business was the leader (82.6%) in the inflow of direct foreign investment in Georgia, followed by small business at 10.7% and medium-sized business at 6.7%. In 2014, small and medium business accounted for 18% of the total business sector turnover, 19.8% of overall output of products, and 43.8% of the people employed in the manufacturing sector (http://www.geostat.ge/). It can be said that the development of small and medium business in Georgia is gaining strength and it is expected that the recent reforms implemented by the government in this direction will result in some positive outcomes.

Economic development of the country is impossible without the development of its real sector, and particularly the manufacturing sector. In 2014, the turnover of the manufacturing sector exceeded 9 billion GEL, which is 16% higher than the corresponding figure from 2012. In addition, the production value of the manufacturing sector amounted to 8201.5 million GEL, which is 12% higher than in 2012. According to the data on this period, the number of people employed in the manufacturing industry increased by 1725 (the rate increased by 1.1; thus, total number of employees was 116,568); 114,843 people were employed in 2012. The number of the people employed in this sector accounted for 19.6% of all the people employed in any business. The dynamism of this sector is driven mainly by the processing industry, which accounted for 80% of industrial production (6611.7 million GEL) — 18% higher than the corresponding figure from 2012. The increase in the processing industry over 2012 was mainly determined by the increase in food and tobacco production (by 27%) and the increase in the production of metallurgical and metal wares (by 6%), caused by growth in both domestic and foreign demand for ferroalloys, metal wares, and food products. Ferroalloys hold the second position (at 10%) in the export commodity structure of Georgia; significant growth was also observed in the export of juices and canned fruits and vegetables.

The production and distribution of electricity, gas, and water accounted for 14.4% of industrial production (1058.7 million GEL), which is 8.9% higher than the corresponding figure from 2012. The growth in this sector was determined by a 14% increase in electricity production (http://www.geostat.ge/). Georgia is one of the richest countries in hydroelectric energy resources in the region and in the whole world, and the richest of the former Soviet countries. By increasing hydropower production, the country can become a major exporter to Turkey.

The mining industry accounted for 4.9% (402.2 million GEL) of the total industrial production—10% higher than in 2012. The growth in this sector was driven by the increase in the production of crude oil and natural gas by 24%, and of metal ore extraction by 22%, caused by the growth of both domestic and foreign demand for crude oil and metal ore. Copper ores and concentrates were at the top of the list of Georgian exports in 2015 (at 12.3% of the country's total export).

In 2014, food, beverage, and tobacco production accounted for the largest share (48%) of the processing industry in Georgia; these sectors were followed by metallurgy and the production of steel wares (17%), nonmetallic mineral products

(12%), and chemical production (8%). The impact of industries such as textile and shoe manufacturing is minimal. The production of textile and textile products, leather, leather products, and footwear amounted to 117 million GEL (1.6%) (http://www.geostat.ge/). Light industry played an important role in the economy of Georgia in the 1980s and accounted for 20.2% of the total manufacturing production. Georgia was famous for the production of silk (49.2 million meters of length in 1980), cotton (60.1 million meters of length), and wool (5.17 million meters of length) (Soviet Georgian Encyclopedia 1991). Nowadays, production of these has ceased. Georgia has particularly favorable conditions for the development of light industry. There is good experience and the potential for the production of cocoon, wool, and leather materials in the country.

It is worth noting that there is a great potential of unused natural resources in the Georgian manufacturing sector, including forests, which constitute a truly important resource. Forests provide a variety of valuable products and raw materials (wood, bark, branches, blackberry leaves, firs, pinecone, sweetbrier, sallow thorn, nettle, licorice, cyclamen bulbs, mushrooms, etc.). Almost all the forests (97.7%) in Georgia are located on mountain slopes. The total area of forests is 2005.6 thousand hectares, and the timber stock is 451,700,120 cubic meters, and 30–40% of the stock is available for recycling (Natural resources of Georgia and protecting environment, statistical publication 2014). There is both domestic and foreign demand for industrial timber. Before Georgia regained its independence, forestry accounted for 4–5% of the country's gross domestic product, as parts of the wood processing industry (69%), cellulose and paper production (17%), and the production of raw forest materials (14%). According to official statistics, the current share of forestry in the gross domestic product of Georgia is quite low compared to the preindependence period, amounting to only 0.90% in 2012. In addition, much has changed in the forestry revenue structure, which is basically represented by timber raw materials and primary production products (90–95%), which should be assessed negatively from the point of view of industrial development (Kandelaki 2015). For Georgia, it is important to develop the domestic processing of timber and to produce end products.

Along with timber production, the production and processing of nontimber forest materials is also possible: 20–22 tons of high-quality fir seeds are annually exported to western European countries and to the USA to grow Christmas trees. One kilogram of Caucasian fir seeds is exported for 35–40 US dollars. "Production and processing of nontimber forest materials has the potential to become one of the most important niche export sectors in Georgia. The European Union represents the largest market for such products, which increases by 8–10% annually and amounts to 50 billion Euros if measured in monetary terms. Despite the growing international demand for this kind of products and the huge potential Georgia has in this direction, this sector is completely underdeveloped and requires special attention to be paid, as it may become a significant source of income for people living in rural areas of the country. In addition, exporting of this product will be a significant source of foreign currency inflow for the country and will contribute to increasing the employment rate and improving social conditions" (The non-timber forest products of Georgian forest development Forum 2015). Development of this sector will also significantly contribute to the promotion of the reputation of Georgia as a producer of ecologically friendly and high-value products. "Based on the proper management of nontimber resources, forestry can play a decisive role in the development of a green economy, create additional jobs, particularly in rural areas, and significantly contribute to the reduction of poverty. For sustainable management of forests and the introduction of the principles of the green economy, first of all, improvement in the legal framework and attraction of foreign investment is needed. However, this does not imply merciless destruction of forests, leaving further generations without any forest resources and promoting ecological disasters" (Kandelaki 2015).

Georgia is one of the richest countries in the world in terms of water resources. There are many rivers, lakes, swamps, glaciers and underground watercourses in the country. Fresh drinking water is one of the most expensive and scarce raw materials in our times. According to the United Nations (The Millennium Development Goals Report 2008; Tvalchrelidze et al. 2011), approximately 2.8 billion people lack good-quality drinking water. Due to the gradual exhaustion of the drinking water supply, Europe is beginning to face this very pressing problem. By 2025, shortages of drinking water will spread throughout whole Europe and will be especially crucial in southern Europe and the Mediterranean region in general (Lalzad 2007). The stock of underground drinking water known so far in Georgia is 573 m^3/s. The maximum amount that can be legally extracted is 301 m^3/s (26 trillion liters per day). Such resource provides an opportunity to provide 17.5 billion liters of the total world demand for fresh drinking water, taking into consideration bottling and transportation capacities and the daily amount of water required physiologically per person, without posing any danger to the bioeconomic environment of the resource. The large and rich European market has opened for Georgia after conclusion of the Association Agreement with the European Union. As mentioned above, the European market also faces the shortage of mineral resources. Georgia is located centrally to a number of countries facing acute drinking water shortages, and the demand for water is steadily increasing. Georgia has good opportunities to become a leading producer and exporter of high-quality industrial water on the global market.

Mineral water can be used in the production of medicines and beauty products, such as soaps, shampoos, gels, unguents, perfumes, etc. Most such products available in Georgia have been imported. It is acknowledged that the mineral composition of Borjomi mineral water is similar to that of French Vichy mineral water, which is used in the production of expensive world-famous beauty products. By implementing of research, Georgia has good opportunities for developing production in this sector (Gagnidze 2015).

Georgia has significant resources of raw materials for the development of mining and metallurgical industries. Among these raw materials, manganese remains its importance. The manganese ores in Chiatura are worth mentioning (a reserve of 176 billion tonnes). In Georgia, there are also ores of rare metals and elements (copper, gold, silver, barium, arsenic, lead, zinc, sulfur, clay (ascanite and gumbrini), andesite, calcite, antimony) of world importance. These ores will contribute to the development of nonferrous metallurgy and chemical production. In addition, auxiliary raw materials, such as dolomite, limestone, and others needed for metallurgical production are available in the country (Okrostsvaridze 2014).

Georgia has significant source of raw materials for the production of construction materials. Raw materials, such as like inert and paving materials, natural stone blocks, limestone (for cement production), quartz sand, refractory clay, diatomite, and agate are available in Georgia. There is a perlite ore in Paravani, too (Natural resources of Georgia and protecting environment, statistical publication 2014), which has a wide range of uses, including in the food industry, the production of building materials, and other fields. The export demand for these minerals is also high. Paving stones from Georgia are distinguished by high quality and production values; the largest deposits are in Kursebi (Teschenitic), Bolnisi (Tuff), Moliti, Sadakhlo and Salieti (marble and marble limestone). Significant amounts of gypsum, plaster, ceramic clays, chalk, and other construction materials are found in Georgia. As can be seen, Georgia is rich in deposits of construction materials with unique qualities, but these are presently not being properly exploited. Construction materials of poor quality are imported in large quantities from Iran, China, and Turkey, while luxury construction materials are imported from Germany and Spain. Only construction blocks and cement are produced in Georgia. However, large quantities of cement are also imported from Heidelberg in German. Despite the excellent physical and mechanical properties of Georgian paving stones, such stones are mainly imported from Iran. It is necessary to restore the production of construction materials in Georgia, but this will be possible only by changing the deposit licensing policy and through supportive measures from the state.

Analysis shows that the country has significant reserves of natural resources that could be used to develop the Georgian industrial sector. The elimination of poverty and increases in the living standards of the population will be impossible unless the country uses its natural resources. The most important natural resources in Georgia for promoting industrial development are underground mineral waters, forests, fuel and energy resources, and metals and rare metals—the last of which are used in jewelry manufacturing, in metallurgy, and as inert and construction materials, and so on. Industrial development will promote economic growth, increase employment, and improve social conditions for the population.

The agricultural sector in Georgia has very old and rich traditions. From the point of view of its agricultural properties, Georgia is a country of global importance, having an extremely long history of cultivating both wheat and grapevines. Grapevines are considered a very important part of Georgian culture, which is evident in Georgian Christianity: Georgians used to make the symbol of the cross from vine stems, and grapevines were seen as a symbol of faith. Georgia played a role in the beginnings of agricultural civilization, and agriculture was not the only an economic activity for the ancient Georgians, a determining factor in their way of life and mentality (Tvalchrelidze et al. 2011).

The population of Georgia is 3.720 million (2016) and the country covers a territory of 69,700 square kilometers. It is located at the crossroads of Europe and Asia, in the south-west Caucasus. The Caucasus mountains divide the region into two parts: a southern part, called Transcaucasia, a northern part. Georgia is situated in the western part of Transcaucasia. A variety of relief creates specific microclimates in the country. Due to the natural barriers of the country—such as the Caucasus mountains and the Black Sea—almost every type of subtropical climate zone is found in Georgia. Soil accounts for almost half of the country's natural wealth (Natural resources of Georgia and protecting environment, statistical publication 2014). About 43.3% of total area of the country (over 3 million hectares) is considered useful for agricultural activities, including pastures and meadows. Thirteen percent of the total area is in the form of plains, 33% is covered by foothills, and the remaining 54% is covered by mountains. Due to this diversity and the fact that Georgia is bordered by the Black Sea, the country has is a wide range of ecological and climate zones. This creates favorable conditions for growing agricultural crops characteristic of temperate and subtropical zones, including grains, early and late vegetables and greens, potatoes, grapes, subtropical crops, and a wide variety of fruit. Livestock and poultry production is quite widespread in towns and villages, and surrounding areas of about 1,800,000 hectares are allocated to pastures and hayfields (Agricultural development strategy of Georgia 2012).

During Soviet times, the Georgian agricultural sector "successfully" managed to find its niche, as the climate conditions of the country were drastically different from the 14 other Soviet republics. Accordingly, the agricultural sector developing in Georgia in those times had no competitors (Khaduri 2012). Georgia was a supplier of subtropical crops, fruits, vegetables, and other food products to the former Soviet republics. "Georgia has favorable climatic and natural conditions conducive to the development of agriculture. However, within the past decades, Georgian agriculture and food production has been lagging well behind other sectors of the economy" (Agricultural development strategy of Georgia 2015). During the last two decades, the agriculture sector was the Cinderella of development assistance; however, this was not only due to the lack of any defined state policy or strategy for the sector. The Government abandoned the sector (not to be confused with a *laissez-faire* approach), paying only lip service to its strategic priority for the economy. This approach was accompanied by a continuing decline in agricultural production, expressed as the decline in the sown area of arable lands and the reduction in production of primary agriculture products (The European Union's Neighborhood Program 2012). However, providing food and ensuring the economic security of the country and the social importance of agriculture, while taking into account the high level of dependence on natural conditions and other external factors, leads to the need for the active involvement of the government in this sector (Shaburishvili 2012). As a result of government efforts and cooperation with the private sector and donor organizations, some positive trends were observed in 2013–2014—in particular, growth in production, expansion of export markets, and the attraction of investment to agricultural sector. In the 2013 state budget, 227.4 million GEL was allocated for agriculture (2.8% of the budget); in 2014, the allocation increased to 263.5 million GEL (2.9%) in 2015, the corresponding figure was 292.9 million GEL (3.1%). Most of this amount (82.5%) was spent on agricultural and rural development programs, followed by food security and plant protection (9%) and the development of viticulture and wine-making (7.9%). In 2014, the turnover of agricultural production exceeded 249.1 million GEL, which is 26% higher than the corresponding figures for 2012. In addition, agricultural output exceeded 3583.2 million GEL, which is 18% higher than in 2012. Goods to the value of 4.5 million GEL were produced as a result of the processing of agricultural products in 2014. The total output of the agribusiness sector was 10% higher than in 2013. This was mainly determined by the growth of the processing sector (13.8% growth). In the reporting period, the number employed in the agricultural sector grew by 2855 people (a 135% increase) over 2012. The average monthly salary of those employed in agricultural sector amounted to 500 GEL, which was 18% higher than the corresponding figure for 2012. In 2014, foreign direct investment in agriculture significantly increased over previous years. Foreign direct investment to the tune of 19.1 million USD was made in agriculture in 2014. This amount exceeds by 61% the corresponding figure of the previous year. The production of grapes, walnuts, nuts, milk, eggs and meat increased in 2014 compared to 2012, though production of wheat, potato, citrus, and tea reduced. In 2014, agriculture accounted for a small share of the GDP (9.2%), but was nonetheless 0.6% higher than in 2012 (http://www.geostat.ge/; Ministry of Agriculture of Georgia, Annual Report 2014).

In 2014, the export of agricultural products increased by 6.7% over 2012. According to the 2014 data, agricultural products worth 825.9 million USD were exported from Georgia. The export of agricultural products in that year accounted for 29% of the total exports of the country. The main exported products were nuts (22%), wine (22%), mineral and still waters (17%), other alcoholic drinks (12%), cattle (4%), and carbonated soft drinks (3%). In the same period, imports of agricultural products increased by 1.1%. According to data for the same year, agricultural products worth 1.3 billion USD were imported into Georgia. The trade deficit amounted to 4.741 million USD and 57% of the total trade turnover. Imports of agricultural products account for 15.2% of total imports to the country. The main imported goods are wheat (12%), tobacco (9%), and poultry (6%), as well as sugar, alcohol drinks, vegetable oil, fish, and others. In 2014, the trade deficit reduced by 7.3% compared with the 2013 value and by 37% compared with the 2012 value (Ministry of Agriculture of Georgia, Annual Report 2014). Analysis shows that the food products market in Georgia is saturated with imported products. In Georgia, there are favorable conditions for growing many of the agricultural products that are imported in high quantities. However, due to high production costs, locally produced Georgian products cannot compete with imported goods.

Food security implies availability and physical and economic access to vital food products, as well as production of such products in sufficient quantities. Physical accessibility depends on the existence of the product in sufficient quantity and quality. Economic accessibility means that individuals should have enough income to satisfy their minimum demands for food (Tchitanava 2015). According to studies by Oxfam, residents of Georgia spend more than half their income (54%) on food, while people in developed countries spend between 10% and 15%. Most food consumed in Georgia is imported, which worsens the situation with the ongoing currency crisis and depreciation of Lari. Daily consumption of bread and bakery products among the residents of Georgia is 1.8–2.0 times higher than the generally recommended amounts. Most Georgian traditional cuisine consists of starch products, and due to low purchasing power, Georgian people mainly consume bread and other related products. Therefore, 62% of calories consumed in Georgia come from bread and similar products, while in developed countries this indicator does not exceed 15% (Food Security as Concept for Policy Planning 2015). The Oxfam report also indicates that, in mountainous regions of Georgia, not only are there problems of physical access to food, but economic access is also limited as well, on account of poverty. Forty-three percent of inhabitants of mountainous areas surveyed fear that food may become unaffordable to them, due to their lack of material and other resources; 49% cannot afford a variety of the food and microelements necessary for health; 25% are forced to eat less food than they want; while 13% confirmed that they often suffer from hunger due to a lack of financial or other resources.

Food security faces serious risks in Georgia. According to the UN resolution, the food security of a country is endangered if over 20% of the food consumed is imported. The amount imported in Georgia is 70–80% (Shaburishvili 2012; Tchitanava 2015). Reduction of this risk requires the creation of a business environment that will promote the development of agriculture, growth of the production of high-quality goods, and will ensure food security. Georgia can not only satisfy the demand of its own residents for food products, but should also be able to become an exporter of agricultural products. The country has great potential to achieve this goal (Kadagishvili and Seturidze 2016). The geographical and geopolitical location of the country, when considered in the light of the Deep and Comprehensive Free Trade Agreement (DCFTA) signed with the European Union and the agreement signed with the European Free Trade Association (EFTA), provides a good opportunity for Georgia to deepen its trade relations with European countries and to encourage enterprises to enter European markets.

There is great potential for the development of small and medium enterprises in the tourism sector. From the point of tourism, Georgia is a unique country. The rich natural and cultural resources of Georgia are also present in a wide variety. There are over 12,000 historical and cultural monuments in the country, four of which are included in the UNESCO World Heritage List. The country has well-developed mountain, sea, and spa resorts. The Caucasus Mountains are very important part of the tourism potential of Georgia. In addition, Georgia is the home of over 2000 mineral water springs, 1300 caves suitable for speleology (Krubera cave, the world's deepest cave, is located in Abkhazia, Georgia and has a depth of 2190 m), 26,060 rivers with a total length of 58,957 km, 860 lakes, 688 glaciers (which are not evenly distributed throughout the country, most being located in the basins of four rivers: the Kodori, Inguri, Rioni, and Tergi), waterfalls, 87 different categories of protected areas—including 14 national reserves, 41 natural monuments, 11 national parks, 19 wilderness areas, and 2 protected landscapes (Natural resources of Georgia and protecting environment, statistical publication 2014). Georgia offers its visitors outstanding cuisine and wine, live music and traditional dances. All this creates opportunities for the development of all types of tourism in Georgia.

The role of tourism in the social and economic development of Georgia is gradually increasing. Tourism is recognized by the state as one of the priority sectors, and due to policies implemented in recent years, the dynamics of tourism development has fundamentally changed. The growth rate of international arrivals in Georgia during the last 5 years has been much higher than the world average. Statistical data show that 5,515,559 visitors arrived in the country in 2014—24% higher than the number in 2012. In 2015, the number of visitors continued to grow and amounted to 5,897,685 people. Both local and international tourism play significant roles in the economy of Georgia. In 2014, most international visitors (4,863,165 or 88% of total international arrivals) were from neighboring countries, with only 652,394 (12%) coming from other countries. Turkey is the leader, with 1,442,695 visitors to Georgia. Azerbaijan had the highest increase in the number of people arriving in Georgia. In 2014, the number of visitors from European countries amounted to 232,558 people. European visitors thus account for 4% of the total number of visitors, with an 11% increase compared with the previous year. The spending of foreign visitors has significant impact on the balance of payments. About 59% of the service export revenues come from tourism sector. International tourism receipts have been steadily increasing. In 2015, tourism receipts from foreign visitors were 1.79 billion USD, while the international tourism spending of Georgian residents amounted to 0.30 billion USD. As a result, the balance of foreign tourism in Georgia totaled 1.49 billion USD (4% growth). The number of tourism-related jobs reached 195,100 in the fourth quarter of 2014. Most of these jobs are in the transportation sector (60%) and in hotels and restaurants (13%). In 2014, the contribution of tourism to total employment was 11%. Tourism accounts for 6% of GDP, more than in 2012. The World Travel and Tourism Council report, 2016 puts Georgia in the seventeenth in terms of the direct contribution of tourism to GDP and in the 25th place for the total contribution among 184 countries. Three point 3% of total investments in Georgia are made in travel and tourism industries. There are 1000 accommodation units in Georgia, consisting of 35,000 beds. As the average demand for beds exceeds the current supply, these numbers are not satisfactory. Tbilisi and Adjara regions have the leading positions in the accommodation industry in Georgia. Hotels account 63% of beds, followed by family hotels and guesthouses (16% for each). As there has been an increasing trend in the number of visitors in recent years, optimistic forecasts may be made in respect to the need for the construction of new hotels. A few international hotels chains are already operating in Georgia, including Radisson Blue Iveria, Tbilisi Marriott, Courtyard Marriot, Sheraton Metekhi Palace, Holiday Inn, Citadines, and others.

Air transport infrastructure is crucially important for the development of tourism in the country. There are three international (Tbilisi, Batumi, and Kutaisi) and three local (Mestia, Natakhtari, and Telavi) airports in Georgia. Due to the increase in tourist flows to Georgia, the number of passengers using Georgian international airports has also increased. In 2014, Georgian airports served to 2,008,171 passengers, which is 9.51% (174,364 passengers) higher than in 2013. The number of passengers increased in all three Georgian international airports in 2014. In the same year, 1,575,386 passengers passed through Tbilisi international airport—9.7%

(139,340 passengers) higher than in the previous year (Kadagishvili 2016b). In 2014, air transportation of passengers in the Georgian aviation market was carried out by three Georgian lines (Georgian Airways, Vista Georgia, and Air Caucasus) and 32 foreign airline companies. Over the last year, four foreign companies, Air Arabia, Yanair, Dniproavia, and Air Cairo, began carrying out regular flights from Georgia. Since October 27, 2014 regular flights between Georgia and Russia resumed. Flights between Tbilisi and Moscow are performed by Georgian Airways and by the Russian lines S7 Siberia, Transaero, and Aeroflot (The Civil Aviation Agency Annual Report of 2014). Georgian airports are well-connected with a range of different countries through transit flights. However, one of the main priorities of the country is developing direct flights, which will support tourism development in the country and have a positive impact on the development of economic relations between countries. Georgia already has some strategic directions, but needs some help in this regard. These directions are Italy, Germany, France, Great Britain, Netherlands, Spain, Switzerland, and Belgium, as well as Romania, Bulgaria, Slovakia, China, India, and Japan (Kvirikashvili 2015). In turn, an increase in the number of airlines operating in the market will create a competitive environment and promote the growth of foreign visitors.

Georgia has been included in lists of the ten safest countries for traveling. It has won some achievements in international relations. The National Tourism Administration of Georgia has participated in various fairs and exhibitions in the tourism sector. "Modern, up-to-date technologies have been introduced, the speed of information dissemination has increased, the use of the internet has spread widely in both business and social activities. This has simplified business activities and at the same time provided an opportunity for the whole world to become familiar with the culture, history, and geography of Georgia. World famous international hotels have been built in Tbilisi, Batumi, Bakuriani, Anaklia, Bazaleti, etc., which has ultimately created favorable conditions for the development of the tourism business" (Kadagishvili 2015). In May 2015, Georgia hosted the European Bank for Reconstruction and Development (EBRD) business forum. EBRD is the largest investment institution in Georgia, having invested over 2.6 billion USD in over 178 projects. In June of the same year, the Youth Summer Olympic Festival was held in Tbilisi. The increase in marketing activities is also worth mentioning. In particular, Georgia has been advertised in nine target markets (Azerbaijan, Turkey, Ukraine, Kazakhstan, Russia, Belarus, Hungary, Latvia, and Israel), as well as through the world's top-rated channels (CNN and Euronews), which will help increase the popularity of the country throughout the world.

Despite the above factors, the country cannot fully utilize its resources. The reasons for this are both subjective and objective. Despite the government's liberal policy, there are some issues that need to be decided if the tourism industry is to be effectively and sustainably developed (Khokhobaia 2016). To achieve effective and sustainable development of the tourism industry, it is necessary to "improve the quality of service, develop infrastructure, develop tourism capacities, and to promote environmental diversity (planning and development of new forests, parks, botanical gardens) and institutional development and organization of the tourism sector" (Erkomaishvili 2016).

The development of tourism should continue in the future. This will contribute to the inflow of additional foreign currency. Tourism development will promote the development of other tourism-related sectors, such as hotels, agriculture, the food industry, the transport and telecommunications sector, education (involving tourism-related training). All this will contribute to the growth of employment and income, which is among the best ways to eliminate poverty.

4.4 State Policy for Supporting the Development of Entrepreneurship

The development of entrepreneurship would be impossible without state support in the first stage of the transition to a market economy. That experience demonstrated that "the modern state in not beyond the market or above the market, but is organic organically built into the market and is a major player on the market, fully responsible for the realization of the interests of the whole community" (Mekvabishvili 2009).

Creating favorable conditions for entrepreneurial activities and the development of the private sector is one of the main tasks for the government of Georgia. According to the World Bank, the private sector creates nine out of ten jobs in the global economy. The government of Georgia is implementing reforms to prepare for the development of entrepreneurship. In March 2014, the Enterprise Development Agency was established, and in June of the same year, a new government program called *Produce in Georgia* was launched (Ministry of Economy and Sustainable Development of Georgia). The basic goal of this reform program is to develop entrepreneurship, supporting the establishment of new enterprises, improving the competitiveness and export potential of the private sector. In addition, the government has added a new component to the Produce in Georgia program, aiming at the development of micro and small enterprises in the region. On February 19, 2014, the Innovations and Technologies Agency of Georgia was established with the support of the World Bank. The purpose of establishing this agency was to support the development of knowledge-based and innovation-based economy and innovative ecosystems, promoting the commercialization of knowledge and innovations and development of high speed internet. The main functions of the agency include promoting the commercialization of knowledge and innovation and developing innovative entrepreneurship, including start-ups. In July 2015, the EU approved the first transfer of a 6 million euro tranche as part of the Deep and Comprehensive Free Trade Area Facility for Small and Medium Enterprises. The EU has allocated 45 million euro for this program, which clearly shows the readiness of the EU to support the implementation of the Association Agreement and the Deep and Comprehensive Free Trade Area agreement in Georgia, while at the same time promoting the development of small and medium enterprises as a basis for sustainable economic development and inclusive growth. The Association

Agreement signed between Georgia and the EU is important for both the political and economic development of Georgia. "It can be said that, by means of the above-mentioned agreement, it will be possible to strengthen different administrative and institutional structures in the country, and also to harmonize Georgian legislation with European standards, which will make it easier for Georgian business subjects to operate in the European market" (Khokhobaia 2015). Implementation of the Association Agreement, including the Deep and Comprehensive Free Trade Area, which represents a general plan for the integration of Georgia with Europe, will increase the country's attractiveness in terms of foreign direct investment, which will facilitate the introduction of modern technologies into Georgia, will help create new jobs, and will provide opportunities to Georgian citizens.

In the process of economic development, the government of Georgia is paying special attention to the development of small and medium enterprises and improving their competitiveness. In order to facilitate the development of small and medium businesses, in 2016, the government of Georgia developed its SME Development Strategy 2016–2020. The strategy is based on the main principle of Think Small First and aims to improve the competitiveness of small and medium enterprises, which in turn will create a solid basis for inclusive and sustainable economic growth. The aim the strategy should be achieved by 2020. According to the strategy document, the number of people employed in small and medium enterprises should increase by 15%, productivity by 7%, and the output of small and medium enterprise by 10% annually.

Agriculture has been recognized as a strategic direction in Georgia in recent years. The Funding of the Ministry of Agriculture has increased in order to intensify production and food security. The budget of the Ministry of Agriculture has also increased; special attention is being paid to improving systems, buying and applying agricultural equipment, and implementing a special program for small farm owners. The Law on Agricultural Cooperatives has been adopted by the parliament of Georgia, a Project Management Agency has been established, and funding of the agricultural sector has significantly increased through the activities of this agency and the support of the banking sector. The Agricultural Research Center has been created to support development of the agricultural sector and the production of food products, protecting and maintaining the biodiversity of birds and animals (Agricultural development strategy of Georgia 2015). As a result of the above activities, by 2015 the state had approved 106 projects (including 84 industrial projects and 22 agricultural projects) with a total investment volume of more than 267 million dollars. State-owned property has been given to 42 beneficiaries, and commercial banks have been allocated credits of over 133 million GEL. In 2015, the government of Georgia developed a Strategy for the Development of Agriculture in 2015–2020. The agricultural development strategy covers issues that will help to improve the competitiveness of the agriculture sector, steadily increasing the production of high-quality goods. The first practical steps have already been taken for agricultural development in the country, and the first positive signs have also appeared. However, the future will show whether this approach bears fruit.

The national tourism strategy is one of the more important reforms of 2015. This strategy sets out the vision of the tourism sector until 2025—a 10-year vision for the development of tourism. The strategy includes significant areas, such as tourism marketing, tourism products, tourism policy, infrastructure, and others. The strategy is a dynamic document that will be periodically reviewed. The main goal of the strategy is to introduce Georgia to the world as a high-quality tourist destination for all seasons, with in its own unique culture, cultural heritage, and national tradition of hospitality. The National Tourism Administration of Georgia is planning to increase the number of tourists to 8.4 million visitors by 2025. According to the estimates of the Agency, if this is achieved, the number of people employed in tourism sector will increase from 180,000 to 270,000, while spending per visitor will increase from 320 US dollars to 365 US dollars, while the volume of investments will increase from 183 million GEL to 874 million GEL.

Despite these reforms, there is still a lot to be done in the country, as the economic reforms implemented in Georgia, despite its many advantages, cannot fully ensure the successful regulation of economic and social processes to meet the interests of individuals and of society as a whole. Accordingly, the living standards of the majority of the population remain very low.

Government, scientists, economists, and entrepreneurs agree that one of the main factors that will contribute to the development of entrepreneurship is raising the level of professional knowledge. There is low level of accessibility to entrepreneurial education in Georgia. The country needs more highly qualification personnel who can respond to the challenges of entrepreneurship. The socioeconomic development strategy set out by the government of Georgia indicates that state policies should be directed to improving human resource capacities. It should be noted that the main goal of Enterprise Development Agency (19 February, 2014) is to support the introduction of mechanisms that make it easier for enterprises and start-ups to have access to information, finance, and education, and to promote the development of a high entrepreneurial culture. The agency will deliver training to 6000 people during the 26-month training program, and 3000 business ideas will be funded. In addition, the higher educational institutions in Georgia offer educational programs in Business Administration; a new model of accession to and funding of vocational education has been elaborated. This is an opportunity for everyone to learn and obtain a profession (Millennium Development Objectives in Georgia: National Report 2014). Twenty-six vocational educational centers are planned in different regions of the country. This will widen the geographical area of accessibility to vocational education (Regional Development Program 2015). Despite the above measures, the educational and vocational education systems require continuous reform and comprehensive development, as programs in "Entrepreneurship" can be found neither among the higher education curriculums nor in vocational programs. Development of entrepreneurial thinking is impossible if only fragmented tasks are dealt with. The latter implies that training is required at all levels of education—general, vocational, higher, and lifelong learning (Lekashvili 2014)—to ensures closer ties and cooperation between the education system and the labor market, employers, and employees.

4.5 Conclusions and Recommendations

Entrepreneurship has seen difficult and controversial days from Independence to the present. The political, economic, and legal environment in the country was not able to ensure the rapid development of business, but overall an increasing trend is still observed.

Therefore, we would like to draw attention to some of the measures that should be implemented to ensure the future development of entrepreneurship: Further deepening of economic liberalization, encouraging the development of entrepreneurship through various tax mechanisms, budget financing, targeted state programs and other financial, economic and organizational mechanisms; continuing the development of favorable legal, economic, investment, technological, and infrastructural environments; the use of funds in ways that have been well tested in global practice (financial, insurance, venture capital funds, leasing companies, etc.); efficient usage of natural resources of industrial importance and the maintenance of natural ecosystems at the same time; the development of processing industry; the production of local food products and reducing the risks to food security; encouraging the formation of farm unions (cooperatives); improving accessibility to agricultural equipment; providing farmers information about modern technologies in the agricultural sector; developing the tourism infrastructure; making international travel to Georgia easier; raising international awareness of Georgia as a country with European democracy; improving state policy to establish close links between business, universities, and scientific and research centers.

Implementation of the above measures will significantly contribute to the development of entrepreneurial activities and will eventually have a positive impact on economic growth and the competitiveness of the country.

References

Agricultural development strategy of Georgia 2012–2022, Government of Georgia, Tbilisi 2012. https://matsne.gov.ge/ka/document/view/2280820

Agricultural development strategy of Georgia 2015–2020, Ministry of Agriculture of Georgia, Tbilisi. 2015. moa.gov.ge/Download/Files/46

Asatiani, R. (2015). *Conceptual analysis of the world economy in the twentieth century and economic portrait of Georgia* (p. 182). Siahkle: Tbilisi.

Erkomaishvili, G. (2016). *Priorities of the development economic policy of Georgia* (p. 107). Tbilisi: Universali.

Food Security as Concept for Policy Planning, EENPARD. Tbilisi, 2015. http://enpard.ge/ge/food-security-as-a-crosscutting-concept-for-policy-making-in-georgia/

Gagnidze I. (2015). Entrepreneurial University: The most important player of the effective policy of education and science. *Journal of Economics and Business 4*, (Vol. 7, p. 128). Tbilisi: TSU.

Hisrich, R., & Peters, M. (1994). *Entrepreneurship* (p. 20). Meridiani: Kutaisi.

National Statistics Office of Georgia. (2015). *Entrepreneurship in Georgia*. Tbilisi: Statistical publication. http://www.geostat.ge/

Jibuti, M. (2013). *Modern social and economic challenges to Georgia and the best ways to overcome them, Academy of economic sciences of Georgia, collection of papers* (p. 140). Siakhke: Tbilisi.

Kadagishvili L. (2015). *Economic integration and the new challenges of Georgia*. No. 107, Series: Administracja I Zarzadzanie [Administration and Management] (34). Siedlce University of Natural Sciences and Humanities, Siedlce, Poland, p. 113. http://www.tstefaniuk.uph.edu.pl/zeszyty/archiwalne/107-2015_10.pdf

Kadagishvili L. (2016a). *Systematic approach to develop small and medium-sized businesses in Georgia*. Paper presented at the Third International Scientific and Practical Conference on Strategic Imperatives of Contemporary Management, 17–18 March 2016 (p. 210). Kiev: KNEU.

Kadagishvili, L. (2016b). Development prospects for transit potential of Georgia. *US–China Law Review, 13*(7), 518.

Kadagishvili L., & Seturidze R. (2016). Agriculture as the priority of the economic development of Georgia, Governing Business Systems. Theories and Challenges for Systems Thinking in practice, 4 Business Systems Laboratory International Symposium, Mykolas Romeri University, Vilnius, August 24–26, p. 212, http://bslab-symposium.net

Kandelaki, T. (2015). Forest resources and forestry in the economy of Georgia. Journal of Sustainable Management of Forests for the Development of the Green Economy in Central Asia and Caucasus, *3*. http://www.rec-caucasus.org/files/publications/pub_1450374259.pdf

Khaduri, N. (2012). *The role of the agricultural sector of Georgia in achieving macroeconomic stability, first international conference sustainable development priorities of agriculture, conference proceedings* (p. 549). Tbilisi: TSU.

Khokhobaia, M. (2015). Tourism policy challenges in Post-Soviet Georgia. *International Journal of Social, Behavioral, Educational, Economic, Business, and Industrial Engineering, 9*(3), 986–989.

Khokhobaia, M. (2016). From rational policy of tourism development to the effective policy. *California Business Review, 4*(1), 11.

Kvaratskhelia, M. (2013). *Ilia Chavchavadze and the contemporary world, Academy of economic sciences of Georgia, collection of papers 11* (p. 275). Siakhke: Tbilisi.

Kvirikashvili G. Ambassadorial of diplomatic representatives of Georgia abroad, 2015 (03.09.15) http://www.economy.ge/uploads/news/2015/ambasadoriali/ministris_sitkva-ambasadoriali.pdf

Lalzad A. (2007). *An overview of global water problems and solutions* (p. 36) London. in Tvalchrelidze A., Silagadze A., Keshelashvili G., & Gegia, D. (2011). *The socioeconomic development program of Georgia* (p. 203). Nekeri Publishing House: Tbilisi

Lekashvili E. (2014). Entrepreneurial thinking and its development problems in Georgia. *Journal of Economics and Business*, *6*, 69. Tbilisi: TSU.

Mekvabishvili, E. (2009). *Globalization of economy: Trends, challenges and prospects* (p. 144). Tbilisi: Universali.

Meskhia, I. (2015). *Economic reforms in Georgia: Analysis, challenges, forecasts, Journal Economics and Business 2, volume VIII* (p. 50). TSU: Tbilisi.

Millennium Development Objectives in Georgia: National Report (prepared by the government of Georgia in cooperation with UN office in Georgia), (2014). Tbilisi http://www.ge.undp.org/content/dam/georgia/docs/publications/GE_UNDP_MDG_Report_Georgia_2014.geo.pdf

Ministry of Agriculture of Georgia, Annual Report 2014. http://www.moa.gov.ge/Ge/Public/Reports

Ministry of Economy and Sustainable Development of Georgia. http://www.economy.ge/

Natural resources of Georgia and protecting environment, statistical publication, Tbilisi, 2014. http://www.geostat.ge/cms/site_images/_files/georgian/agriculture/Garemo_2014.pdf. Last accessed on 20 Mar 2016.

Okrostsvaridze A (2014). *Development dynamics and modern conditions in the mining sector of Georgia*. Tbilisi. http://eprints.iliauni.edu.ge/usr/share/eprints3/data/3498/1/A.O.CENN%20Project.pdf

Papava V., Tapladze L., & Gegeshidze A. (participants) (2015). *Georgia's economy: Reforms and pseudo-reforms* (p. 40). Tbilisi: Intelekti.
Regional Development Program in Georgia in 2015–2017. http://gov.ge/files/381_43285_728272_1215-1.pdf
Shaburishvili S. (2012). Foreign experience in the agricultural sector insurance and Georgia; First International Conference on Sustainable Agricultural Development Priorities. Conference proceedings. Tbilisi: TSU, p. 494.
SME development strategy of Georgia 2016–2020. gov.ge/files/439_54422_706524_100-1.pdf
Social and economic development strategy of Georgia 2020. www.mrdi.gov.ge/ge/news/actionplan/5302260e0cf298a857ab7dce
Social Protection and Social Inclusion in Georgia: Executive summary, European Commission, Institute of Social Studies and Analysis (ISSA), Tbilisi, p. 3. ec.europa.eu/social/BlobServlet?docId=6886&langId=ka
Soviet Georgian Encyclopedia. (1991). *Editor in chief I. Abashidze* (p. 131). Tbilisi.
Tchitanava, N. (2015). *Agriculture in Georgia: Transformation, problems, prospects* (pp. 84–64). Iverioni: Tbilisi.
The Civil Aviation Agency Annual Report of 2014. http://www.gcaa.ge/geo/annualreport.php
The European Union's Neighborhood Program: agriculture and rural development sectors in the Eastern Partnership countries, Georgia. (2012). Tbilisi. http://eeas.europa.eu/delegations/georgia/documents/virtual_library/cooperation_sectors/georgia_assesment_final_ka.pdf
The Millennium Development Goals Report. (2008). New York: United Nations Department of Economic and Social Affairs, p. 56.
The non-timber forest products of Georgian forest development Forum, June 26, 2015, the EU for Georgia. enpard.ge/ge/
Tvalchrelidze, A., Silagadze, A., Keshelashvili, G., & Gegia, D. (2011). *The socioeconomic development program of Georgia* (p. 121). Nekeri Publishing House: Tbilisi.

Chapter 5
Towards Discovering the Limits of Smart Grid Communication Infrastructure

Miroslav Kadlec, Jan Rosecky, Filip Prochazka, Barbora Buhnova, and Tomas Pitner

Abstract The concept of Smart Grid enforces standard power grid with intelligent devices and communication network to add new functionality to the power distribution system. The concept builds upon enormous volumes of metering and monitoring data, and thus also a robust communication infrastructure. Apart from pilot projects, modeling and simulation plays an important role in smart grids design, since it provides an opportunity to effectively benchmark and compare particular technologies, especially for its communication infrastructure.

In this paper, we summarize the specifics of communication in smart grids. Then, we provide an extensive review on particular approaches to smart grids simulation, which are analyzed and compared. Finally, we present GridMind, a new Smart grid simulation software that enhances the quality and usability of executed simulations, describe its features and the simulation process, and discuss its application in real projects.

Keywords Smart grid • Communication • Modeling • Simulation

M. Kadlec (✉) • B. Buhnova • T. Pitner
Faculty of Informatics, Masaryk University, Brno, Czech Republic
e-mail: miroslav.kadlec@mail.muni.cz; buhnova@mail.muni.cz; tomp@mail.muni.cz

J. Rosecky
Faculty of Informatics, Masaryk University, Brno, Czech Republic

Mycroft Mind, a.s., Brno, Czech Republic
e-mail: j.rosecky@mail.muni.cz

F. Prochazka
Mycroft Mind, a.s., Brno, Czech Republic
e-mail: filip.prochazka@mycroftmind.com

G. Dominici et al. (eds.), *Governing Business Systems*, Springer Proceedings in Business and Economics, DOI 10.1007/978-3-319-66036-3_5

5.1 Introduction

As the amount of electricity consumption has risen over the last century, the negative impact of the power generators on the environment became hot topic to search a solution for. While incorporation of renewable sources may help to reduce the environmental issues of electricity distribution infrastructure, it also brings technical challenges. Although the photovoltaic and wind power generators are able to provide significant power production under optimal conditions, it is mainly unstable and can not be predicted accurately. Though, searching for the ways to incorporate aforementioned power sources in spite of the negative impact of production variability is an important task. Nowadays, the concept of smart cities represents one approach to build an eco-sustainable community through energy optimization and sharing within the particular area, while preserving the high comfort for the inhabitants. In order to achieve effective electricity management, having up-to date data about power grid state is essential. The concept of smart grid presents standard electricity distribution network enhanced with information and communication technology (ICT), in which, the data collected from the entire architecture may be used to react to and compensate power outages. In the greater scale, Energy distribution companies are motivated to deploy smart grids in order to minimize energy losses in the power grid. Though, smart grids research became a subject of investments from both electricity distributors and governments. Since no extensive review on simulations of communications in smart grids has been conducted, this paper aims to summarize particular approaches used in the scope of this topic. First, specifics of communication technologies potentially usable in smart grids are summarized. Then, a review of published simulation tools and approaches is presented. In the final part, GridMind, a tool for general modeling and simulating Smart grid dynamics is described.

5.2 Background

Since the concept of smart grid is being developed by many institutions and research groups simultaneously, rather than being defined by a centralized authority, concrete approaches may differ in various aspects. Despite of particular effort, smart grids lack on standardization of concrete hardware and software technologies to be used. Nevertheless, the high level structure might be considered similar along different approaches. In Trefke et al. (2013), a complete conceptual view of smart grid was proposed, describing the whole infrastructure as a multi-layered model divided into several domains and zones, see Fig. 5.1. Each layer represents particular level of interoperability providing support to layers located higher. Since for example the business layer includes business-specific aspects of information exchange, the function layer describes logical functions and services as well as the relations among them from a technical perspective to realize respective business aspects defined in the top level. According to this model, having up-to-date, accurate and complete

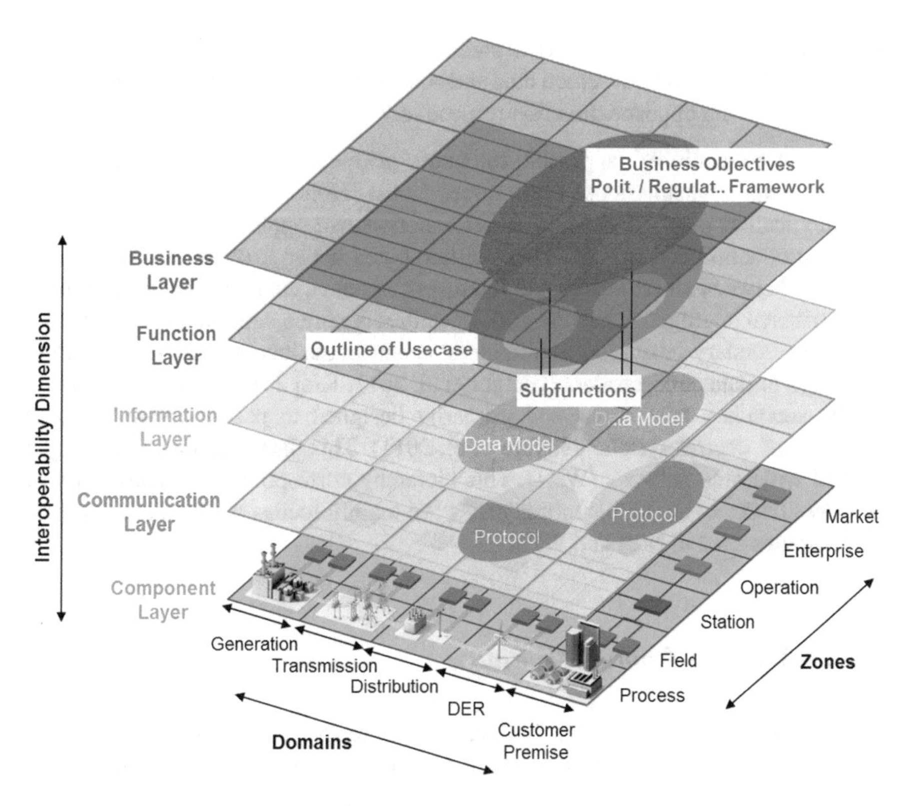

Fig. 5.1 A multi-layered conceptual model of smart grid

data is crucial for achieving the goals mentioned in the introduction part. Hence, serious attention must be paid to measuring and detecting mechanisms as well as distribution of relevant data to other grid agents. The latter implies the need for a solid communication and information-technology infrastructure developed along with the energy distribution network. Although the smart grid communication infrastructure is rather complex and potential implementation may vary in detail, generally, several types of communicating objects may be identified. In Vyas and Pandya (2012), the generic entities participated in smart grid applications are described as follows:

- **Smart meters** are devices located in households, that sense electricity (or generally water, gas, etc.) usage. In addition, smart meters enable communication with other in-home electric devices.
- By **user electricity appliances**, any other devices connected to smart meter are usually addressed, e.g. water heaters, electric cars or small power generators.
- **Central office** is a server deployed in the infrastructure, that collects, aggregates and processes all the data obtained from smart metering. Its purpose is to execute the computational part of smart grid appliances.

- **Data concentrators** serve as a mediators between smart meters and central servers. They pass both sensed data and control commands from meters to central offices and the opposite direction respectively.

The aforementioned approach to smart grid communication infrastructure divides data transmissions into three areas. Home area network (HaN), communication platform used by smart meters, smart appliances and devices for power production and storage. Neighborhood area network (NaN) maintains data transfers between smart meters and intelligent systems, enabling the incorporation of distributed intelligence into the grid. Localities are often delimited as areas fed by a single secondary substation. Distributors' agents in the localities are referred-to as gateways or data concentrators (Gungor et al. 2011; Krej 2014), often incorporated in the secondary substations and primarily designed to pass measured data to distributors' central systems (Niyato et al. 2011). This data exchange is already a part of wide area network (WaN). This hierarchy corresponds to "zones" axis of SGAM (Trefke et al. 2013). In this paper, we mainly focus on the communication technologies used in NaN and WaN.

5.2.1 *Wireless Communication*

Since the deployment costs are significant measure for choosing the most suitable infrastructure, wireless technologies are commonly considered for WAN, reading the data from concentrators or gateways (common communication alternatives involve installation of optic fibers or high-voltage PLC). In opposition to wireline technologies, wireless approaches bring several advantages. As there is no necessity to install physical communication lines, material savings may be significant in the large scale smart grid deployment. Additionally, the overall costs may be reduced by using a wireless infrastructure, that is already deployed, e.g. the cellular networks owned by telecommunication companies.

Within the context of wireless communications in smart grids, there are several approaches, including GPRS/EDGE, 3G network, LTE (Pham 2013), or alternatives like ZigBee or WiMax. All these technologies are described and compared in Usman and Shami (2013). In Rengaraju et al. (2012), Rengaraju et al. compare WiMax and LTE, conducting simulations on data up-link and emphasizing the importance of the feature for smart grid applications. Islam et al. (2014) argue that since WiMax contains integrated mechanisms providing QoS, it is a suitable technology for Smart grid applications, and conducts supportive simulations in OPNET. Recently, a novel technology, referred-to as LORA (Alliance 2015) is being developed. The approach is closely related to sensor networks and the Internet of Things, where Smart grids are more and more considered to belong (Zaballos et al. 2011).

Growing number of smart grid devices communicating via wireless networks becomes a serious issue (Kouhdaragh et al. 2015). Based on field measurements,

Madueno et al. (2013) analyzes the number of smart meters that can fit into a GSM cell and proposes a way of providing for much finer GSM cell granularity and thus extensively boosting the capacity of the system.

5.2.2 Powerline Communication

Powerline communication (PLC) uses electric signal modulation to simultaneously carry both data and alternating current over electrical wiring. PLC represents the natural way of developing communication infrastructure on existing power infrastructure (both low and high voltage). The main advantage of this technology is in its usability for every household connected to power distribution network. In the scope of central-European networks, it will almost certainly be used for NaN communication. Powerline communication represents a rather noisy channel, whose quality depends on a wide range of factors including current power load of the wires, external electromagnetic disturbances or powerline traffic on close wires. For longer distances, signals needs to be amplified, which is why smart meters act as signal repeaters (Yadav 2015) in majority of existing installations. Several standards are relevant in central-European area: older narrow-band, BPSK-based Meters-and-More technology (Meters and Alliance 2015); newer narrow-band OFDM-based PRIME, G3 and IEEE-1901.2; and broadband over powerline (BPL) (Tonello and Zheng 2009).

A number of generic low-level modeling and simulation approaches has been proposed, among others (Canete et al. 2011; Tonello and Versolatto 2010, 2011; Prasanna et al. 2009; Andreadou and Pavlidou 2010; Atayero et al. 2012; Lu et al. 2013; Razazian et al. 2010; Tonello and Zheng 2009), most concentrating on OFDM, particularly PRIME or G3. While Hoch (2011) considers G3 more powerful in his Matlab-simulated comparison with PRIME, experiments set up in Skrek (2015) proved PRIME technology faster for the scenarios.

Major technologies have been extensively tested in on-field experiments conducted as a part of OPEN Meter initiative (Open meter 2015), Sendin et al. also published results form large field tests of PRIME-based meters in Spanish Iberdrola grid (Sendin et al. 2012). López et al. (2015) studies PLC (and GPRS) technology behavior under various conditions, with respect to previously proposed (López et al. 2012) modeling methodology. Wolkerstorfer et al. (2016) provides valuable long-term measurements of PLC behavior in various environments, together with simulation methodology taking into account low-level protocol overhead.

Unfortunately, the presented simulation approaches were only dealing with point-to-point communication, not taking into account repeater-enabled communication hops. In fact, none of them was focused on modeling end-to-end behavior on application level. As for models of higher levels of ISO/OSI layers over PLC infrastructure, Kim et al. (2008) presented a simulation setting with repeaters using Network Simulator 2, Bauer et al. (2009) has analyzed the effects of employing IPv6 over low-speed PLC and finally Matanza et al. (2013) proposed to model network effects of the low-level power-line processes using BER and then pass it to high-level network protocols.

5.2.3 *Communication Protocols*

Since standardization is playing an important role in smart grid development, many domain-specific communication protocol on various ISO/OSI layers have emerged (summarized in De Craemer and Deconinck 2010). Device Language Message Specification and COmpanion Specification for Energy Metering (DLMS/COSEM) is an open set of standards for metering data exchange. DLMS itself standardizes the methods to represent and transfer metered data and energy meter functions. COSEM is a part of DLMS suite that defines the rules for data exchange with energy meters based on existing standards. The meters are modeled as sets of logical devices, whereas each logical device represents a subset of the functionality of metering equipment.

DLMS/COSEM is now basically considered a standard in the last mile (G1) communication, beating legacy protocols like SML and IEC 61850 (Feuerhahn et al. 2011). DLMS/COSEM specification is fully covered in so-called "colored books", excerpts of which are freely-available (Association 2014a,b, 2015, 2003). Apart from the limited-access full colored books, message specifications are available at Taylor and Kmethy (2010). Regarding the use of DLMS over PLC networks, several communication profiles have been introduced. Whereas Meters and More technology uses HDLC-based approach, OFDM meters use TCP/IP networks, UDP in case of G3 (Kmethy 2014).

Solely Zaballos et al. (2009) has simulated transfers of DLMS messages over PLC in order to compare the standard with IEC 60870-5. Interesting work has been conducted by Armendariz et al. (2014), connecting OPNET System-in-the-Loop module to Adruino Uno and Raspberry Pi nodes simulating metering devices. The nodes ran GURUX (2016) implementation of DLMS server so the exchanged messages were respecting the standard.

5.3 Modeling Communication in Large-Scale Smart Grid Setups

Apart from the pilot projects, a significant effort has been made to employ simulation into the problem of Smart grids development in order to improve the design and create a platform for testing potential solutions. Simulation of Smart grid dynamics provides an opportunity to effectively compare and to identify bottlenecks and possible risks of particular approaches, technologies and strategies potentially usable in the final solution. As long as running simulation process brings incomparably lower expenses than deploying examined technology in a pilot project, it may be considered an effective way to point out the most suitable technologies and enhance the smart grid design. In Li and Zhang (2014), Li states that "The smart grid will generate billions of data points from thousands of system devices. This in turn requires a robust, large-bandwidth communication infrastructure that can cope with the enormous volume of data that will be constantly exchanged. In addition, the communication network will need to be reliable, scalable, and extendable to future smart grid services and applications. It must be protected and made resilient against failures and attacks in order to assure cyber security. In Wang et al. (2011), Gungor et al. (2013) potential Smart grid applications are summarized along with their communication requirements. Satisfying this demanding set of challenges for the next generation power grid system requires a better understanding of the future design methods of the smart grid and identification of its key features." According to Rinaldi (2004), modeling smart grid as an interdependent critical infrastructure should involve: time scales; geographic scales; cascading and higher order effects; social/psychological elements; operational procedures; business policies; restoration and recovery procedures; government regulatory, legal, policy regimes; and stakeholder concerns.

Extensive review (Mets et al. 2014) concluded that the growing importance of simulating smart grid dynamics is mostly driven by two needs: to evaluate either (1) demand-response strategies in local communities, so-called smart grid cells, or (2) overall wide-area monitoring, protection and control architecture.

In order to analyze different types of demand control strategies and evaluate their influence on overall grid cell sustainability, various agent-based energy and communication infrastructure co-simulation tools have been introduced. Mentioned systems generally consist of both power dynamics and communication infrastructure simulator, performing these simulations simultaneously. Real-time Mosaik (Schütte et al. 2012) simulator is a powerful modular Python-based simulation environment, enabling an integration of existing simulators in order to simulate the power dynamics of areas comprising thousands of nodes. Kosek et al. (2014) present the comparison of two power and communication grid co-simulation frameworks (MasSim resp. JadeSim and IPSYS-DE), orchestrated in Mosaik. Mets et al. (2011) present a comprehensive simulation environment using the OMNET++ simulator as a development platform. The Coupled Simulator (Bergmann et al. 2010) is built on Network Simulator NS-2 and the commercial Siemens' Power System Simulation (PSSTM) as a benchmark to newly developed communication and control techniques. In Godfrey et al. (2010), Godfrey et al. present a co-simulation framework built on OpenDSS and NS-2 mainly for grid load balancing applications. Bhor et al. (2016) conducted a similar work using OMNET++, instead of NS-2.

The wide-area monitoring, protection and control simulators aim to test the influence of real-time sensor data availability on the ability of the supervisory control and data acquisition (SCADA) systems to provide global grid stability. EPOCHS (Hopkinson et al. 2006) combines continuous PSCAD/EMTDC power simulator and discrete NS2 network simulator in a co-simulation, connected together with the Runtime Infrastructure (RTI). Another approach, based on the High-Level Architecture (HLA), is presented in Georg et al. (2012), where DIgSILENT PowerFactory and OPNET network simulator are coupled together as HLA federates. Recent work of Albagli et al. (2016) has proposed a similar framework, and as a side effect also a sketch of ontology of smart grid elements. Lin et al. (2011, 2012) combines Positive Sequence Load Flow (PSLF) and NS-2 into one discrete, event-driven environment. They use a common interface, referred-to as Service Interface Function Blocks, similarly as in Pang et al. (2014).

Lévesque et al. (2014) introduced a preliminary implementation of a HLA-based simulator with the ambition to cover all the three smart grid perspectives, as presented in IEEE (2011): the power systems, the grid communications and the related information technology. The time-stepped co-simulator implementation integrates OMNET++ with Java processes generating IEC 61850 communication protocol messages.

5.3.1 Our Approach: The Grid Mind Simulation Tool

In this section, a novel tool written in Prolog for general modeling and simulating Smart grid dynamics called GridMind (Rosecky et al. 2015) is presented. Primarily, the tool was used to estimate the abilities of a given infrastructure to collect and provide particular types of data, analyzing the data freshness, completeness and reliability, rapidly changing with the number of concurrently executed data transfer jobs.

In order to perform simulation of a specific infrastructure, first, a statistical model of transport layer characteristics, e.g. application data throughput; window sizes; packet loss; duration of connection initialization and termination. To achieve this, a set of OMNET++ simulations is performed. The simulation setups are validated through actual measured data from pilot projects. These statistical models serve as inputs of GridMind modeling tool. According to the quantity of consumption points, setup of technical processes and used communication protocols, both, a realistic communication topology and traffic is generated. Along the generated network, agent-based discrete-event simulations of the grid communication is executed using state machine models of individual agents and processes. Message delivery times estimations are based on computed transport layer characteristics under particular conditions. These estimations are dynamically recomputed after infrastructure conditions changes, for example when a new data transfer starts or a running transfer finishes. The simulation outputs are then provided in the form of terms of satisfaction of individual communication requests. Regarding to the structure of GridMind platform, the whole system consists of several parts. In the Storage component, the models are stored represented as orientated graphs. Between separate model elements, particular relations described in the further section are defined, see Fig. 5.2. Through **abstraction**, various levels of specificity and detail may be expressed. Rather than classifying elements into categories, more generic entities are defined to model a class of more specific ones. Element A is considered

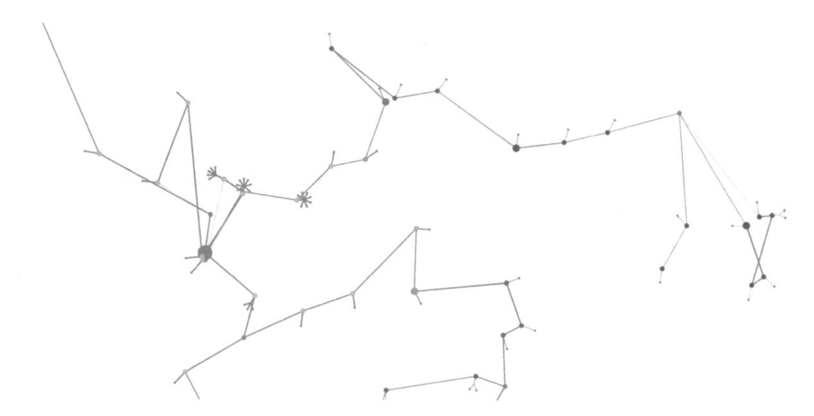

Fig. 5.2 A visualization of communication topology model used in GridMind

to be an abstraction of another element B, if A holds all attributes of B. To give an example, generic `secondary_substation` may be intuitively viewed as an abstraction of a concrete substation_1234 element. Beside abstraction, **roles** are second instrument to create relations between two elements, or an element and a general term. In the scope of GridMind relations, value V plays *role* R for element E if E has a property named R with value V. Since roles are also considered to be elements, role ontologies may be possibly defined and through structuring the roles into contexts, additional mechanism of role polymotphism is provided. **Contexts** are created in order to specify sub-models of particular problems, e.g. procedures related to a data reading process. In the latest version of GridMind, the role a particular element plays in a given context may be defined. For the simulation process, **causalitites** are defined in GridMind to model reactions to particular events creating additional events in the future. Apart from explicit relations, so-called **lambda elements** provide an opportunity to create potential and stochastic relations by defining them implicitly. This mechanism is called intension—the more relations of an element is realized through lambdas, the more intensive it is considered to be.

The actual simulation is performed through cooperation of three tools called solvers. The purpose of the **Extension solver** is extension generation, meaning construction of explicit forms of given elements. The rules to generate extensions are defined by labdas of particular intensive elements. The **Context Generator** represents an approach to element or general term generation, mainly used for the data exports. Iterative rules contain lambdas determining which records will be added to the output collection based on its current content. Finally, the **Consequence Generator** maintains the simulation process itself. Events are sorted by their timestamps and stored into a queue to form a simulation timeline. Intensionally-defined registered actions may react to the processed events, producing another output events to be put back into the timeline.

5.3.2 Applications of GridMind

At the moment, GridMind is used in two projects executed by PRE and E.ON, the two of three major electricity distributors in Czech Republic. The main task is describe and analyze specifics of potential technical solutions in power distribution grids. In scope of these projects, GridMind identifies problematic spots of communication network, where PLC technology is not effectively usable (e.g. because of long distance between secondary station and the endpoint consumer). Another technology, like cellular network, may be employed for these special cases, since it is more suitable for them.

5.4 Conclusion

The main purpose of this paper is to provide an extensive review on simulation approaches for smart grids. First, the motivation to use simulation tools in smart grid environment is described. Then existing approaches are analyzed and compared and the simulation tool called GridMind is presented. Regarding the GridMind, the modeling and simulation process is specified and its application in currently running projects is mentioned.

5.4.1 On-Going Work and Future Directions

Statistical models of communication channels have been created for several wireless technologies under various conditions including signal quality class, external traffic class or amount of concurrent transfers. Similar analysis covering various implementations of PLC is still in progress. The problem for PLC appears to be much more complex, as the condition state-space is much larger (involving amount of repeater nodes, crossings, wire types and more).

In relation to the existing functionality, further specifications, particularly more extensive analysis of the influence of starting a new transfer or finishing an old one on other on-going transfers may be needed. Moreover, the whole approach will be validated against net-flow monitoring records from in-the-field measurements.

References

Albagli, A. N., Falcão, D. M., & de Rezende, J. F. (2016). Smart grid framework co-simulation using HLA architecture. *Electric Power Systems Research, 130*, 22–33.

Alliance LoRa. (2015). Lora technology. Accessed 2015-21-12.

Andreadou, N., & Pavlidou, F.-N. (2010). Modeling the noise on the OFDM power-line communications system. *IEEE Transactions on Power Delivery, 25*, 150–157.

Armendariz, M., Chenine, M., Nordstrom, L., & Al-Hammouri, A. (2014). A co-simulation platform for medium/low voltage monitoring and control applications. In *2014 IEEE PES, Innovative Smart Grid Technologies Conference (ISGT)* (pp. 1–5). New York: IEEE.
Association, D. U. (2003). COSEM glossary of terms.
Association, D. U. (2014). COSEM interface classes and OBIS identification system.
Association, D. U. (2014). DLMS/COSEM architecture and protocols.
Association, D. U. (2015). DLMS/COSEM conformance testing process.
Atayero, A. A., Alatishe, A., & Ivanov, Y. A. (2012). Power line communication technologies: Modeling and simulation of prime physical layer. *World Congress on Engineering and Computer Science, 2*, 931–936.
Bauer, M., Plappert, W., Wang, C., & Dostert, K. (2009). Packet-oriented communication protocols for smart grid services over low-speed PLC. In *IEEE International Symposium on Power Line Communications and Its Applications, 2009. ISPLC 2009*, March (pp. 89–94).
Bergmann, J., Glomb, C., Gotz, J., Heuer, J., Kuntschke, R., & Winter, M. (2010). Scalability of smart grid protocols: Protocols and their simulative evaluation for massively distributed DERs. In *2010 First IEEE International Conference on Smart Grid Communications (Smart-GridComm)*, Oct (pp. 131–136).
Bhor, D., Angappan, K., & Sivalingam, K. M. (2016). Network and power-grid co-simulation framework for smart grid wide-area monitoring networks. *Journal of Network and Computer Applications, 59*, 274–284.
Canete, F. J., Cortés, J., Díez, L., Entrambasaguas, J. T., & et al. (2011). A channel model proposal for indoor power line communications. *IEEE Communications Magazine, 49*, 166–174.
De Craemer, K., & Deconinck, G. (2010). Analysis of state-of-the-art smart metering communication standards. In *Proceedings of the 5th Young Researchers Symposium.*
Feuerhahn, S., Zillgith, M., Wittwer, C., & Wietfeld, C. (2011). Comparison of the communication protocols DLMS/COSEM, SML and IEC 61850 for smart metering applications. In *2011 IEEE International Conference on Smart Grid Communications (SmartGridComm)*, Oct (pp. 410–415).
Georg, H., Wietfeld, C., Muller, S., & Rehtanz, C. (2012). A HLA based simulator architecture for co-simulating ict based power system control and protection systems. In *2012 IEEE Third International Conference on Smart Grid Communications (SmartGridComm)*, Nov (pp. 264–269).
Godfrey, T., Mullen, S., Dugan, R. C., Rodine, C., Griffith, D. W., & Golmie, N. (2010). Modeling smart grid applications with co-simulation. In *2010 First IEEE International Conference on Smart Grid Communications (SmartGridComm)* (pp. 291–296). New York: IEEE.
Gungor, V., Sahin, D., Kocak, T., Ergut, S., Buccella, C., Cecati, C., & Hancke, G. (2011). Smart grid technologies: Communication technologies and standards. *IEEE Transactions on Industrial Informatics, 7*, 529–539.
Gungor, V. C., Sahin, D., Kocak, T., Ergut, S., Buccella, C., Cecati, C., & Hancke, G. P. (2013) A survey on smart grid potential applications and communication requirements. *IEEE Transactions on Industrial Informatics, 9*, 28–42.
GURUX. (2016). Gurux open source community. Accessed 2016-01-11.
Hoch, M. (2011). Comparison of PLC G3 and PRIME. In *IEEE International Symposium on Power Line Communications and Its Applications (ISPLC 2011)* (pp. 165–169).
Hopkinson, K., Wang, X., Giovanini, R., Thorp, J., Birman, K., & Coury, D. (2006). Epochs: A platform for agent-based electric power and communication simulation built from commercial off-the-shelf components. *IEEE Transactions on Power Systems, 21*, 548–558.
IEEE. (2011). IEEE guide for smart grid interoperability of energy technology and information technology operation with the electric power system (EPS), end-use applications, and loads. *IEEE Std 2030-2011* (pp. 1–126).
Islam, M., Uddin, M. M., Al Mamun, M. A., & Kader, M. (2014). Performance analysis of AMI distributed area network using wimax technology. In *2014 9th International Forum on Strategic Technology (IFOST)* (pp. 152–155). New York: IEEE.

Kim, M.-S., Son, D.-M., Ko, Y.-B., & Kim, Y.-H. (2008). A simulation study of the PLC-MAC performance using network simulator-2. In *IEEE International Symposium on Power Line Communications and Its Applications, 2008. ISPLC 2008*, April (pp. 99–104).

Kmethy, G. (2014). IEC 62056 DLMS/COSEM seminar – communication profiles. Accessed 2016-01-05.

Kosek, A., Lunsdorf, O., Scherfke, S., Gehrke, O., & Rohjans, S. (2014). Evaluation of smart grid control strategies in co-simulation 2014; integration of IPSYS and mosaik. *Power Systems Computation Conference (PSCC), 2014*, Aug (pp. 1–7).

Kouhdaragh, V., Tarchi, D., Vanelli-Coralli, A., & Corazza, G. E. (2015). Smart meters density effects on the number of collectors in a smart grid. *2015 European Conference on Networks and Communications (EuCNC)* (pp. 476–481). New York: IEEE.

Krejčí, L. (2014). *Programové vybavení datového koncentrátoru AMM sítě [online]*. Masters thesis, Czech Technical University. Available at http://is.muni.cz/th/325292/fi_m/.

Lévesque, M., Béchet, C., Suignard, E., Maier, M., Picault, A., & Joós, G. (2014). From co-toward multi-simulation of smart grids based on HLA and FMI standards. arXiv preprint arXiv:1412.5571.

Li, W., & Zhang, X. (2014). Simulation of the smart grid communications: Challenges, techniques, and future trends. *Computers & Electrical Engineering, 40*, 270–288.

Lin, H., Sambamoorthy, S., Shukla, S., Thorp, J., & Mili, L. (2011). Power system and communication network co-simulation for smart grid applications. In *2011 IEEE PES Innovative Smart Grid Technologies (ISGT)* (pp. 1–6). New York: IEEE.

Lin, H., Veda, S. S., Shukla, S. S., Mili, L., & Thorp, J. (2012). Geco: Global event-driven co-simulation framework for interconnected power system and communication network. *IEEE Transactions on Smart Grid, 3*, 1444–1456.

López, G., Moreno, J., Amarís, H., & Salazar, F. (2015). Paving the road toward smart grids through large-scale advanced metering infrastructures. *Electric Power Systems Research, 120*, 194–205.

López, G., Moura, P. S., Custodio, V., & Moreno, J. I. (2012). Modeling the neighborhood area networks of the smart grid. In *2012 IEEE International Conference on Communications (ICC)* (pp. 3357–3361). New York: IEEE.

Lu, X., Kim, I. H., & Vedantham, R. (2013). Implementing prime for robust and reliable power line communication (PLC). *Texas Instruments White Paper*.

Madueno, G. C., Stefanovic, C., & Popovski, P. (2013). How many smart meters can be deployed in a gsm cell? In *2013 IEEE International Conference on Communications Workshops (ICC)* (pp. 1263–1268). New York: IEEE.

Matanza, J., Alexandres, S., & Rodriguez-Morcillo, C. (2013). Automatic meter-reading simulation through power line communication. In *2013 IEEE 21st International Symposium on Modeling, Analysis Simulation of Computer and Telecommunication Systems (MASCOTS)*, Aug (pp. 283–287).

Meters and Alliance, M. (2015). Technology | meters and more. Accessed 2015-12-11.

Mets, K., Ojea, J. A., & Develder, C. (2014). Combining power and communication network simulation for cost-effective smart grid analysis. *IEEE Communications Surveys Tutorials, 16*, 1771–1796.

Mets, K., Verschueren, T., Develder, C., Vandoorn, T., & Vandevelde, L. (2011). Integrated simulation of power and communication networks for smart grid applications. *2011 IEEE 16th International Workshop on Computer Aided Modeling and Design of Communication Links and Networks (CAMAD)*, June (pp. 61–65).

Niyato, D., Xiao, L., & Wang, P. (2011). Machine-to-machine communications for home energy management system in smart grid. *IEEE Communications Magazine, 49*, 53–59.

Open meter. (2015). Report on final test results and recommendations. Accessed 2015-11-06.

Pang, C., Vyatkin, V., & Mayer, H. (2014). Towards cyber-physical approach for prototyping indoor lighting automation systems. In *2014 IEEE International Conference on Systems, Man and Cybernetics (SMC)* (pp. 3643–3648). New York: IEEE.

Pham, G. T. (2013). Integration of IEC 61850 MMS and LTE to support smart metering communications.

Prasanna, S. G., Lakshmi, A., Sumanth, S., Simha, V., Bapat, J., & Koomullil, G. (2009). Data communication over the smart grid. In *IEEE International Symposium on Power Line Communications and Its Applications, 2009. ISPLC 2009* (pp. 273–279). New York: IEEE.

Razazian, K., Umari, M., Kamalizad, A., Loginov, V., & Navid, M. (2010). G3-PLC specification for powerline communication: Overview, system simulation and field trial results. In *2010 IEEE International Symposium on Power Line Communications and Its Applications (ISPLC)* (pp. 313–318). New York: IEEE.

Rengaraju, P., Lung, C.-H., & Srinivasan, A. (2012). Communication requirements and analysis of distribution networks using wimax technology for smart grids. In *2012 8th International Wireless Communications and Mobile Computing Conference (IWCMC)* (pp. 666–670). New York: IEEE.

Rosecky, J., Prochazka, F., & Buhnova, B. (2015). Grid mind: Prolog-based simulation environment for future energy grids.

Rinaldi, S. M. (2004). Modeling and simulating critical infrastructures and their interdependencies. In *Proceedings of the 37th Annual Hawaii International Conference on System Sciences, 2004* (pp. 873–880). New York: IEEE.

Schütte, S., Scherfke, S., & Sonnenschein, M. (2012). Mosaik-smart grid simulation API. In *Proceedings of SMARTGREENS* (pp. 14–24).

Sendin, A., Berganza, I., Arzuaga, A., Pulkkinen, A., & Kim, I. H. (2012). Performance results from 100,000+ prime smart meters deployment in Spain. In *2012 IEEE Third International Conference on Smart Grid Communications (SmartGridComm)* (pp. 145–150). New York: IEEE.

Skrášek, T. (2015). *Úzkopásmová PLC komunikace se standardy G3-PLC, PRIME a IEEE-1901.2 [online]*. Masters thesis, Brno University of Technology. Available at http://hdl.handle.net/11012/39956.

Taylor, D. & Kmethy, G. (2010). 61968-9 message profiles for DLMS/COSEM. Accessed 2015-19-11.

Tonello, A. M., & Versolatto, F. (2010). Bottom-up statistical PLC channel modeling - Part II: Inferring the statistics. *IEEE Transactions on Power Delivery, 25*, 2356–2363.

Tonello, A. M. & Versolatto, F. (2011). Bottom-up statistical PLC channel modeling - Part I: Random topology model and efficient transfer function computation. *IEEE Transactions on Power Delivery, 26*, 891–898.

Tonello, A. M., & Zheng, T. (2009). Bottom-up transfer function generator for broadband PLC statistical channel modeling. In *IEEE International Symposium on Power Line Communications and Its Applications, 2009. ISPLC 2009* (pp. 7–12). New York: IEEE.

Trefke, J., Rohjans, S., Uslar, M., Lehnhoff, S., Nordstrom, L., & Saleem, A. (2013). Smart grid architecture model use case management in a large european smart grid project. In *4th IEEE/PES Innovative Smart Grid Technologies Europe (ISGT EUROPE), 2013* (pp. 1–5). New York: IEEE.

Usman, A. & Shami, S. H. (2013). Evolution of communication technologies for smart grid applications. *Renewable and Sustainable Energy Reviews, 19*, 191–199.

Vyas, D., & Pandya, H. (2012). Advance metering infrastructure and dlms/cosem standards for smart grid. *International Journal of Engineering Research, 1*. e-ISSN: 2278-0181.

Wang, W., Xu, Y., & Khanna, M. (2011). A survey on the communication architectures in smart grid. *Computer Networks, 55*, 3604–3629.

Wolkerstorfer, M., Schweighofer, B., Wegleiter, H., Statovci, D., Schwaiger, H., & Lackner, W. (2016). Measurement and simulation framework for throughput evaluation of narrowband power line communication links in low-voltage grids. *Journal of Network and Computer Applications, 59*, 285–300.

Yadav, A. (2015). Cypress powerline communication (PLC) repeater implementation. Accessed 2015-11-13.

Zaballos, A., Vallejo, A., Majoral, M., & Selga, J. (2009). Survey and performance comparison of AMR over PLC standards. *IEEE Transactions on Power Delivery, 24*, 604–613.

Zaballos, A., Vallejo, A., & Selga, J. M. (2011). Heterogeneous communication architecture for the smart grid. *IEEE Network, 25*, 30–37.

Chapter 6
Exploiting Internet-of-Things: Platforms and Business Models

Tindara Abbate, Fabrizio Cesaroni, Maria Cristina Cinici, and Massimo Villari

Abstract Internet-of-Things (IoT) is expected to play a key role in the near future due to the possibility it shows to spur processes of economic growth by fostering differentiated business applications. To exploit several possibilities, firms need to define and adopt appropriate business models. By analyzing the case of FIWARE, we discuss which business models can be adopted by different actors involved in the development and usage of a cloud-based platform enabling IoT solutions. We show that such platform represents a general purpose technology, which allows innovative forms of division of labor among technology suppliers and technology users, with positive revenues for involved actors.

Keywords General purpose technology • Internet-of-Things • Open business model • IT platform • FIWARE

6.1 Introduction

The advent of Internet-of-Things (IoT) cloud-based solutions has represented a relevant technological breakthrough, whose benefits will be fully revealed and realized in the next future. IoT is expected to generate a strong impact on the firms' activities and operations, on the relationships among various agents (both firms and public institutions), and eventually on the way in which citizens (customers) interact among them within the society. Therefore, an increasing number of firms and governments have started to invest heavily in the development of such technologies, in order to obtain a leading position that might guarantee in the future the exploitation of a sustainable competitive advantage.

T. Abbate (✉) • F. Cesaroni • M.C. Cinici
Department of Economics, University of Messina, via dei Verdi, 75, 98122, Messina, ME, Italy
e-mail: abbatet@unime.it

M. Villari
Department of Engineering, University of Messina, Contrada di Dio, 1, 98166, Messina, Italy

G. Dominici et al. (eds.), *Governing Business Systems*, Springer Proceedings in Business and Economics, DOI 10.1007/978-3-319-66036-3_6

To fully exploit the technology and benefit from it, firms need to pursue a business model (that is, to organize all the activities, from value proposition to value delivery) (Teece 2010; Zott and Amit 2010) that perfectly fits its inner characteristics and totally exploits its specific features. Indeed, similarly to past technological breakthroughs (e.g., the advent of electricity or, more recently, that of biotechnologies), which have been studied by historicists of technology (Rosenberg 1976), new technological paradigms often impose firms to think at a different organization of labor and at a diverse way of designing and creating value propositions (Amit and Zott 2001). In the case of IoT cloud-based computing, a similar process is, therefore, to be expected.

Accordingly, this study addresses the following research question: which business models might be pursued by firms to benefit from the advantages offered by IoT cloud-computing?

To answer this research question, it analyzes the practical case of FIWARE, a recently funded EU initiative, which has seen the involvement of different actors (from large IT operators to small software developers) with the objective of developing an IT-based platform for potential business purposes. By examining the case of FIWARE, it thus explores the features that IoT cloud-based open business models should have. In doing so, while it also considers the perspective of large firms involved in the development of the IT platform, it mainly focuses on small software operators involved in the development of subsequent applications.

In the next section, it starts by providing a theoretical framework needed to address the empirical analysis. In Sect. 6.3, it explains the methodological approach it has followed to perform the analysis, whose results are shown in Sect. 6.4. Finally, Sect. 6.5 concludes the paper by discussing the managerial and theoretical implications of this study.

6.2 Theoretical Framework

6.2.1 General Purpose Technologies and Open Innovation

During the last decades, prior research on Open Innovation (Chesbrough 2003) has shown that firms may benefit from collaborations with external partners by allowing the in-flow of external technologies and technological competences. In fact, external technologies may be integrated with the internal technological base in order to generate new products/services and enhance the firm's ability to create value. This process of technology in-flow may be undertaken along the entire process of innovation development, since the initial stages of basic research, to the latter stages of product and service design.

Apart from internal strategic consideration, two main conditions may limit the firms' possibility to exploit an Open Innovation approach: (1) the lack of adequate absorptive capacities (Cohen and Levinthal 1990; Zahra and George 2002); and, (2) the difficulty to set-up strong appropriability mechanisms that protect partners' intellectual property from uncontrolled deployment by third parties (Cohen et al. 2000). As for the former, firms need to invest in both scientific and technological research that allow them to monitor the external technological environment, identify the owners of complementary technological skills and competences, integrate external technological knowledge with the internal knowledge base, and eventually convert the potentialities offered by external technologies into actual products and services capable of generating a competitive advantage. As for the latter, firms both need to protect their technologies with patents and other forms of intellectual property rights, and to negotiate with potential partners the allocation of property rights on exchanged technologies.

Only once these two conditions are met and difficulties associated to their implementation overcome, firms may take full advantage of collaborations with external technology suppliers. Traditionally, firms that have undertaken such an approach have pursued an open business model (Teece 2010; Zott and Amit 2010; Chesbrough 2006) characterized by a strict control over the core elements of the technology to be embedded into innovative products and services, while external technology acquisitions have been limited to marginal and complementary technological components, often customized by the external supplier for the benefits of the potential technology user. In other words, technologies and technological knowledge exchanged in innovative collaboration processes are often specialized and (co-)developed *ad-hoc* to solve contextual problems.

However, when technologies object of exchange are General Purpose Technologies (GPTs), as in the case of IT platforms analyzed in this study, different forms of open business model may be pursued by partners, with advantages for both technology suppliers and technology users. Indeed, as prior research has shown (Helpman 1998; Gambardella and McGahan 2010), GPTs allow a different configuration of division of labor at the industry level and a different organization of the innovative process. A simple comparison between the business models based on Specialized Technologies (STs) with respect to business models focused on GPTs allows to fully get the sense of the advantages provided by GPTs. As shown in Fig. 6.1a), in the case of an ST setting, the external technology is developed to fully respond to the potential user's application needs and to be fully integrated into its internal knowledge base. In this situation, the development costs of the specialized (that is, customized) external technology are totally incurred in by the technology supplier, while the technology user only incurs in the indirect costs of developing an absorptive capacity and of securing internal intellectual assets. Adaptations costs of external technology to internal needs, albeit not absent, can be supposed to be limited, given the fact that it is the technology supplier mainly in charge of providing a technological solution that fits context-dependent conditions.

By contrast, in the case of a GPT setting (Fig. 6.1b), the technological solution developed by the technology supplier does not respond to any specific (context-dependent) application condition, but is intended to satisfy a large number of possible application needs, not necessarily closely related one to the other. Indeed, the more general the technology is, the larger the number of application domains that can be served by the same GPT. In this case, albeit a ST solution implies a customization effort, the cost to develop a GPT is likely to be higher than that of a

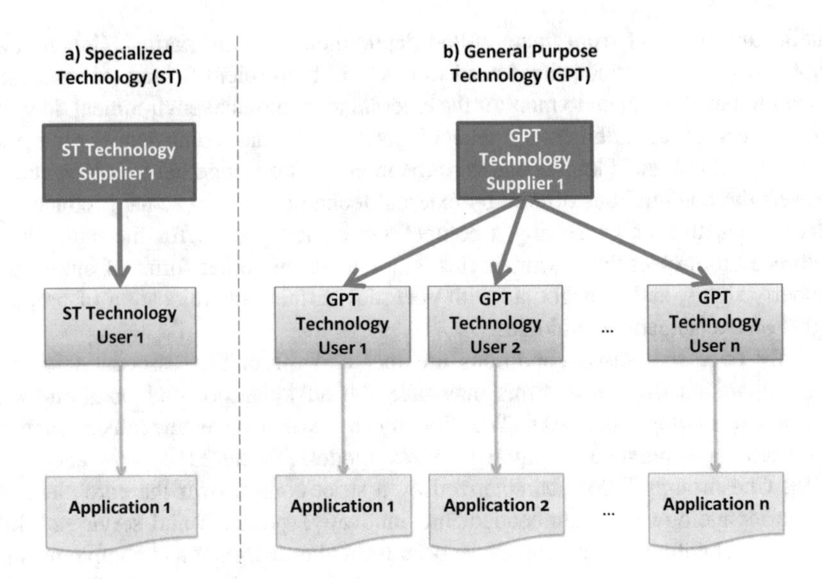

Fig. 6.1 (**a**, **b**) ST vs. GPT user-supplier interaction

ST, provided that it requires to overcome the limited context-dependent conditions of a narrow application domain. Furthermore, the development of GPTs is often associated to the development of *ad-hoc* toolkits (Von Hippel and Katz 2002), which the technology supplier provides to users in order to facilitate the adaptation of the GPT to their local conditions.

Provided that such toolkits avoid adaptation costs to be excessively high for the users, both technology suppliers and technology users may benefit from a GPT setting: with respect to a ST setting, technology suppliers may more than compensate the extra costs of generalization of the technology by selling it to a larger number of customers (application domains); and technology users may benefit from a more stable technology, which has been already applied to other technological domains, without incurring in excessive adaptation costs.

6.2.2 General Purpose Technologies, Technical Platforms and Ecosystem Innovation

Since they are usually depicted as an interface between different groups of suppliers and users that facilitate value-creation exchanges (Evans 2003; Gawer 2010; Rochet and Tirole 2006), IT platforms are meant here as a perfect example of GPTs. In particular, they build on the modularizations of complex systems in which certain components (the platform itself) remain stable, while others (the complements) are encouraged to vary in cross-section or over time (Baldwin and Woodard 2009). In any platform system, there are three types of components: (1) the "complements", which exhibit high variety and high rates of change over time; (2) the "core components", which remain stable as the complements change; and (3) the "interfaces", which are the design rules that allow the core and the complements to operate as one system. Both the core components and the interfaces are relatively long-lived, hence part of "the platform."

Long-established research (Gawer and Cusumano 2013) has defined two pre-dominant types of platforms: "internal" or "company-specific" platforms, and "external" or "industry-wide" platforms (i.e., the main subject of this paper). Whereas internal (company or product) platforms are conceived as a set of assets organized in a common structure from which a company can efficiently develop and produce a stream of derivative products, external (industry) platforms are conceived as products, services, or technologies that act as a foundation upon which external innovators, organized as an innovative business ecosystem, can develop their own complementary products, technologies, or services. Additionally, while internal platforms allow their owner to achieve economic gains by re-using or re-deploying assets across families of products developed by either the firm or its close suppliers, industry platforms facilitate the generation of a potentially very large number of complementary innovations by tapping into the innovative capabilities of many external actors, and function as a technological foundation at the heart of innovative business ecosystems.

To perform this industry-wide role and convince other firms to adopt the platform as their own, the external platform must (1) perform a function that is essential to a broader technological system, and (2) solve a business problem for many firms and users in the industry. While necessary, these conditions alone are not sufficient to help firms transform their products, technologies or services into industry platforms, nor indicate how platform leaders can stimulate complementary innovations by other firms, including some competitors, while simultaneously taking advantage of owning the platform (Gawer and Cusumano 2002).

The most critical distinguishing feature of an industry platform is the potential creation of network effects (Iyer et al. 2006). These are positive feedback loops that can grow at exponentially increasing rates as adoption of the platform and the complements rise. The network effects can be very powerful, especially when they are "direct" between the platform and the user of the complementary innovation and reinforced by a technical compatibility or interface standard that makes using multiple platforms ("multi-homing") difficult or costly (McIntyre and Subramaniam 2009). For example, Windows applications or Apple iPhone applications only work on compatible devices. The network effects can also be "indirect" or "cross-side," and sometimes these are very powerful as well (Clements and Ohashi 2005). These occur when, for example, advertisers become attracted to the Google search engine because of the large number of users.

Industry platforms guide technological innovation trajectories and stimulate innovation on complements. In order to do so they need to address two different sets of strategic issues (Gawer 2008): (1) developing a core function to encourage other companies to develop complementary applications that grow the platform ecosystem (coring); and (2) shaping market dynamics by gaining control over an installed base to win platform competition (tipping). Recently authors has started to considering that multiple platform strategies can coexist (Cennamo and Santalo 2013, 2015) because of: (1) asymmetric or local network effects (Eocman et al. 2006); (2) modest costs of adopting multiple platforms (Eisenmann 2006); or (3) differentiated consumer preferences (Armstrong and Wright 2007).

We build on the above streams of research to theoretically demonstrate that multiple business models can coexist within technical platforms and empirically examine this phenomenon among the developers and the users of the same IT platforms. IT platforms are an excellent laboratory for empirically analyzing the business models adopted by solvers and users for several reasons. First, other studies have documented that IT platform has become a strategic option for software vendors who expect to benefit from value co-creation with partners by developing complementary components and applications (Giessmann and Legner 2016; Hartmann and Bosch 2016). Second, because multiple actors coexist in the industry, we can exploit heterogeneity in the way those distinct actors manage their activities and the relationships with third-parties. Finally, IT platform usually change over time (even the core components can evolve, only the interfaces need to be stable), allowing us to analyze the strategies pursued by the different involved actors.

6.3 Research Design

The objective of this research is that of analyzing which business models can be effectively pursued by firms to benefit from the advantages offered by IoT. To achieve this objective we performed a descriptive-interpretative qualitative research (Denzin and Lincoln 2000), aiming to provide a useful description, explanation and interpretation of the phenomenon under investigation. We have chosen this research method because its purpose is to examine a phenomenon that is occurring at a specific place and time, including the conditions, practices and relationships that exist, processes that are going on, or trends that are evident (Strauss and Corbin 1998). Therefore, we carried out an Internet search to select a successful project, focused on IoT cloud-computing and characterized by the involvement of multiple actors with different roles, competences and objectives. To identify a potential case study, we referred to the European cloud platform oriented "to advance Europe's competitiveness in Future Internet technologies and to support the emergence of Future Internet-enhanced applications of public and social relevance" (www.ec.europa.eu). In turn, we selected the FIWARE platform for different reasons: (1) it is an EC project that is included in the Future Internet Private Public Partnership (FI-PPP) program, oriented to improve the effectiveness of business processes and infrastructures supporting applications; (2) it can be used by a range actors – large firms, small-medium enterprises, public administrations, software houses, etc. – to validate innovative technologies in the context of smart applications and to prove their ability to support user driven innovation schemes; and, (3) finally, it facilitates the collaborations between business and academics.

Then, we proceeded to an accurate data gathering about FIWARE by using different types of materials, methods and investigators (Denzin 1978). Firstly, we conducted desk research to identify and acquire information that already existed in documents, internal reports, dossiers, and articles in order to obtain a good understanding of the FIWARE. We also examined the descriptive material and other documents available on the European website. Second, we performed field research through different rounds of in-depth interviews with developers of FIWARE (Deshpande and Farley 2004) in order to explore aspects related to this platform, such as its characteristics, reference architectures, functionalities, applications and services offered, potential development and etc. The interviews were conducted in March 2016, and each interview lasted approximately 2 h, following the methodological prescriptions on data collection through personal interviews (Lee 1999).

The information obtained by interviews was transcribed, codified and analyzed using text mining and lexical analysis. For validating our qualitative analysis, we presented the results to the respondents in order to obtain their feedback and corrections (Elliott 1999). The results of this case analysis are reported in the next section.

6.4 FIWARE Architecture and Philosophy

In a context in which cloud computing, big data, and IoT are enabling key technologies for the Internet of the Future, the European Commission (EC) envisioned the possibility to foster the wide adoption of such systems, in total openness, avoiding vendor lock-in and simplifying the composition of new services. The EC understood the need to find the right compromise between academic and industrial fields. To this end, the EC has started the Future Internet Private Public Partnership (FI-PPP) program that has brought to the delivery of a new complex European cloud platform, named FIWARE. The aim of FIWARE is to yield an open standard platform and an open, sustainable, global ecosystem. The FIWARE Reference Architecture includes a set of general-purpose platform functions (Building Blocks), available through APIs, called Generic Enablers (GEs). GEs gather advanced and middleware interfaces to networks and devices, advanced web-based user interfaces, application/services ecosystems and delivery networks, cloud hosting, data/context management, IoT service enablement, and security. FIWARE considers GE Open Specifications (that are public and royalty-free) and their implementations (GEi). There might be multiple compliant GEi(s) of each GE open specification. At least, there is one open source reference implementation of FIWARE GEs (FIWARE GEri(s)) with a well-known open source license.

FIWARE can thus be considered a de Facto Standard of future complex systems, at least in Europe, where clouds and IoT might be applied in various scenarios such as eHealth, Smart Cities and so on. By adopting such a standard, private companies (Specific Enablers) can make their businesses developing customized solutions able to satisfy needs of individuals and SMEs by connecting new IoTs and devices.

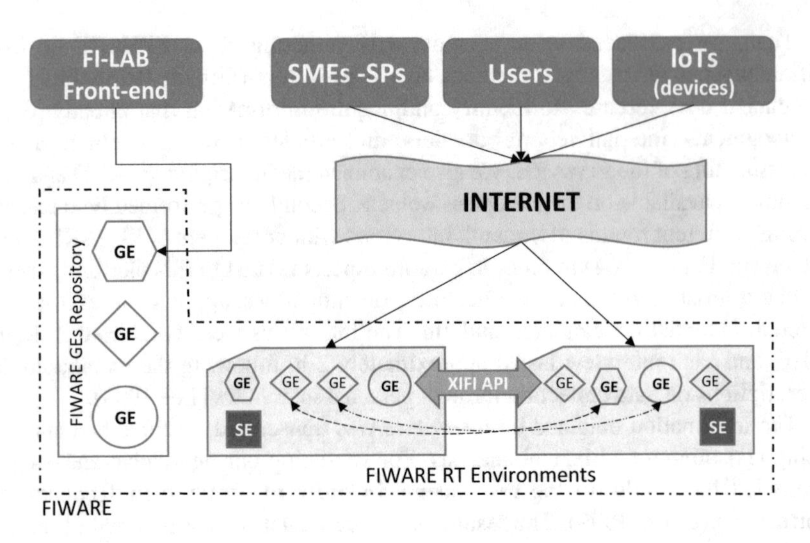

Fig. 6.2 FIWARE EcoSystem

6.4.1 *The FIWARE EcoSystem*

The FIWARE Ecosystem is shown in Fig. 6.2 (see Fazio et al. 2015). Starting from the left part of the picture, in FIWARE, a common and well-known GEs repository is defined (that is the static part of FIWARE). The different geometric shapes of each GE remark the possibility offered by FIWARE of hosting and executing (see the RunTime Environment – RT of it, which is the dynamic part) any type of GE. Below the repository there is the platform itself that is a composition of more federated platforms that can easily interact each other thanks to the XIFI agreement (FIWARE). In the picture each RT shaped cradle shows how more platforms are able to host GEs in different contexts/companies. Indeed, GEs can be seamless moved from RT shaped cradle to another and vice versa (see the dashed-lines). FIWARE allows this, thanks to the openness of its platform and APIs. Here Users, SMEs (Small and Medium-sized Enterprises, named also Local Players), SPs (Service Providers) and IoTs can interact through the Internet with the same kind of platforms and protocols, for different purposes but in a same way. FI-LAB Front-End in the picture depicts this common abstraction for interacting with FIWARE. To this FIWARE is representing a Standard de Facto of future complex systems, at least in Europe, where clouds and IoTs need to be used in any scenario as eHealth, Smart Cities and so on. Figure 6.2, inside the shaped cradle also shows a few rectangular small elements labeled SE. They represent the Specific Enabler developed by each company. Companies can make their businesses developing customized SPs able to satisfy needs of Users and SMEs and for connecting new IoTs and devices.

Figure 6.3 shows four different shaped cradle systems identifying four business IT companies (Big Players), named: (A), (B), (C) and (D). Each RunTime Envi-

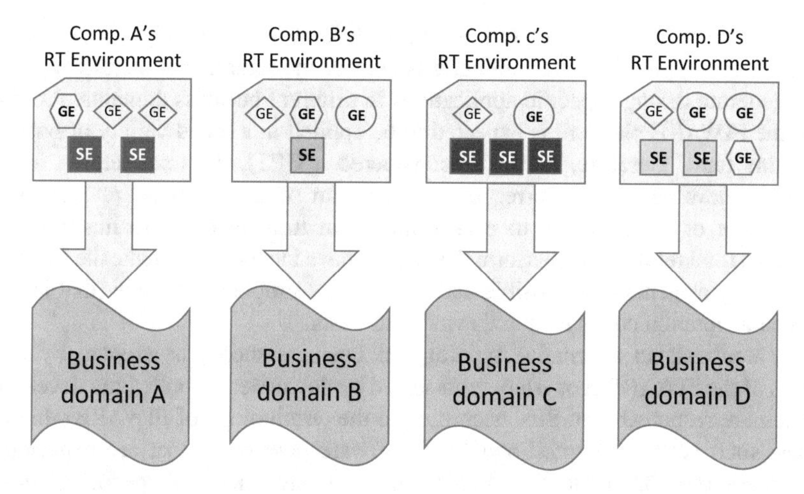

Fig. 6.3 FIWARE business domains

ronment (RT) is able to execute any Generic Enabler of FIWARE (see triangle, pentagon, exagon, etc.., shapes), however the portfolio of Specific Enablers (see rectangular shapes) for each companies is different each other. The portfolio of SPs along with their users' customizations represents the compelling offerings of each company. Hence, business scenarios might be differentiated in terms of number of GEs, SEs and customizations.

6.4.2 Identifying Business Models of Participants to the FIWARE Initiative

The FIWARE ecosystem depicted so far reveals that different agents participate in the co-development of the initiative, playing different roles, contributing with specific resources and competences, pursuing different goals, and being subject to different motivations. Within this complexity of roles and resources, we could however identify at least two common patterns that we characterized in terms of different business models adopted by the different categories of actors.

A first typology of business model is adopted by those Big Players (that is, large IT operators) that play a key role in the development of the system and in the definition of its inner characteristics. To such actors (that are responsible for the different GEs) it is demanded the relevant task of providing and developing the technological knowledge, skills and competences that are needed to make the system work. This task implies a relevant effort, both in terms of financial and human resources and technological capabilities. In principle, these actors do not participate in the development of downstream applications, and therefore the returns for their effort mainly arise from the licensing of the (usage of the) open platform to downstream operators. In this sense, such large firms mainly act as external technology suppliers, which indirectly benefit of the returns that technology users will generate through specific applications in different business domains. Provided that the FIWARE platform is expected to be applied in a broad variety of business domains (and, therefore, it can be considered a GPT), the total returns for the platform developers will correspond to the sum of the marginal returns of the application of the platform to each domain. In turn, in order to maximize the expected total returns, the platform developers have incentives to make the FIWARE technology as general as possible and its usage as simple as possible (that is, with limited adaptation costs) for the downstream users.

By contrast, an alternative typology of business model is adopted by those actors of the FIWARE ecosystem represented by downstream application developers (which are responsible of SEs, according to the terminology of FIWARE). In most cases, such actors are small and local software developers that are expected to design and develop applications to solve the contextual needs of specific groups of customers. These smaller, downstream software developers are therefore adopting an open business model. On the one side, the business model is open upward, to let the inflow of technology (the FIWARE platform) from large technology developers. On the other side, the business model is open downward, to let final customers participate in the co-development of the specialized application. In turn, the amount of value created through this business model results from the difference between the (high) value offered to final customers for the specialized and customized solutions, and the (low) cost of technology acquisition from upstream suppliers.

To better explore the way by which downstream application developers leverage the possibilities offered by the FIWARE platform, we analyzed more in details those SMEs that applied to the sub-unit of FIWARE focusing on smart cities (Frontier Cities project). The list of analyzed firms is shown in Table 6.1.

All companies listed in Table 6.1 are small firms (often start-ups) aiming at deploying IoT cloud-computing technology made available through FIWARE. They are software developers specialized in one or few application fields, which develop applications to solve needs and problems related to the field. Albeit the service they offer is strongly technology-based, their main aim is to satisfy their specific customers' needs. Therefore, they need to have a strong linkage with downstream market, being able to properly assess potential customers' characteristics and to translate often latent needs in explicit applications. Their vision is, therefore, customer oriented, as Table 6.2 seems to reveal.

In performing their task, however, they largely benefit of technological solutions (and standards) offered by the FIWARE platform. In this sense, they consider FIWARE as a repository of available general purpose component technologies, that they combine together in a creative manner to develop a (set of) device(s)/service(s) that satisfies customers' specific needs. Since components offered by FIWARE are standardized, their combination and recombination can be obtained at relatively reduced cost, that is, without the need to develop specific interfaces that allow the different components to interact among them.

Table 6.1 SMEs participating to FIWARE-frontier cities

SME	Country	Sector of activity	Main product	Web-site
Any solution	Palma de Mallorca, Spain	Smart cities	SmartLock	www.anysolution.eu/
Ares2T	Rome, Italy	Smart cities	Charge advisor	www.ares2t.com/en/web/ca.php
Breeze	Hamburg, Germany	Smart cities	Breeze	www.projectbreeze.eu
Ecogriddy	Trento, Italy	CleanTech and smart cities	Cortex	www.ecogriddy.com
Everimpact	France	Smart cities	Everimpact	www.everimpact.org
Fi-Guardian	Rio de Janeiro, Brazil	Smart cities	Fi-Guardian	
Floud	Florence, Italy	Smart cities	Floud	www.floud.eu
HealthBail	Athens, Greece	Smart cities	HealthBail	http://www.ilab.atc.gr/projects/healthbail
Koiki	Madrid, Spain	Smart cities and social learning	Koiki	www.koiki.eu
Mejora Tu ciudad	Madrid, Spain	Smart cities	ImproveYourCity	http://www.improveyourcity.org/
OpenMove	Trento, Italy	Smart cities and transportation	OpenMove	www.finodex-project.eu
Sensape	Germany	Smart cities	Chimp	www.sensape.com
SmartAppCity	La Rioja, Spain		SmartApp City	www.smartappcity.com/en/
Spero	Coimbra, Portugal	Smart cities	Spero.City	www.spero.systems/one-page/
TalkyCar	Malaga, Spain	Smart cities	TalkyCar	www.talkycar.com

Table 6.2 Elements of SMEs' business models

SME	Vision	Value proposition	Goals in FIWARE	Use of FIWARE technologies
Any solution	To develop strategic methodologies and projects in the field of tourism, smart cities and destinations and emergencies	To give people and businesses access to an application and a lock that will let them control WHEN and WHO can really enter their homes/offices	Fuding; mentoring services and business support	IoT cloud with mobile devices
Ares2T	To be the next generation charging experience for plug-in electric vehicles drivers	To develop novel future internet and clean technologies ready for the market, with particular focus on smart electro-mobility	Product development and and market scaling; contact wih industry players	Integration of several FIWARE solutions (smart charging; smart navigation services; dedicated mobile apps)
Breeze	To provide actionable insights for a more livable environments	To provide partners with actionable insights to make cities, buildings and communities more livable and healthier	Usage of several FIWARE components; interaction with a community of indstrial partners	Smart sensor networks and intelligent environmental data analytics (cloud APIs; openData platform; CitySDK data models)
Ecogriddy	Tu support energy hungry manufacturing companies that manage more than one production site and that want to run their processes in a more data-driven way	To provide a an efficient energy data management solution to business customers	Support to product development; Provsion of non-equity funds; usage of open data; networking	Fully integrated IoT architecture, mae of: (1) monitoring hardware/sensors; (2) a cloud layer; (3) an interface layer that allows users' interacton
Everimpact	Everimpact aims at solving air quality issues in cities, by measuring and monetizing their CO2 emissions	To provide cities with a real-time map of their emissions at street and building level, in order to help them target key areas of interventions	Use of FIWARE's enablers and freely available repository of applications. Product development; networking; linkage to potential partners	(1) Cosmos GE for big data analysis; (2) Geoserver/3D as GIS data provider; (3) 2D–UI GE library to build application-like interface

Fi-Guardian	To provide a smart monitor for adverse events, that is any kind of events that impact the citizens' quality of life or expose them to conditions of risks	To develop solutions to assist citizens and government to face, together, adverse circumstances such as natural disasters	Availability of key technologies in the form of generic enablers; provision of an easy, integrated and accessible cloud computing environment for developers	Generic enablers: Publish/subscribe context broker; BigData analysis-cosmos; complex event processing (CEP); stream-oriented components; application mashup; identity management
Floud	To provide an innovative, flexible and low-cost platform for road-traffic data collection and analysis	To support the development of smart environments (public and private spaces) by leveraging on existing technical and physical infrastructure	To develop initial prototype and final product	
HealthBail	To develop a platform that would enable adopters of a healthy behaviour to seek advice from online sources in an efficient and rather timely effective way	To develop a platform that offers services to virtually connect among professionals and with healthy behaviour adopters	To use generic enabling technologies	
Koiki	To change the usual concept of home delivery service by empowering the recipients to choose the day and time of delivery		Focus on open data	Usage of generic enablers: Publish/subscribe context broker; complex event processing; software deployment and configuration
Mejora Tu Ciudad	To provide different channels and communication tools, both for citizens and for city councils	To develop a communication platform between citizens, city council and technicians and utilities	Integration of several technologies available and supported by FIWARE	Generic enablers will us to improve our product in two different ways: Improving tghe design of existing architecture, adding new functionality to platform.

(continued)

Table 6.2 (continued)

SME	Vision	Value proposition	Goals in FIWARE	Use of FIWARE technologies
OpenMove		To offer an online platform for mobile ticketing including the whole range of means of transport available within a given urban area	Access to international network; use of FIWARE technology; availability of business coaching	Six generic enablers integrated in the cluster architecture of OpenMove
Sensape	To revoltunize the way brands advertise their product using artificial intelligence	Offering of marketing and sales tools with artificial intelligence in the B2B segment, by delivering a totally new and interactive way to get in contact with the customer	Availability of technology, business support, coaching and mentoring	Cloud IaaS GE, the object storage GE and KeyRock.
SmartAppCity	To bring together all the city services, boosting the commercial sector, generating value to citizens and tourist, and improving the quality of life	Support municipalities in serving citizens, and city shops and businesses in offering products and services	Provision of a standard technology and a set of open tools (generic enablers); networking	Generic enablers: BigData analysis; identity management; publish/subscribe context broker; data visualization and analysis; application mashup
Spero	To support citizens and IoT reporting and connections to social networks	To offer an integrated web-based report and decision support system for occurrences in urban space	To leverage Fiware's scalability opportunities; networking; Partcipation in the ecosystem	Generic enablers: Big data; complex event processing; object storage; POI data provider; context broker; identity manager
TalkyCar		TalkyCar connects vehicles with smartphones to track trips	To ensure the compatibility with Smart-City environments and IoT Fiware platfrom	Various technological contents available in Fiware

An example may help clarify how the system works. The Italian company Ecogriddy has developed a solution, named Cortex, that allow manufacturing companies to manage their production sites and maintain energy costs under control. Cortex makes use of different FIWARE technological components. Specifically, it is built on three layers interconnected in a classical IoT architecture fully integrated and available to customers without extra efforts from them (end-to-end solution): (1) a physical layer that consists in monitoring hardware/sensors (industrial grade); (2) a cloud layer, which collects, analyzes and elaborates further the data received by the gateways and by other contextual sources; (3) an interface layer that allows the users to interact with the energy data and to learn from them. All these components are offered by FIWARE, and the only (and main) effort made by Ecogriddy has been that of thinking at an original and creative way to combine them to solve a specific practical problem. In doing so, they have developed an organizational design that potentially offers scalability, modularity, resiliency, and compliance to open standards and edge computing capabilities that an IoT approach can offer.

Furthermore, for most SMEs participating to the initiative, absent the FIWARE platform, the planned business model could not be implemented. In the words of managers of Everimpact, a France SME developing air quality solutions for cities, "As a newly created startup, the financial support was of course really a great help to take a giant leap in our development. But where FIWARE is making a difference compared to other accelerators is on the support. Instead of starting to develop our application from the ground up, we could rapidly use the FIWARE enablers. I just can't help thinking about all the money that has been saved by the EU by providing this huge 'app store' to startups and SMEs. (. . .) Practically the technical experts and support we received saved us months of development. It is difficult to compete with such value proposition in my opinion. And it is reassuring for investors to see that your company has a solid platform to lean on."

6.5 Discussion and Conclusions

Received literature on platforms have usually associated technological platforms with a positive impact on innovation (Thomas et al. 2014). The positive effect stems from the fact that, by offering unified and easy ways to connect to common components and foundational technologies, platform leaders help reduce the cost of entry in complementary markets, and provide demand for complements, often fuelled by network effects. Platforms offer therefore a setting where it is in the interest of both private firms to elicit and encourage innovation by others. Despite these arguments the existing literature on platforms does not address the different strategies and or business models that actors involved in the platforms can pursue. This study addresses this issue and contributed contextual evidence of the strategies adopted by actors involved in a successful case, namely the FIWARE platform.

The analysis of the FIWARE case has clearly shown how the development of an IT platform that exploits the possibilities offered by IoT cloud computing can provide advantages to different types of organizations and public institutions. Our analysis revealed that the various actors that contribute to the development and usage of the platform adopt GPT-based business models that confer to them a potential competitive advantage. Therefore, it results important to discuss under which conditions such business models may offer a benefit with respect to more traditional (non GPT-based) business models.

As far as the first typology of cloud-based business models adopted by the Big Players is concerned, we saw that the more general the upstream technology (i.e., the GEs embedded into the FIWARE platform) is, and the simpler is its usage for downstream application developers, the higher the incentives for the Big Players are, since they may distribute their technological developments to a larger share of potential users. As such, this situation is quite different from traditional approaches adopted by firms in the IT sector, which were used to develop specialized technologies for each application domain and gain returns from the proprietary exploitation of the same technologies. By contrast, the division of innovative labor among the various actors involved in the FIWARE ecosystem and implied by the technology represents a new model of industry organization. Within this new model, the large firms acting as technology developers are therefore required to pursue a business model in which the value proposition is mainly defined by the offering of a general purpose technology to a diversified plethora of downstream users that may adopt the technology in contexts that are unknown *ex-ante* to the original developers.

As for the second typology of business model (adopted by downstream operators responsible of specific SEs), what makes it more or less advantageous with respect to traditional business models is the existence of two independent conditions: (1) the upstream platform (the GEs) has to be general enough to be easily and cheaply applied to differentiated business domains, which mainly depends on how the upstream system developers have designed it; and, (2) the amount of absorptive capacities (Cohen and Levinthal 1990; Zahra and George 2002) possessed by the downstream software developer, and therefore its experience, know-how and technological competences, along with its ability to understand and respond to the (latent) needs of final customers. If both conditions are satisfied, that is, if upstream operators have made the platform general enough and if downstream operators are in possess of adequate absorptive capacities, then the cost of technology adaptation that downstream software developer have to incur in to apply the GPT to the specific application need is expected to be lower than the cost that the same software developer should incur to totally develop the application in-house, if the GPT platform (FIWARE) were not present. As such, in the presence of an industry structure organized around a IoT cloud-based GPT, also downstream operators have incentives to adopt an open business model.

Finally, it is worth noticing that also governments may benefit from the development of IoT cloud-based platforms such as FIWARE. The advantage to them is not obviously economical in nature. Rather, as in the case of the European Commission that has partly funded FIWARE, governments are often required to spend public financial resources under the form of research grants to promote the development costs of the platform. The grant may also cover the whole amount of financial resources needed to the full development of the platform, thus leaving it open and freely available to downstream operators. Nevertheless, the social benefits of similar technologies are expected to overcome the share of public funds devoted to their development, mainly because the existence of the technology and the possibility for downstream users to benefit from it should favor its application to various business domains thus boosting the economy. In this respect, platforms such as FIWARE represent physical infrastructures available to many actors. And, as other general purpose technologies, such infrastructures are expected to become engines for economic growth (Helpman 1998).

The richness of our data set has allowed for the use of a fine-grained qualitative analysis. Nevertheless, our work is not free of limitations. The empirical evidence we provide in favor of our theoretical framework may be industry-specific. A second limitation is that in developing our analysis of the business models actors adopt in IT platform we are aware that multiple levels of analysis come into play. This paper does not explore the theory and practice of platform concepts beyond the level of the firm, although we have alluded to industry and sectorial level analysis. Limitations aside, this paper has the merit to focus scholar's attention on the heterogeneous, even successful, behaviors actors involved in a IT platform can adopt.

References

Amit, R., & Zott, C. (2001). Value creation in e-business. *Strategic Management Journal, 22*(6/7), 493–520.

Armstrong, M., & Wright, J. (2007). Two-sided markets, competitive bottlenecks and exclusive contracts. *Economic Theory, 32*(2), 353–380.

Baldwin, C. Y., & Woodard, C. J. (2009). The architecture of platforms: A unified view. In A. Gawer (Ed.), *Platforms, markets and innovation* (pp. 19–44). London: Edward Elgar.

Cennamo, C., & Santalo, J. (2013). Platform competition: Strategic trade-offs in platform markets. *Strategic Management Journal, 34*(11), 1331–1350.

Cennamo, C., & Santalo, J. (2015). How to avoid platform traps. *MIT Sloan Management Review, 57*(1), 12–15.

Chesbrough, H. W. (2003). *Open innovation: The new imperative for creating and profiting from technology*. Boston, MA: Harvard Business School Press.

Chesbrough, H. W. (2006). *Open business models: How to thrive in the new innovation landscape*. Boston, MA: Harvard Business School Press.

Clements, M. T., & Ohashi, H. (2005). Indirect network effects and the product cycle: Video games in the U.S., 1994–2002. *Journal of Industrial Economics, 53*(4), 515–542.

Cohen, W. M., & Levinthal, D. A. (1990). Absorptive-capacity: A new perspective on learning and innovation. *Administrative Science Quarterly, 35*, 128–152.

Cohen, W. M., Nelson, R. R., & Walsh, J. (2000). *Protecting their intellectual assets: Appropriability conditions and why us manufacturing firms patent (or not)*. Cambridge, MA: National Bureau of Economic Research (NBER).

Denzin, N. K. (1978). *The research act: A theoretical introduction to sociological methods*. New York: McGraw-Hill.

Denzin, N. K., & Lincoln, Y. S. (2000). *Handbook of qualitative research* (2nd ed.). Thousand Oaks/London/New Delhi: Sage Publication.

Deshpande, R., & Farley, J. U. (2004). Organizational culture, market orientation, innovativeness, and firm performance: An international research odyssey. *International Journal of Research in Marketing, 21*(1), 3–22.
Eisenmann, T. R. (2006). Internet companies' growth strategies: Determinants of investment intensity and long-term performance. *Strategic Management Journal, 27*(12), 1183–1204.
Elliott, R. (1999). Editor's introduction to special issue on qualitative psychotherapy research: Definitions, themes and discoveries. *Psychotherapy Research, 9*, 251–257.
Eocman, L., Jeho, L., & Jongseok, L. (2006). Reconsideration of the winner-take-all hypothesis: Complex networks and local bias. *Management Science, 52*(12), 1838–1848.
Evans, D. S. (2003). Some empirical aspects of multi-sided platform industries. *Review of Network Economics, 2*, 191–209.
Fazio, M., Celesti, A., Marquez, F. G., Alex Glikson A, & Villari, M. (2015) Exploiting the FIWARE cloud platform to develop a remote patient monitoring system. *20th IEEE Symposium on Computers and Communications (ISCC15)*, Larnaca, Cyprus, IEEE Computer Society, July, 2015.
FIWARE. Building Blocks as in the original architecture. www.fiware.org
Gambardella, A., & McGahan, A. M. (2010). Business-model innovation: General purpose technologies and their implications for industry structure. *Long Range Planning, 43*, 262–271.
Gawer, A. (2010). *Platforms, markets and innovation*. Northampton, MA: Edward Elgar.
Gawer, A., & Cusumano, M. A. (2002). *Platform leadership: How Intel, Microsoft, and Cisco drive industry innovation*. Boston, MA: Harvard Business School Press.
Gawer, A., & Cusumano, M. A. (2008). How companies become platform leaders. *MIT Sloan Management Review, 49*(2), 28–35.
Gawer, A., & Cusumano, M. A. (2013). Industry platforms and ecosystem innovation. *Product Innovation Management, 31*(3), 417–433.
Giessmann, A., & Legner, C. (2016). Designing business models for cloud platforms. *Information System Journal, 26*(5), 551–579.
Hartmann, H., & Bosch, J. (2016). Towards a multi-criteria decision support method for consumer electronics software ecosystems. *Journal of Software, 28*(6), 460–482.
Helpman, E. (1998). *General purpose technologies and economic growth*. Cambridge, MA: The MIT Press.
Iyer, B., Lee, C., & Venkatraman, N. (2006). Managing in a "small world ecosystem": Lessons from the software sector. *California Management Review, 48*(3), 28–47.
Lee, T. (1999). *Using qualitative methods in organizational research*. Thousand Oaks, CA: Sage.
McIntyre, D. P., & Subramaniam, M. (2009). Strategy in network industries: A review and research agenda. *Journal of Management, 35*, 1494–1517.
Rochet, J. C., & Tirole, J. (2006). Platform competition in two-sided markets. *Journal of the European Economic Association, 1*, 990–1029.
Rosenberg, N. (1976). *Perspectives on technology*. Armonk, NY: M.E. Sharpe.
Strauss, A., & Corbin, J. (1998). *Basics of qualitative research: Techniques and procedures for developing grounded theory* (2nd ed.). Thousand Oaks, CA: Sage.
Teece, D. J. (2010). Business models, business strategy and innovation. *Long Range Planning, 43*(2), 172–194.
Thomas, L., Autio, E., & Gann, D. (2014). Architectural leverage: Putting platforms into contexts. *Academy of Management Perspectives, 28*(2), 198–219.
Von Hippel, E., & Katz, R. (2002). Shifting innovation to users via toolkits. *Management Science, 48*, 821–833.
XIFI: the project of the European Public-Private-Partnership on Future Internet (FI-PPP) programme. https://www.fi-xifi.eu/about-xifi/what-is-xifi.html
Zahra, S. A., & George, G. (2002). Absorptive capacity: A review, reconceptualization, and extension. *Academy of Management Review, 27*, 185–203.
Zott, C., & Amit, R. (2010). Business model design: An activity system perspective. *Long Range Planning, 43*(2), 216–226.

Chapter 7
The Leadership Competencies and Intuitive Decision-Making of Top and Middle Level Managers in the Automotive Industry

Ivan Erenda, Aleksej Metelko, Vasja Roblek, and Maja Meško

Abstract The main purpose of the study was to identify the presence of intuitive decision-making by top and middle managers in the Slovenian automotive industry, to identify the influence of their behavioural competencies and emotional intelligence on intuitive decision-making, to identify their level of intuitiveness and, on the basis of theoretical and empirical research, to establish competencies and factors of the model of leadership competencies based on intuitive decision making.

As a quantitative research method, a questionnaire was used as the primary measuring instrument. It contained the following structure: (1) demography, (2) emotional intelligence (SSEIT–Schutte Self-report Emotional Intelligence Test), (3) decision-making styles (GDMS–General Decision Making Style) and (4) intuitiveness (AIM Survey–Agor Intuitive Management Survey).

Statistical data analysis was carried out using SPSS program version 21 and MS Excel version 2007, and the model was created using the program Pajek version 3. The following methods were used for research data analysis: descriptive statistics, factor analysis, regression analysis and variance analysis.

Results of the performed quantitative research show that respondents are often directed by intuition when making important decisions (79.3% make decisions based on intuition), while statistically significant differences occur (1) regarding sex, as women on average rely slightly more on intuitive decision-making than men, and (2) regarding leadership experience: respondents with the least leadership

I. Erenda
TPV d.o.o, Novo mesto, Slovenia,
e-mail: ivan.erenda@gmail.com

A. Metelko
Tiskarna Vesel d.o.o., Novo mesto, Slovenia,
e-mail: aleksej.metelko1@gmail.com

V. Roblek (✉)
Reflecta GmbH, Klagenfurt am Wörthersee, Austria
e-mail: vasja.roblek@gmail.com

M. Meško
University of Primorska, Faculty of management Koper, Slovenia
e-mail: maja.mesko@fm-kp.si

G. Dominici et al. (eds.), *Governing Business Systems*, Springer Proceedings in Business and Economics, DOI 10.1007/978-3-319-66036-3_7

experience think they are not led by intuition, while all other respondents think they are led by intuition (more than a fourth). The research findings indicate that behavioural competencies do not have any significant impact on intuitive decision-making and the same is true for emotional intelligence. Another more significant research finding shows a relatively high level of intuitiveness, as the average result is 7.1 out of 12 points. Moreover, the research indicates that level of intuitiveness increases with years of leadership experience and with higher level of education.

Keywords Management • Behavioural competencies • Emotional intelligence • Intuition • Intuitive decision-making • Automotive industry

7.1 Introduction

The automotive industry is one of the most significant sectors of industry in the world, as it has significant economic power and influence. Bilas et al. (2013) specify that according to the OICA (French: *Organisation internationale des constructeurs d'automobiles*), the automotive industry would be the world's sixth largest economy if it were an independent country. In 2011, worldwide car production stood at exactly 80,092,840 cars. In terms of size, the automotive industry is one of the largest employers worldwide and as such is directly or indirectly responsible for every ninth job in developed countries. Development of different technologies and increasing innovativeness are key factors of success in the automotive industry. The automotive market has become global – global changes are dictating the guidelines and the rate of operation as well as the entire supply chain, irrespective of the place of business. Therefore, this line of business, as specific and demanding as it is, requires specific knowledge and highly educated, motivated and innovative personnel, in particular as managers. In order to highlight the specificity of the managers' role and leadership in the automotive industry in comparison with comparable levels of managers in other lines of business, we point out some specific conditions and principles.

Naturally, the level of a leadership position along with its field are of significant importance, however we can generalise regarding the following features, which are to a great extent common to all levels or fields:

- Target-oriented activities. The system in the entire supply chain is extremely targeted. Targeted activities represent an operating principle adopted by an individual supply chain member, classifying the system of goals in both the horizontal and vertical direction – so-called goal setting in a "top-down" manner and reporting in the opposite direction, i.e. "bottom-up" manner. The key performance indicators (KPI) are clearly defined at the strategic and operational level. The system of reporting and acting is normally structured in a precise manner: (1) the content of reporting (KPI), (2) frequency of reporting (from daily to yearly), (3) manner of reporting (system of meetings, visualisation, data entry in the supporting information system) and (4) people responsible for a given area and their competent substitutes.

- Project activities. In the automotive industry, project activities are a manner of operating that results from a continuous cycle of changing car models and the resulting cyclical changes of projects and subprojects in the supply chain. A project can be treated as a sequence of actions and tasks with a defined time frame. The objective of these actions performed throughout several functions in the company has to be achieved within the requirements using different resources, e.g. human, financial. Interdisciplinarity is one of the essential features of projects (Kerzner 2009) and risk is an inherent feature of project activities, especially with development projects.
- Continuous development of competencies and mentoring. This is a property that is becoming more and more true for all industries and lines of business and not only for the automotive industry. We can say with certainty that continuous development of competencies and mentoring in the automotive industry are explicitly present and are becoming an established way of operating.
- Change management, responsiveness and flexibility. Dynamic levels of change and a significant role of time horizon in the process of change management or in the battle for competitiveness are strongly expressed in the automotive industry, reflected in the operating principle at all management levels.
- Risk management. Supply chain in the automotive industry is subject to several problems and risks that hinder its smooth functioning and therefore threaten the effectiveness of individual projects as well as the performance of companies involved in the supply chain. This is one of the reasons the automotive industry pays particular attention to risk management or occurring threats. For this reason, some organisations implement actions for identification, assessment of probability of occurrence and possible effects of risks based on previously determined processes of risk management. These are followed by determination of a plan to reduce the possibility of risk occurrence and its negative effects. Managers from all three levels play a crucial role in risk management, as through their experience, knowledge and available information, they can identify on time a possible risk occurrence and minimise or eliminate it with an early and appropriate action.

As shown in the short outline of the industry and the operating principles adopted by management in the automotive industry, which have been shaped on the basis of the said distinctive features, the need to search for a new approach to identification and understanding of the functioning of manager competencies is extremely highly expressed. The combination of circumstances in which the automotive industry management operates is especially challenging where it involves decision making, because the circumstances are increasingly difficult, which results in a higher degree of risk.

7.2 Leadership Competencies

The term competence is widespread and used in many scientific disciplines from management (e.g. competence management) to law (e.g. competence of courts and witnesses) (Mulder et al. 2009), which is the reason for their being a number of different definitions of the concept. Boštjančič (2011) states that what most definitions have in common is that they define different levels of awareness of individuals or organisations in view of achieving the desired efficiency level. Study and implementation of competencies are becoming increasingly widespread. Competencies have even spread to the extent that they no longer represent any competitive advantage but have become more of a standard mode of operation. Appropriate competencies have a particularly significant role in the development of appropriate management personnel both in the economic and non-economic sector. Namely, standard competencies acquired through full-time education are often not sufficient for effective management of continuous changes within the organisations in their wider influential environment, which leads to the extreme importance of identifying, measuring and developing key competencies of employees.

Looking back at more recent history and the concept of competencies in the sense of having a substantial connection with the general definition of the word as used today, we are taken back to the year 1959 and to R. H. White, who defined a competence as an essential need for acquiring: knowledge, skills control, and a need for research or qualification (Mulder et al. 2009). In 1967, M. Argyle, together with his colleagues, defined the factors of skilled performance (Argyle and Kendon 1967).

Then, in the year 1973, D. McClelland published, in the American Journal *American Psychologist*, an article called "Testing for Competence rather than Intelligence", where he uses the term competency as criteria for grading in the higher education system. He advocates replacing the IQ tests with a test of competencies and establishes the term competency as a feature of individuals connected with their above average performance. He also argues that above average performance is not dependant only on knowledge but also on persistence, an individual's personal characteristics and motivation. The above mentioned article was followed by several studies and research works on competencies in different areas, including teachers' education, vocational education, management and human resource management (Hsieh et al. 2012).

Gilbert (1978) defines a correlation between competencies and efficient implementation of improvements. Boyatzis (1982) carried out a study examining managers' effective performance in relation to the characteristics they have to have in order to perform different managerial jobs in different organisations effectively. Zemke (1982) extends the use of the term competencies to all aspects of training and development of employees. McLagan (1989) developed competence profiles for self-assessment and development. The competency framework for managers established by authors Quinn et al. (1996) shows the importance of thinking in terms of collective competencies of a team (team or group) and the importance or even need for various competencies inherent in team members. Prahalad and Hamel (1990) develop a concept of core competencies at the organisational level. They realise that organisations that have identified their own core competencies and have implemented them in the strategic development of their organisations achieve better results.

Classifications of competencies as well as their definition are not unified or they have not converged into a single classification. As a result, there exist several classifications or differentiations of competencies. According to one such differentiation, there are individual and organisational competencies. Sanchez (2003) defines organisational competencies as the ability of an organisation to achieve objectives considering the available resources and capabilities. Organisational competencies are based on (1) management and coordination of available resources and capabilities, (2) special-purpose integration and use of resources and capabilities for the purpose of achieving specific objectives and (3) achievement of objectives that are the basic motive and the driving force in an organisation. Spencer and Spencer (1993) define individual competencies as visible and hidden (disguised) characteristics of an individual reflected in the degree of their performance in a certain job. The listed authors identify five (5) competency characteristics, as follows: (1) motives (what motivates an individual to undertake an activity), (2) specific traits (which are psychical, such as the way of reacting in certain specific situations), (3) self-concept (intertwining of values, moral and other views, convictions and self-confidence shaping the individual's self-concept), (4) knowledge (in certain fields) and (5) skills (various skills to perform certain tasks).

Classification or differentiation of competencies into managerial or leadership competencies on one hand and technical competencies on the other is a very common undertaking that is often applicably used in profit and non-profit organisations. In view of our research, primarily focussed on intuitive decision-making or largely defined regarding the competencies of acting intuitively, we can state that this is about a relatively new way of classifying this soft and relatively unexamined competency.

7.3 Intuitive Decision-Making

"Until recently, managers felt uneasy to admit publicly that when making a decision about dozens or thousands of employees and with billions at stake, in spite of everything they have to ultimately rely on their intuition. In this scientific trait era of quantification of everything, they found it extremely inconvenient to refer to this human ability that is not appreciated at all within the professional circles of experts" (Jelovac 2009). Kralj (2003) mentions that originally intuition was used more due to poorly developed knowledge, but later on knowledge grew and therefore became strongly dominant. He says further on that the use of intuition is above all effective in different crisis situations when there is a need to make on-the-spot decisions that also represent solutions to the problem. He also points out that the use of intuition is effective when making a decision on minor issues, as the costs and possible damage resulting from a wrong decision are lower than when using other types of decision-making.

Patton (2003) came to a similar conclusion, saying that intuitive decision-making plays an important role when responding to crisis situations, especially when making a decision involving some elements of uncertainty. Several researchers (Agor 1984a, 1989; Barnard 1938; Dane and Pratt 2007, 2009; Dean and Mihalasky 1974; Hodgkinson et al. 2009; Hogarth 2001; Klein 2004; Simon 1987; Sinclair and Ashkanasy 2005; Sinclair et al. 2009) discuss the role intuition plays in making a decision. We can often find statements that people who rely on intuition are especially those who occupy hierarchically higher positions, have more complex and difficult issues to sort out and are pressed for time (Dörfler and Ackermann 2012).

Van Den Berg and Hoekzema (2006) argue that directness in intuitive decision-making renders the decisions important. Agor (1986) claims that intuition is a brain skill particularly useful for making important decisions in leadership, especially in the following circumstances: (1) when there is a high degree of uncertainty; (2) when there have been few previous cases; (3) when variables of the problem are not scientifically predictable; (4) when facts are limited; (5) when facts do not give a clear vision on which direction to go to find a solution; (6) when there are time restrictions and pressure to make the right decision; and (7) when the solution needs to be chosen from among more or less equal options. We can find similar statements in Jelovac (2009), who says that when making decisions, managers use intuition especially in the following circumstances and situations: (1) when it is not possible to get along without a clear vision for the future; (2) when new ideas need to be involved in the existing system; (3) when there is great uncertainty; (4) when there is little previous knowledge; (5) when facts are limited and do not present a clear and accurate direction of activities; (6) when analytical data are irrelevant; (7) when there is a dilemma in choosing among several alternative solutions; (8) when there is big time pressure; (9) when the decision is about people (HRM issues); and (10) when business discussions and negotiations take place.

In the past, several studies on intuitive decision-making were conducted. Their range was very broad; they covered different fields and dealt with various study issues. For instance, Sadler-Smith (2004) found in his study that in small and medium sized companies there is a positive relationship between the intuitive style of decision-making and favourable financial and non-financial indicators of a company's good performance. It is worth mentioning that Brockmann and Anthony (2002) found that managers make faster and better decisions when they rely on their intuition. They also assert that this finding is true for team decision-making (Bourgeois and Eisenhardt 1988; Eisenhardt 1989, 1990) as well as individual decision-making (Agor 1984b, 1985, 1989; Parikh et al. 1994).

The main purpose of the study was to identify the presence of intuitive decision-making among top and middle managers in the Slovenian automotive industry, to identify the influence of their behavioural competencies and emotional intelligence on intuitive decision-making, to identify their level of intuitiveness and, on the basis of theoretical and empirical research, to establish competencies and factors of the model of leadership competencies based on intuitive decision-making.

7.4 Methodology

7.4.1 Sample

The target population consists of individual "elements" that represent a basic unit of research (Kalton and Vehovar 2001). In our case, the elements of the target population are represented by managers fulfilling all the following criteria: (1) managers acting within the framework of the geographical borders of the RS, (2) managers working in companies whose core business is the automotive industry, (3) managers acting in companies with more than ten employees and (4) managers whose position is at a top or middle management level. In a broader sense, our target population of the research was represented by top and middle managers in Slovenian companies whose core business is the automotive industry.

The research covered 138 respondents, 81.3% of whom were male. Most respondents were from 31 to 40 years old (44.4%), followed by the age category from 41 to 50 years (33.3%). Most respondents had one to 5 years of experience (30.6%), followed by those with 6–10 years (27.6%) and those with 16 years or more (19.4%). A little more than half of respondents (52.7%) have the 7th level of education. A little less than half of respondents (49.3%) hold a position of department or project manager.

7.4.2 Description of Measuring Instrument

In our case, the measuring instrument is a survey questionnaire consisting of four research items: (1) demography, (2) emotional intelligence, (3) decision-making styles and (4) intuition.

The first item covering the demographic aspect consists of six closed questions referring to the following: (1) gender, (2) age, (3) years of leadership experience, (4) education, (5) workplace and (6) number of employees in the company.

The second item of the measuring instrument measured emotional intelligence by means of the SSEIT (Schutte Self-report Emotional Intelligence Test) questionnaire. It is based on Salovey and Mayer's questionnaire (1990) assessing one's own emotions, other people's emotions, expression of emotions, balancing one's own emotions and the emotions of others and use of emotions in problem solving (Schutte et al. 2009).

The SSEIT questionnaire has been used in several studies of emotional intelligence, and a lot has been written about it. Schutte et al. (2009) report that in the PsycINFO database there are more than 200 publications cited an article from Schutte et al. (1998), which represents a demonstration text of the use of the SSEIT questionnaire. In this way, the psychometric data related to the SSEIT questionnaire are available in the article regarding deployment of this questionnaire as well as in articles on several further studies made on the basis of the SSEIT questionnaire. The mentioned survey questionnaire comprises 33 statements and answers may be given within a five-point scale as follows: 1 (never), 2 (rarely), 3 (occasionally), 4 (often) and 5 (always). The total number of answers is used to determine the level of emotional intelligence of each respondent. The total scores can range between 33 and 165, and the greater the score, the higher the level of emotional intelligence.

The third item of this measuring instrument was intended to determine different decision-making styles through the GDMS (General Decision Making Style) questionnaire. This questionnaire was designed to assess how individuals approach decision-making. Five decision-making styles are pointed out as follows: (1) rational (logical evaluation of alternative options), (2) avoidant (avoiding and postponing decision-making), (3) dependent (searching for advice and directions from others), (4) intuitive (relying on instincts and feelings) and (5) spontaneous (direct decision making with a desire to make it as quick as possible). It consists of 25 statements and answers may be given within a five-point scale as follows: 1 (never), 2 (rarely), 3 (occasionally), 4 (often) and 5 (always). We used this questionnaire to examine different decision-making styles, and in accordance with the scope of our research, we were mostly interested in the intuitive decision making style. The psychometric data of the GDMS questionnaire are outlined in the initial article (Scott and Bruce 1995) and in several further studies (Baiocco et al. 2009; Bruine de Bruin et al. 2007; Dalal and Bonaccio, 2010; Galotti et al. 2006; Gambetti et al. 2008; Gati et al. 2010: Parker et al. 2007; Thunholm 2009).

The fourth and last item of the measuring instrument was intended to determine level of intuition, and for this purpose we used the questionnaire Intuitive Management Survey, often called the AIM survey, which is short for Agor Intuitive Management Survey. It was designed based on the MBTI (Myers and McCaulley 1985) questionnaire and consists of 17 closed questions (in two questions, when replying with "yes", an additional explanation is requested), four half-open questions with several alternative answers and one open question. Based on the first 12 replies to the closed questions, we can calculate the intuition points. A respondent can collect from 0 to 12 points, it being understood that a higher number of points means a higher level of intuition. Sinclair and Ashkanasy (2005) claim that at the time of their research, the AIM Survey was the most quoted measuring instrument for measuring intuition.

7.4.3 *Process*

We chose the online survey as the mode of data collection. Two main reasons for choosing this mode from among other alternatives (different types of surveys, interviews...) were the economy of carrying out the survey on one hand and adjustment of the method to the respondent's general way of acting on the other. We identified possible weaknesses of the chosen method, which are above all respondents' refusal to reply and incomplete answers to the survey questions. These two risks proved to be accurate, as they came true to an acceptable extent.

7.5 Research Results

Hypothesis 1 There is a statistically significant correlation between behavioural competencies and intuitive decision-making of top and middle management in the automotive industry.

In order to test the effect of behavioural competencies on intuitive decision-making, we used regression analysis (enter method) with the dependent variable being represented by the calculated variable of "intuitive decision-making" and the independent variables were all variables from the behavioural competencies group.

With the help of predicted variables, we can provide an explanation for 30.6% of the variation of the intuitive decision-making variable (see Table 7.1).

Regression model is statistically significant ($\alpha < 0.05$) (see Table 7.2).

Among all the variables included, only the variable 12v "I often make decisions spontaneously." has a statistically significant effect on intuitive decision making ($\alpha = 0.011$). Therefore, the frequency of spontaneous decisions does affect intuitive decision-making.

Table 7.1 Regression summary in accordance with the enter method for H1

Model	R	R^2	Adjusted R^2	Standard error of estimate
1	0.553	0.306	0.124	0.61989

Table 7.2 ANOVA in accordance with the enter method for H1

Model		Sum of squares	df	Average square	F	Sig.
	Regression	14.899	23	0.648	1.686	0.044
1	Residual	33.815	88	0.384		
	Total	48.714	111			

Although the regression model is statistically significant, we cannot deem the hypothesis confirmed, as only one out of 23 variables included has a statistically significant effect.

Hypothesis 2 There is a statistically significant correlation between the emotional intelligence and intuitive decision-making of top and middle management in the automotive industry.

In order to ascertain whether emotional intelligence has any effect on intuitive decision-making, we performed regression analysis using the enter method. As the dependent variable, the factor of intuitive decision-making was considered, whereas all variables for measuring emotional intelligence were considered as the independent variables.

With the help of predicted variables, we can provide an explanation for 36.6% of the variation of intuitive decision-making (see Table 7.3).

Regression model is not statistically significant ($\alpha = 0.238$) (see Table 7.4).

We also attempted performing regression using the stepwise method. This resulted in two regression models.

We can provide explanation for 10.5% of variation with the former and 14.3% of variation of the dependent variable with the latter. Due to the fact that, based on the coefficient of determination, the second model is more appropriate, we only consider the latter (see Table 7.5). Table 7.6 ANOVA using the enter method for H2.

Model 2 is statistically significant ($\alpha = 0.000$) (see Table 7.6).

Only the variables "Emotions are one of the things that make life worth living." and "By listening to the tone of voice, I can discern people's feelings." were included. Both of them have a statistically significant effect.

Table 7.3 Regression summary in accordance with the enter method for H2

Model	R	R^2	Adjusted R^2	Standard error of estimate
1	0.605	0.366	0.067	0.946

Table 7.4 ANOVA in accordance with the enter method for H2

Model		Sum of squares	df	Average square	F	Sig.
	Regression	36.101	33	1.094	1.223	0.238
1	Residual	62.625	70	0.895		
	Total	98.726	103			

Table 7.5 Regression summary using the stepwise method for H2

Model	R	R^2	Adjusted R^2	Standard error of estimate
1	0.323	0.105	0.096	0.931
2	0.378	0.143	0.126	0.915

Table 7.6 ANOVA using the enter method for H2

Model		Sum of squares	df	Average square	F	Sig.
1	Regression	10.330	1	10.330	11.920	0.001
	Residual	88.396	102	0.867		
	Total	98.726	103			
2	Regression	14.079	2	7.040	8.400	0.000
	Residual	84.647	101	0.838		
	Total	98.726	103			

The hypothesis therefore cannot be deemed confirmed, as it only applies to two out of 33 variables in total.

Hypothesis 3 Intuitive decision-making among top and middle management in the automotive industry in Slovenia can be defined with the subspaces of the leadership competencies variables.

In order to test the hypothesis, we first transcoded the variable "intuitive decision-making" by placing the respondents with a variable value of 2.5 or lower into the group "low intuition", whereas the respondents with a variable value higher than 2.5 were placed into the group "high intuition". The former group included 6.6% of respondents and the latter included the remaining 93.4%. Next, we performed the discriminant analysis in which we attempted to split the respondents into two groups: those with low and those with high intuition in decision-making, based on the variables from the emotional intelligence section and the section on styles of decision-making (we excluded the questions based on which the variable "intuitive decision-making" was calculated). Initially, we used the enter method, but the model was not statistically significant, so we repeated the process using the stepwise method. Three variables were included in the model, specifically: one from the emotional intelligence section (Q10ar "When I see people's facial expressions, I can recognise the emotions they feel.") and two from the section on styles of decision-making (Q12e "When making decisions, I consider different options based on the specific goal." and Q12s "I usually make important decisions at the very last moment."). Canonical correlation coefficient is 0.445; the value of Wilks' lambda is 0.802 and it is statistically significant ($\alpha = 0.000$). Among the variables included in the model, the variable Q10ar "When I see people's facial expressions, I can recognise the emotions they feel." had the highest value of structural weight, whereas the variable Q12e "When making decisions, I consider different options based on the specific goal." had the lowest value of structural weight.

The value of the canonical correlation coefficient is 0.445 (Table 7.7).

The value of Wilk's lambda is 0.802, and it is statistically significant ($\alpha = 0.000$) (see Table 7.8).

Among the variables included in the model, the variable Q10ar "When I see people's facial expressions, I can recognise the emotions they feel." had the highest

Table 7.7 Eigenvalue and canonical correlation coefficient

Function	Eigenvalue	% variance	of Cumulative %	Canonical coefficient	correlation
1	0.247	100.0	100.0	0.445	

Table 7.8 Wilks' lambda

Function	Wilks' lambda	χ2	Df	sig.
1	0.802	21.988	3	0.000

Table 7.9 Structural weight of the variables included in the model

Function 1
Q10ar_r when I see people's facial expressions, I can recognise the 0.658 emotions they feel. – Inverted value
Q12s_r I usually make important decisions at the very last moment 0.389 – Inverted value
Q12e_r when making decisions, I consider different options based — 0.365 on the specific goal. – Inverted value

value of structural weight, whereas the variable Q12e "When making decisions, I consider different options based on the specific goal." had the lowest value of structural weight (See Table 7.9).

7.6 Model of Leadership Competencies of Intuitive Decision-Making of Top and Middle Managers in the Automotive Industry

Using the Pajek (Spyder) method, we calculate dimensions of centrality showing the most central point in view of the selected criteria. Dimensions of centrality tell us if a certain point is located in the centre, on the edge or somewhere in between. The net also allows us to calculate dimensions of significance along with the dimensions of centrality. Two dimensions of significance are essential: we can measure the structural influence of individual points and the structural support of individual points. The points are considered to be influential in the net where paths of connection start. Points with high support in the net are those where the paths of influence end. Therefore, it is about those points in the net towards which flows the structural prestige or structural trust (Žerdin 2012).

We used this model to examine which variables of emotional intelligence and decision-making styles are most interconnected or most important. First, we calculated the correlation between the variables and further on considered only those pairs of variables whose correlation coefficient was higher than 0.4. We analysed the pairs of variables and their power of connectivity by means of the Pajek programme.

The highest level of importance is assigned to the variables Q10av "I can easily recognise my emotions as I experience them." and Q12q "I postpone decision-making whenever possible.", and they are both connected with five variables. If

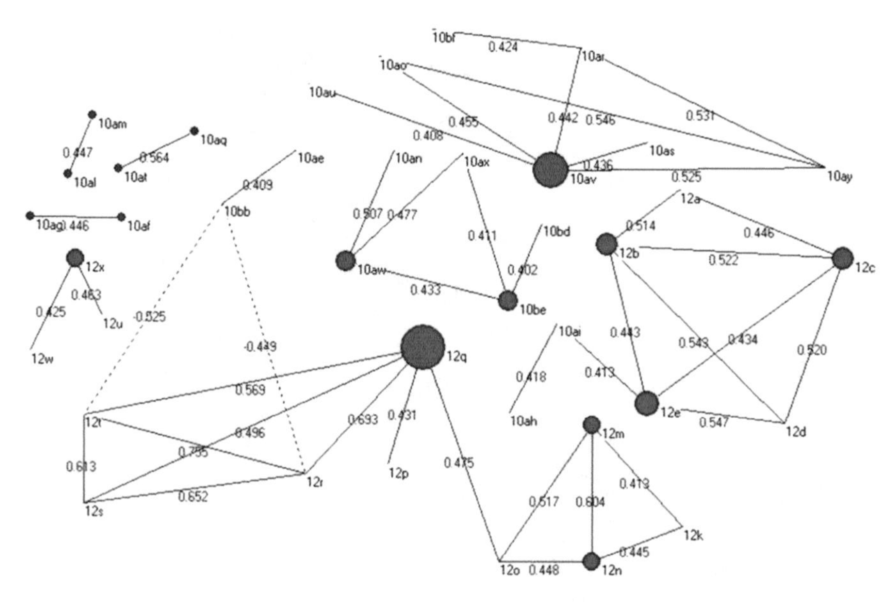

Fig. 7.1 Centre's of connections (Source: Author's work)

we also take into consideration the power of connection (correlation), the most important variable is Q12q "I postpone decision-making whenever possible.", followed by Q10av "I can easily recognise my emotions as I experience them." We also assessed what the central variables are.

The diagram shows the importance (centrality) of variables through the point size. As we have already stated, the most important variable is Q12q "I postpone decision-making whenever possible.", followed by Q10av "I can easily recognise my emotions as I experience them.", Q12e "When making decisions, I consider different options based on the specific goal.", Q12b "I doublecheck my information sources to be sure I have the right facts before making decisions." and Q12c "I make decisions in a logical and systematic way." (Fig. 7.1).

However, we did not show the correlation between the variables for the group having a low level of intuition, as it comprised only 8 units. On the other hand, we showed it for the group having a high level of intuition, namely the correlations (as for all respondents) higher than 0.4.

The highest level of importance is attached to the variables Q10av "I can easily recognise my emotions as I experience them." and Q12q "I postpone decision-making whenever possible.", and they are both connected with five variables. Considering the power of connectivity, the most important variable is Q12q "I postpone decision-making whenever possible.", followed by Q19av "I can easily recognise my emotions as I experience them."

The most important (central) variable is Q12q "I postpone decision-making whenever possible.", followed by Q10av "I can easily recognise my emotions as I experience them.", Q10aw "I motivate myself by imagining a good outcome to

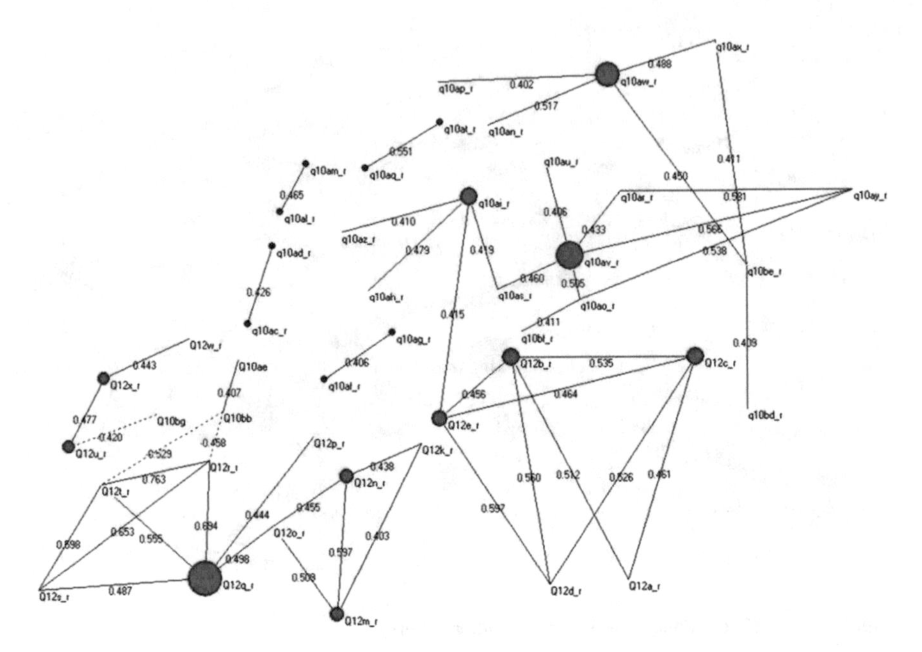

Fig. 7.2 Centres of connections for respondents with high levels of intuition (Source: Author's work)

tasks I take on.", Q10ai "I am aware of my emotions as I experience them – inverse values.", Q12b "I double-check my information sources to be sure I have the right facts before making decisions – inverse values." and Q12c "I make decisions in a logical and systematic way – inverse values." (Fig. 7.2).

When comparing the weighted levels of variables for all respondents and weighted levels of variables for respondents having high intuition, we can see that the level of the variable Q10av "I can easily recognise my emotions as I experience them." is higher for the group of respondents having high intuition (2.370) than in the group of other respondents (2.266). In addition, the weighted level of the variable Q12q "I postpone decision-making whenever possible." is slightly higher in the group of respondents having high intuition (2.678) than in the group of other respondents (2.664). Examining H1, H2 and H3 and data processing using the Pajek method, we have made conclusions about statistically typical variables (attributes) having the most typical effect on intuitive decision-making of top and middle managers in the Slovenian automotive industry. Based on the research conclusions, we can define the model of intuitive decision-making of top and middle managers in the automotive industry by means of two fundamental components and their constituents (see Fig. 7.3) as follows: (1) **emotional components** and (2) **time components** and two influential factors: (1) **experience** and (2) **awareness of intuitive functioning.**

The elements of the emotional component of the model of intuitive decision-making are the following:

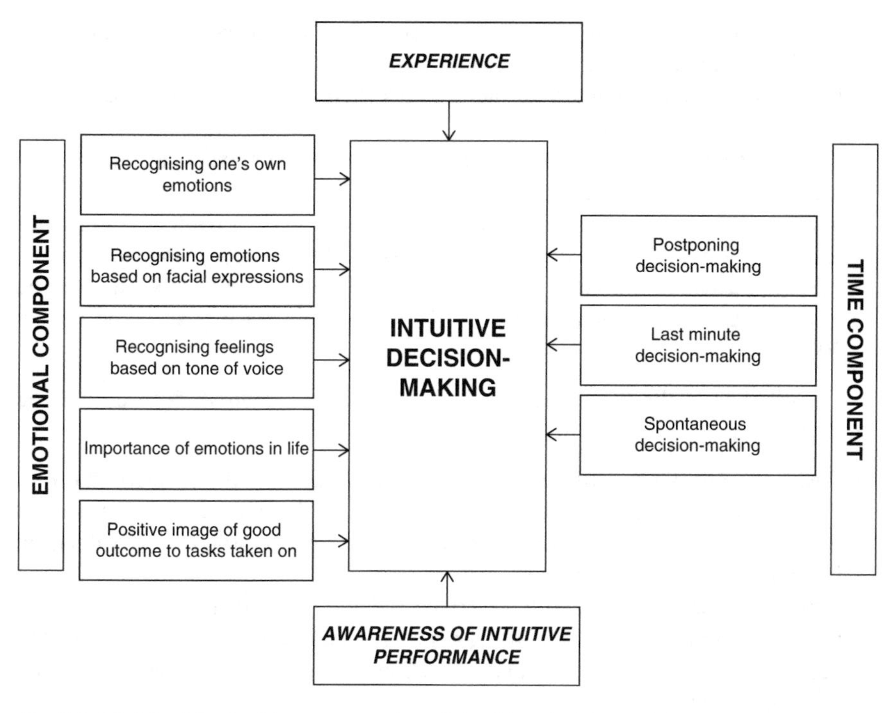

Fig. 7.3 Model of leadership competencies of intuitive decision-making of top and middle managers in the automotive industry (Source: Author's work)

- **Recognising one's own emotions** – self-knowledge, understanding one's own emotions, monitoring oneself and recognising feelings as they happen (Salovey and Mayer 1990). Recognising and awareness of one's own emotions are some of the bases for healthy emotions. Good awareness of emotions has positive effects on people's health condition and their behavioural characteristics.

  Recognising one's own emotions is a precondition for monitoring one's own emotions (positive and negative) and for recognising others' emotions. The ability to monitor emotions, positive as well as negative, represents a starting point on the scale of complexity of emotional processes (Avsec and Pečjak 2003).
- **Recognising (others') emotions based on facial expressions** – ability to identify other people's emotions through their appearance and behaviour represents the second development level of identification, assessment and expression of emotions (Avsec and Pečjak 2003). This is an ability that grows through successful identification of one's own emotions and is usually more developed with managers who meet different people on daily basis.
- **Recognising feelings based on tone of voice** – the findings related to the recognition of emotions based on facial expressions are also true for this element.
- **Importance of emotions in life** – emotions are extremely important for people, as through emotions we receive information on how to react in a given situation.

Besides, emotions are also important for motivation and behaviour of individuals and for maintaining proper relationships with other people, as correct experiencing and expressions of emotions play an important role in friendship, partnership and other social relations.

- **Positive image of good outcome to tasks taken on** – motivation and encouragement of ourselves, use of all our inclinations to pursue our objectives, to submit initiatives, to pursue our wishes to get promoted and to overcome obstacles and disappointments caused by frustrations (Goleman 2001). Besides flexible planning, creative thinking and diverting attention, motivation belongs to the group of emotion regulation within emotional intelligence (Avsec and Pečjak 2003).

Constituents of the time component of the model of intuitive decision-making are as follows:

- **Postponing decision-making** – it is typical of situations where a decision maker is not familiar with all arguments based on which they could make a clear decision, therefore they postpone making a decision, hoping the right decision is eventually given a clear frame.
- **Last minute decision-making** – is connected with postponing decision-making; when the circumstances for making a decision (without all necessary facts) are accompanied by time pressure and a decision maker is forced to make a decision in the last minute.
- **Spontaneous decision-making** – spontaneity is generally defined as a feature or characteristic of an event that happens by itself or freely and unintentionally.

Factors impacting intuitive decision-making:

- **Experience** – the research points out a statistically important influence of experience on intuitive decision-making (respondents with the least leadership experience believe they are not guided by intuition, while those with more work experience think they are guided by intuition).
- **Awareness of intuitive performance** – the level of intuition varies between respondents who consider that in their management function they are often guided by intuition and those who do not share the same opinion. The respondents claiming not to be guided by intuition on average reach a lower level of intuition than those claiming they are often guided by intuition during decision-making.

The constituents of the time component of the model of intuitive decision-making of top and middle managers are closely interlinked, in particular the constituents "postponing decision-making" and "last minute decision-making".

We wrote about the time component and correlation between the time restrictions and intuitive decision-making in the previous chapters, as many authors have reported about this correlation and they are to a great extent united on this matter. The same is true about spontaneity in decision making, which is, under different descriptions, one of the key features of intuitive performance and intuitive decision-making. We can make a similar conclusion about experience and awareness of intuitive performance being two important factors that are, in the model of intuitive decision making, accordingly shown as influential factors in intuitive decision-making of top and middle managers in the Slovenian automotive industry.

7.7 Discussion and Conclusion

The performed research represents a significant contribution to creating of a new knowledge in the field of companies' management and administration. The research raises a fundamental starting point for further in-depth and targeted research regarding other related areas of society. Originality of the research is confirmed by the fact that there is no domestic or foreign scientific literature available to demonstrate any research comprising the elements of operationalisation (examination of relationship between leadership competencies and intuitive decision-making) used in the present research.

Limitations of the research are defined in the following contexts: (1) Limitation of capabilities to give an overall theoretical retrospective review of individual areas covered by the theoretical part of the research. (2) Use of standardised measuring instruments of foreign origin and occurrence of potential differences between the environment where the measuring instruments were designed and the environment where they have been used. (3) Limitations of capabilities of translation of measuring instruments regarding words, collocations and phrases pertaining to original questionnaires for which no adequate Slovenian translations exist. (4) Use of the Pajek method, which was used in past research mostly in the field of natural science and networking, while its use in quantitative research represents a relatively new approach.

Our research has led us to the conclusion that there is no statistically important connection between the emotional intelligence and intuitive decision-making of top and middle managers in the automotive industry. Due to this conclusion, we suggest research in terms of the correlation between certain types of intelligence in the framework of Gardner's taxonomy of multiple intelligences and intuition and intuitive decision-making. The suggested research could in some parts be based on conclusions made by authors Gardner and Moran (2006), who determined correlations between interests and intellectual abilities of individuals. In our opinion, it would be particularly interesting to conduct research in terms of the correlation between social intelligence and intuition of managers in the automotive industry. We can support this suggestion by quoting authors like Boyatzis (1982), Spencer and Spencer (1993), Sanghi (2007) and Yukl (2010), who highlight various competencies successful managers should have and develop, and they point out the ability to create good social relationships first, as this is one of the basic dimensions of social intelligence.

- We believe that it would be interesting to conduct research focussed mainly on different ways the managers make decisions, whether in the automotive industry or elsewhere. The research could go in different directions, such as a comparative assessment of ways of decision-making by management levels or a comparative assessment of ways of decision-making in different departments (development, technology, production, logistics, quality, HRM, etc . . .) or ways of decision-making in different situations. The measuring instrument could be the same as used in the present research, since diverse research issues studied on the basis of information acquired by means of the GDMS questionnaire could serve to form a conceptual framework of a research issue and further on to put together a research plan. Looking into the literature and previous research, we have not found any research conducted using this measuring instrument in the field of the automotive industry.
- One of the most important conclusions of our research, which states that top and middle managers in the automotive industry are often guided by intuition, deserves attention and consideration in view of possible directions of further research. With regard to the finding that there are statistically typical differences among respondents who claim to be often guided by intuition when in a leadership role and those not sharing the same opinion, we suggest conducting research within the framework of a qualitative research concept that may by means of an in-depth study indicate a cause-and-effect framework for the mentioned phenomenon.
- We believe that research focussed on studying correlations between different leadership styles and decision-making styles (rational, avoidant, dependent, intuitive and spontaneous like in our case or using a different measuring questionnaire for the area of decision-making, including intuitive decision-making) would be of great interest.
- We think that research identifying other competencies in connection with intuition in management – competencies of intuitive functioning – would also be of great interest.

With regard to the selection of a paradigmatic approach to research in possible further research identifying the level of intuition (not applying to the manner of decision-making), we suggest to future researchers that they should choose the qualitative paradigmatic approach to research. The reason for this suggestion is the substantial content of the respondents' answers to the question "what kind of feelings they get when they know that a particular decision is right" and to the open question asking the respondents to give an example of a very important decision where they followed their intuition and their decision proved to be the right one. According to these replies, we can determine the level of the respondents' awareness about the existence of the phenomenon called intuition, and the suggested qualitative approach to research could be used to obtain advanced information by means of which we could generate new knowledge on this interesting research area. The second reason to take up the suggested qualitative approach in future research regarding the level of intuition is the relatively high rate of non-responses and incomplete responses we faced during our research. According to Kalton and Vehovar (2001), the main difficulty relating to non-responses is the danger that "respondents participating in the research survey differentiate from other eligible respondents not participating in the research". This statement certainly leads to a careful reflection on the significance of substantial validity of the acquired information before any executive restrictions, which we mostly attach to the quantitative paradigmatic approach to research.

A.1 Appendix: Summary of Results

On average, the respondents are in the upper quarter of emotional intelligence, as they scored 127.9 out of a possible 165. The respondents have a relatively high level of intuition as, on average, they collected 7.1 points out of a possible 12. The level of intuition increases with the years of leadership experience and with education level.

1. The respondents often make decisions intuitively.
2. Respondents are often directed by intuition when making important decisions.
3. Women, on average, make decisions slightly more intuitively than men.
4. Frequency of spontaneous decisions affects intuitive decision-making.
5. On average, respondents who make decisions intuitively to a greater extent recognise emotions based on facial expressions.
6. Importance of emotions in life and knowing the tone of voice are shown as statistically typical predictors of intuitive decision-making.
7. Findings from the survey data processing using the Pajek method show a significant connection between the items feelings recognition and positive image of a final outcome to a specific problem and intuitive decision-making.
8. On average, respondents who make decisions intuitively make important decisions to a greater extent at the last minute.
9. In most cases, respondents identify the right decisions through perception of strong energy and excitement.
10. In most cases, respondents identify wrong decisions through a feeling of anxiety and mixed or conflicting signals.
11. Use of intuition in important decision-making is hindered by stress and haste.
12. More than half of respondents share the opinion that they use intuition in decision-making.
13. Most respondents do not use any special techniques or methods of increasing intuition effectiveness when making difficult decisions.
14. Intuition increases with the level of education.
15. Intuition increases with the number of years of leadership experience.

16. Respondents with the fewest years of experience are not guided by intuition, while respondents with more years of experience are guided by intuition (more than three quarters of them).
17. Respondents estimate that intuition works best at the very beginning, when they try to evaluate the future or the available possibilities.
18. Most respondents do not use any techniques or methods to develop intuitive capability.
19. Behavioural competencies do not have any statistically significant impact on intuitive decision-making.

References

Agor, W. H. (1984a). Using intuition to manage organizations in the future. *Business Horizons, 27*(5), 49–54.

Agor, W. H. (1984b). *Intuitive management: Integrating left and right brain management skills*. Englewood Cliffs: Prentice Hall.

Agor, W. H. (1985). Managing brain skills to increase productivity. *Public Administration Review, 45*(1), 864–868.

Agor, W. H. (1986). How top executives use their intuition to make important decisions. *Business Horizons, 29*(1), 49–53.

Agor, W. H. (1989). *Intuition in organizations: Leading and managing productively*. Newbury Park: Sage.

Argyle, M., & Kendon, A. (1967). The experimental analysis of social performance. *Advances in Experimental Social Psychology, 3*, 55–98.

Avsec, A., & Pečjak, S. (2003). Emocionalna inteligentnost kot kognitivno-emocionalna spretnost. *Psihološka obzorja, 12*(2), 35–48.

Baiocco, R., Laghi, F., & D'Alessio, M. (2009). Decision-making style among adolescents: Relationship with sensation seeking and locus of control. *Journal of Adolescence, 32*(4), 963–976.

Barnard, C. I. (1938). *The functions of the executive*. Cambridge: Harvard University Press.

Bilas, V., Franc, S., & Arbanas, B. (2013). Utjecaj aktualne ekonomske krize na stanje i perspektive razvoja autoindustrije. *Ekonomska misao i praksa, 12*(1), 299–320.

Boštjančič, E. (2011). *Merjenje kompetenc: metoda ocenjevanja centra v teoriji in praksi*. Ljubljana: Planet GV.

Bourgeois, L. J., III, & Eisenhardt, K. M. (1988). Strategic decision processes in high velocity environments: Four cases in the microcomputer industry. *Management Science, 34*(7), 816–835.

Boyatzis, E. R. (1982). *The competent manager: A model for effective performance*. New York: Wiley.

Brockmann, E. N., & Anthony, W. P. (2002). Tacit knowledge and strategic decision making. *Group & Organization Management, 27*(4), 436–455.

Bruine de Bruin, W., Parker, A. M., & Fischhoff, B. (2007). Individual differences in adult decision-making competence. *Journal of Personality and Social Psychology, 92*(5), 938–956.

Dalal, R. S., & Bonaccio, S. (2010). What types of advice do decision-makers prefer? *Organizational Behavior and Human Decision Processes, 112*(1), 11–23.

Dane, E., & Pratt, M. G. (2007). Exploring intuition and its role in managerial decision making. *Academy of Management Review, 32*(1), 33–54.

Dane, E., & Pratt, M. G. (2009). Conceptualizing and measuring intuition: A review of recent trends. *International Review of Industrial and Organizational Psychology, 24*, 1–40.

Dean, D., & Mihalasky, J. (1974). *Executive ESP*. Englewood Cliffs: Prentice Hall.
Dörfler, V., & Ackermann, F. (2012). Understanding intuition: The case for two forms of intuition. *Management Learning, 43*(5), 545–564.
Eisenhardt, K. M. (1989). Making fast strategic decisions in high-velocity environments. *Academy of Management Journal, 32*(3), 543–587.
Eisenhardt, K. M. (1990). Speed and strategic choice: How managers accelerate decision making. *California Management Review, 32*(3), 39–54.
Galotti, K. M., Ciner, E., Altenbaumer, H. E., Geerts, H. J., Rupp, A., & Woulfe, J. (2006). Decision-making styles in a real-life decision: Choosing a college major. *Personality and Individual Differences, 41*(4), 629–639.
Gambetti, E., Fabbri, M., Bensi, L., & Tonetti, L. (2008). A contribution to the Italian validation of the general decision-making style inventory. *Personality and Individual Differences, 44*(4), 842–852.
Gardner, H., & Moran, S. (2006). At the workplace. In H. Gardner (Ed.), *Multiple intelligences: New horizons*. New York: Basic Books.
Gati, I., Landman, S., Davidovitch, S., Asulin-Peretz, L., & Gadassi, R. (2010). From career decision-making styles to career decision-making profiles: A multidimensional approach. *Journal of Vocational Behavior, 76*(2), 277–291.
Gilbert, T. F. (1978). Human competence—Engineering worthy performance. *NSPI Journal, 17*(9), 19–27.
Goleman, D. (2001). *Čustvena inteligenca na delovnem mestu*. Ljubljana: Mladinska knjiga.
Hodgkinson, G. P., Sadler-Smith, E., Burke, L. A., Claxton, G., & Sparrow, P. (2009). Intuition in organizations: Implications for strategic management. *Long Range Planning, 42*(3), 277–297.
Hogarth, R. M. (2001). *Educating intuition*. Chicago: The University of Chicago Press.
Hsieh, S. C., Lin, J. S., & Lee, H. C. (2012). Analysis on literature review of competency. *International Review of Business and Economics, 2*(1), 25–50.
Jelovac, D. (2009). *Izzivi razvoja organizacije*. Ljubljana: Založba Agathos.
Kalton, G., & Vehovar, V. (2001). *Vzorčenje v anketah*. Ljubljana: Fakulteta za družbene vede.
Kerzner, H. (2009). *Project management – A systems approach to planning, scheduling and controlling*. Hoboken: Wiley.
Klein, G. (2004). *The power of intuition: how to use your gut feelings to make better decisions at work*. New York: Doubleday Currency.
Kralj, J. (2003). *Management: temelji manegmenta, odločanje in ostale naloge managerjev*. Koper: Visoka šola za management.
McClelland, D. C. (1973). Testing for competence rather than for "intelligence". *American Psychologist, 28*(1), 1–14.
McLagan, P. A. (1989). Models for HRD practice. *Training and Development Journal, 43*(9), 49–60.
Mulder, M., Gulikers, J., Biemans, H., & Wesselink, R. (2009). The new competence concept in higher education: Error or enrichment? *Journal of European Industrial Training, 33*(8/9), 755–770.
Myers, I. B., & McCaulley, M. H. (1985). *Manual: A guide to the development and use of the Myers-Briggs type indicator*. Palo Alto: Consulting Psychologists Press.
Parikh, J., Neubauer, F. F., & Lank, A. G. (1994). *Intuition: The new frontier of management*. Cambridge, MA: Blackwell.
Parker, A. M., Bruine de Bruin, W., & Fischhoff, B. (2007). Maximizers versus satisficers: Decision-making styles, competence, and outcomes. *Judgment and Decision making, 2*(6), 342–350.
Patton, J. R. (2003). Intuition in decisions. *Management Decision, 41*(10), 989–996.
Prahalad, C. K., & Hamel, G. (1990). The core competences of organizations. *Harvard Business Review, 68*(5), 67–101.
Quinn, R. E., Faerman, S. R., Thompson, M. P., & McGrath, M. R. (1996). *Becoming a master manager*. New York: Wiley.

Sadler-Smith, E. (2004). Cognitive style and the management of small and medium-sized enterprises. *Organization Studies, 25*(2), 155–181.
Salovey, P., & Mayer, J. D. (1990). Emotional intelligence. *Imagination, Cognition and Personality, 9*(3), 185–211.
Sanchez, R. (2003). Analyzing internal and competitor competences, resources, capabilities, and management processes. In D. O. Faulkner & A. Campbell (Eds.), *The oxford handbook of strategy. Volume I: A strategy overview and competitive strategy* (pp. 344–369). Oxford: Oxford University Press.
Sanghi, S. (2007). *The handbook of competency mapping*. New Delhi: Sage.
Schutte, N. S., Malouff, J. M., Hall, L. E., Haggerty, D. J., Cooper, J. T., Golden, C. J., & Dornheim, L. (1998). Development and validation of a measure of emotional intelligence. *Personality and Individual Differences, 25*(2), 167–177.
Schutte, N. S., Malouff, J. M., & Bhullar, N. (2009). The assessing emotions scale. In C. Stough, D. Saklofske, & J. Parker (Eds.), *The assessment of emotional intelligence* (pp. 119–134). New York: Springer Publishing.
Scott, S. G., & Bruce, R. A. (1995). Decision-making style: The development and assessment of a new measure. *Educational and Psychological Measurement, 55*(5), 818–831.
Simon, H. A. (1987). Making management decisions: The role of intuition and emotion. *Academy of Management Executive, 1*(1), 57–64.
Sinclair, M., & Ashkanasy, N. M. (2005). Intuition: Myth or a decision-making tool? *Management Learning, 36*(3), 353–370.
Sinclair, M., Sadler-Smith, E., & Hodgkinson, G. P. (2009). The role of intuition in strategic decision making. *The Handbook of Research on Strategy and Foresight, 6*(4), 393–417.
Spencer, L. M., & Spencer, S. M. (1993). *Competence at work*. New York: Wiley.
Thunholm, P. (2009). Military leaders and followers – Do they have different decision styles? *Scandinavian Journal of Psychology, 50*(4), 317–324.
Van Den Berg, E., & Hoekzema, D. (2006). Teaching conservation laws, symmetries and elementary particles with fast feedback. *Physics Education, 41*(1), 47–56.
Yukl, G. (2010). *Leadership in organizations*. Upper Saddle River: Pearson Prentice Hall.
Zemke, R. (1982). Job competencies: Can they help you design better training? *Training, 19*(5), 28–31.
Žerdin, A. (2012). Vpliv zamenjave politične elite na omrežje ekonomske elite. (Doktorska disertacija). Ljubljana: Fakulteta za družbene vede. Retrieved in May 2016 from: http://dk.fdv.uni-lj.si/doktorska_dela/pdfs/dr_zerdin-aleksander.PDF

Chapter 8
Government Performance, Ethics and Corruption in the Global Competitiveness Index

Davide Di Fatta, Roberto Musotto, and Walter Vesperi

Abstract Public administration efficiency is an up to date topic. More in depth, the crucial point is how it is related, on the one hand, with a disruptive phenomenon like corruption and, on the other hand, with ethics. This study aims to show how public sector performance is affected by ethics and corruption. In order to explain such a relationship, this research run a cross-country analysis, where indices of public-sector performance are juxtaposed with corruption levels.

Using the Global Competitiveness Index (GCI) from World Economic Forum, through a regression analysis on a dataset made by 140 countries in 2014–2015, this paper shed the light on the relationships between public-sector performance, ethics and corruption.

Results show a correlation between government efficiency and ethics. These findings could be an inspiration for government workers and managers in order to establish an ethical culture that can increase public performance.

Keywords Public administration • Ethics • Corruption • Institutions • Government efficiency

8.1 Introduction

Public administration executes policy objectives set by the government. It achieves in practice any plan, program or priority according to specific instructions. This long arm of politics plays a big role when economic institutions have to be put into effect. Hence, the quality of governance has broad consequences in the growth of nations (Olson et al. 2000). It also helps to explain why some countries can grow faster than

D. Di Fatta (✉)
SEAS Department, University of Palermo, Palermo, Italy
e-mail: difatta.davide@gmail.com

R. Musotto • W. Vesperi
University of Messina, Messina, Italy
e-mail: roberto.musotto@unime.it; walter.vesperi@unime.it

G. Dominici et al. (eds.), *Governing Business Systems*, Springer Proceedings in Business and Economics, DOI 10.1007/978-3-319-66036-3_8

others can: because the political action if more effective and efficient than others when productivity has to be stimulated.

Huhtala et al. (2015) studies the associations between ethical organizational culture and engagement: this relation should be a reference point both for private and public workers in order to establish an ethical culture that can increase public performance.

This paper aim to show how public sector performance is affected by ethics and corruption. In order to show such a relationship, we run a cross-country analysis where indices of public-sector performance are juxtaposed with corruption levels. Basically, the intuition is that when public officers and government officials have to apply law, enforce policies and execute orders with a certain degree of discretion bribes and other illicit systems can guide or influence their behavior. Once the bribe is taken, the executive process is enhanced and speeds up.

Data are extracted from 2015–2016 Global Competitiveness Report from World Economic Forum. It presents the rankings of the Global Competitiveness Index (GCI) on 12 different pillars of economics development. This paper explores in a new way this path: while others (Acemoglu and Verdier 1998; Mo 2001) looked on the correlation between those parameters, this manuscript looks out for another possible correlation with the weak ties problem.

The paper is organized as follows: this first section is an introduction. The second one proposes a literature review. Third section explain the research method and the indices structure. Fourth section deals with results and discussion. Fifth section concludes.

8.2 Literature Review

Corruption in public sector in a frequent topic in previous studies, starting from Heidenheimer et al. (1970). This paper aim to provide an international point to view aiming to build a research framework able to capture the relation among government performance, ethics and corruption (Yolles and Di Fatta 2017a).

8.2.1 Government Performance and Corruption

A pivotal study about corruption in the public sector Heidenheimer et al. (1970) identified three different types of corruption: “black corruption” involving abhorrent actions and requiring punishment; “white corruption” related to depreciable acts, but not severe enough to warrant sanction; “grey corruption” in the middle between the two other above mentioned types of corruption.

In general, there is a widespread belief that corruption affects growth and public sector performance (Gould and Amaro-Reyes 1983; Mauro 1995; Jain 2001). However, there is no consensus in the literature if it is a desirable thing or not.

In particular, two different opinions can be found in the past literature on this topic: Mauro (1997) asserted that corruption might be responsible of slow economic growth and lower quality of public services because of rent-seeking issues of governments and bureaucracies.[1] On the opposite point of view, Acemoglu and Verdier (1998) assessed how some corruption might be helpful for public sector performance. And Mo (2001) considered corruption the "lube" that allows smooth bureaucratic operations and helps to raise the efficiency of an economy. Considering this different points of view, this research focus on both side of the features that affect public sector performance: ethics (Sen 1999) and corruption (Heidenheimer et al. 1970).

8.2.2 Global Competitiveness Index (GCI)

For our study, we take into account the structure of the Global Competitiveness Index (GCI), developed by Schwab and Sala-i-Martin (2011) in collaboration with the World Economic Forum.

Each year, since 1979 (Schwab 1979), annual reports "*have examined the factors enabling national economies to achieve sustained economic growth and long-term prosperity*" (Sala-i-Martin et al. 2007, p. 3). The GCI was introduced in 2004 by the World Economic Forum in order to measure and compare national competitiveness among countries taking into account specific components that influence their level of productivity.

National competitiveness has always been an issue for policy makers (Reinert 1995). Starting from simple cross-country comparisons of import and export, nowadays it evolved in intensity and spread, concerning a growing number of policy makers, analysts and enterprises (Lall 2001).

Competitiveness concept and national competitiveness derive from business school literature. The idea is that countries run like enterprises. Therefore, the productivity level sets the prosperity level that can be earned. This concept is influenced by Porter (1990) conceptual framework of competitiveness appeared first in The Competitive Advantage of Nations.

Companies compete for markets and resources, while looking for better strategies in order to improve their performance. Hence, nations should work in a similar way. National economies "*compete with each other, can measure competitive performance, and mount competitiveness strategy*" (Lall 2001, p. 1503).

Sala-i-Martin et al. (2007) define national competitiveness as a set of institutions, policies and factors that determine the level of productivity of a country. This pantagruelic set is based upon 12 Pillars that reflect a different spectrum of reality, allowing comparisons across time and countries.

[1]From this point of view, public corruption is also responsible of lower investments, loss of tax revenues, monetary problems and composition of government expenditure.

National competitiveness approach has been widely criticized. Krugman (1994) calls it a "*dangerous obsession*" that gets into misleading results. In fact, the most common definition of competitiveness requires that "*price or cost indices are expressed in a common currency*" (Krugman 1994, p. 3). This implies that, assuming any other factor constant, countries are somehow competing against each other.

This competing view is not always true when different economies trade with each other; they do not behave like firms in a zero sum competitive arena, but exchanges can be beneficial for both countries.

Despite any criticism moved against such an index, competitiveness analysis is a valid instrument for policy makers because it has the great advantage to spot problems and to show efficiency effects. Indices benchmark national performance and show a path for governments in order to achieve specific objectives. In fact, indices allows studying and evaluating the effects of national policies and reforms that can be corrected through institutional changes.

This is where the Global Competitiveness Index aims to and why it is crucial in order to build a competitiveness strategy: "*to analyze which failures are remediable by policy and whether the government concerned has the ability to undertake such policy*" (Lall 2001, p. 1505).

On such grounds, government efficiency and corruption are analyzed in order to outline a possible path for policy makers that might allow increasing productivity.

8.3 Methodology

This study deals with the structure of the GCI (Schwab and Sala-i-Martin 2011). Specifically, we focused our attention on the report 2014–2015, the first pillar, sub-point A such as public institutions, in order to evaluate a relation among "ethics and corruptions" and "government efficiency" between 140 countries.[2]

[2]Countries involved in this study are: Albania, Algeria, Argentina, Armenia, Australia, Austria, Azerbaijan, Bahrain, Bangladesh, Belgium, Benin, Bhutan, Bolivia, Bosnia and Herzegovina, Botswana, Brazil, Bulgaria, Burundi, Cambodia, Cameroon, Canada, Cape Verde, Chad, Chile, China, Colombia, Costa Rica, Côte d'Ivoire, Croatia, Cyprus, Czech Rep., Denmark, Dominican Rep., Ecuador, Egypt, El Salvador, Estonia, Ethiopia, Finland, France, Gabon, Gambia, Georgia, Germany, Ghana, Greece, Guatemala, Guinea, Guyana, Haiti, Honduras, Hong Kong SAR, Hungary, Iceland, India, Indonesia, Iran, Islamic Rep., Ireland, Israel, Italy, Jamaica, Japan, Jordan, Kazakhstan, Kenya, Korea Rep., Kuwait, Kyrgyz Republic, Lao PDR, Latvia, Lebanon, Lesotho, Liberia, Lithuania, Luxembourg, Macedonia FYR, Madagascar, Malawi, Malaysia, Mali, Malta, Mauritania, Mauritius, Mexico, Moldova, Mongolia, Montenegro, Morocco, Mozambique, Myanmar, Namibia, Nepal, Netherlands, New Zealand, Nicaragua, Nigeria, Norway, Oman, Pakistan, Panama, Paraguay, Peru, Philippines, Poland, Portugal, Qatar, Romania, Russian Federation, Rwanda, Saudi Arabia, Senegal, Serbia, Seychelles, Sierra Leone, Singapore, Slovak Republic, Slovenia, South Africa, Spain, Sri Lanka, Swaziland, Sweden, Switzerland, Taiwan China, Tajikistan, Tanzania, Thailand, Trinidad and Tobago, Tunisia, Turkey, Uganda, Ukraine, United Arab Emirates, United Kingdom, United States, Uruguay, Venezuela, Vietnam, Zambia, Zimbabwe.

8.3.1 Ethics and Corruptions

Ethics and corruptions is a composite indicator capturing three variables: 1-diversions of public funds to companies, individuals, or groups due to corruption, 2-public trust in politicians, 3-irregular payments and bribes. Scores are expressed according to a seven point Likert scale (Dawes 2008): if diversion of public funds is common, indicator is equal to one; if never occurs, it is equal to seven.

With respect to public trust in the financial honesty of politician, the value 1 corresponds to very low trust; 7 = very high.

In a similar way, irregular payments and bribes values is the result of average score across the five components of the following question: in your country, how common is it for firms to make undocumented extra payments or bribes in connection with (a) imports and exports; (b) public utilities; (c) annual tax payments; (d) awarding of public contracts and licenses; (e) obtaining favorable judicial decisions? In each case, the answer ranges from 1 (very common) to 7 (never occurs).[3]

8.3.2 Government Efficiency

Government efficiency is also a composite indicator and it captures five variables: wastefulness of government spending, burden of government regulation, efficiency of legal framework in setting disputes, efficiency of legal framework in challenging regulations and transparency of government policymaking.

Wastefulness of government spending is a measure for how efficiently the government spend public revenue? The answer ranges from 1, meaning extremely inefficient to 7 meaning extremely efficient in providing goods and services.

Burden of government regulation measures how burdensome is for businesses to comply with governmental administrative requirements (i.e. permits, regulations, reporting): it is equal to 1 if it is extremely burdensome; 7 = not burdensome at all.

With respect to the efficiency of legal framework in setting disputes, it is scaled according to how efficient is the legal framework for private businesses in settling disputes: it is equal to 1, if extremely inefficient; 7 if extremely efficient.

Efficiency of legal framework in challenging regulations is computed in relation to the following question: how easy is it for private businesses to challenge government actions and/or regulations through the legal system? If the answer is extremely difficult, the score is 1; if it is extremely easy, the score is 7.

[3]Source: World Economic Forum, Executive Opinion Survey

The last point refers to government efficiency: it explains the transparency of government policymaking, or in other words how easy is it for businesses to obtain information about changes in government policies and regulations affecting their activities. The results ranges from 1, meaning extremely difficult, to 7 meaning extremely easy.[4]

8.3.3 Scatter Plot and Linear Regression

Each model begins with an idea of some kind of relationship among certain variables: in other words, typically starting from observation, the researcher hypothesize that one variable varies with another or is caused by another (Greene 2011). As probably already known, regression is the study of a dependence and a linear regression model is used to study the relationship between a dependent variable and one or more independent variables (Weisberg 2005).

Basically, our idea is that government efficiency varies in relation with ethics and corruption. Before setting the linear regression model, the first step is a graphical representation of the phenomenon through the scatter plot. Scatter graph or scatter plot is a graph in which two (or more) variables in a data set are shown on a Cartesian space (Montgomery et al. 2015). Results will be shown in the next section.

In order to investigate this relation we adopted the Ordinary Least Squares (OLS) regression method. OLS is an optimization technique (or regression) that allows to find a function, represented by a regression curve, which is as close as possible to a set of data (typically points of the plane). In particular, the function must be the one that minimizes the sum of squares of the distances between the observed data and he responses predicted by the linear approximation of the data (residuals).

According to Greene (2011) OLS is the benchmark approach, and often, the preferred method. Gujarati (2009) suggests that OLS method is intuitively appealing and mathematically much simpler than the others. Furthermore, we have also to consider the OLS statistical properties (Davidson and MacKinnon 1993):

1. The OLS estimators are expressed in terms of the observable variables (i.e., X and Y): therefore, they can be easily computed;
2. They are point estimators: each of them will provide only a single point (or value) of the population;
3. Once the OLS estimates are obtained from the sample data, the sample regression line can be easily obtained.

[4]Source: World Economic Forum, Executive Opinion Survey

8.4 Results and Discussion

In our case, having two variables ("government efficiency" and "ethics and corruption"), we must decide which to represent on the horizontal axis (x) and which on the ordinate (y). In order to check our intuition we use government efficiency composite index (above described in the third section) as dependent variable; ethics and corruption composite indicator (above described) is used as independent variable (Fig. 8.1).

As shown in the graph, intuitively Y increases when X increases and Y decreases when X decreases. Then we can suppose that there is a sort of relation among them. Therefore, as suggested by literature aforementioned (Davidson and MacKinnon 1993; Gujarati 2009; Greene 2011) we use OLS regression in order to check linear relation (Fig. 8.2).

The coefficient of determination (R^2) is usually used in classical regression analysis (Stock and Watson 2007; Rao 2009). According to Nagelkerke (1991), it is the proportion of variance explained by the regression model; therefore, it is also a useful measure of success of predicting the dependent variable from the independent variables. In our case $R^2 = 0.83$ and this score confirms a strong linear correlation.

These results are consistent with the findings by Frederickson and Rohr (2015), which studied the relation between ethics and public performance considering also the perception of this phenomenon by citizens.

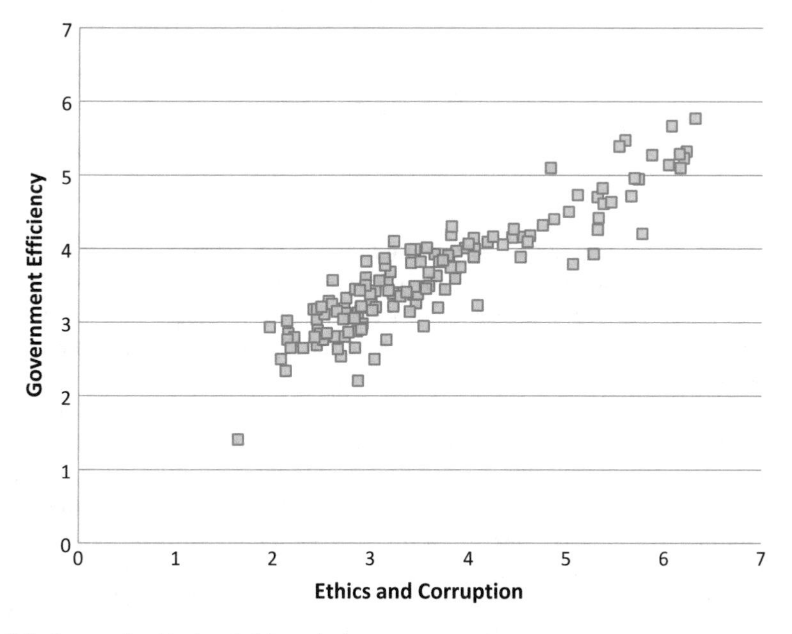

Fig. 8.1 Scatter plot (Authors' elaboration)

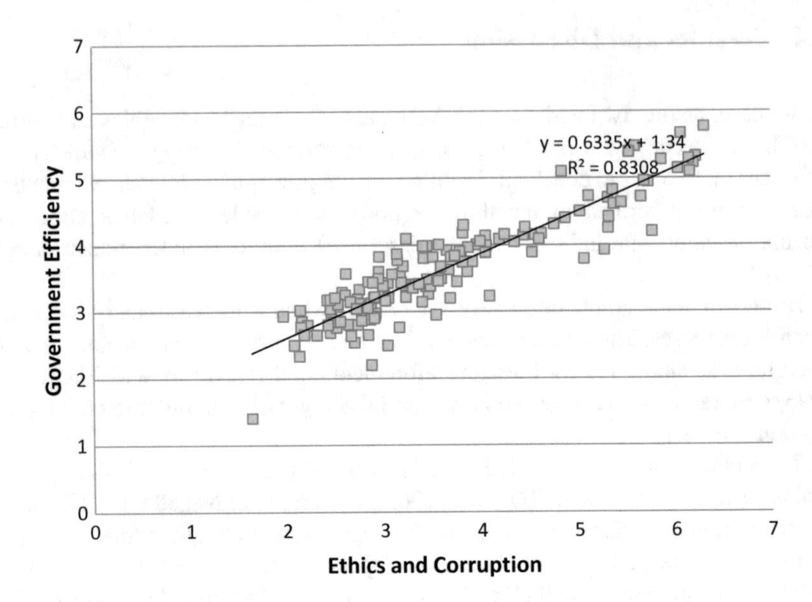

Fig. 8.2 Linear regression (Authors' elaboration)

Table 8.1 Scores (Authors' elaboration)

	Ethics and corruption	Government efficiency
1°	Singapore 6.3	Singapore 5.8
2°	Finland 6.2	Qatar 5.7
3°	New Zeland 6.2	Hong Kong 5.5
…	…	…
138°	Brazil 2.1	Argentina 2.3
139°	Paraguay 2.0	Italy 2.2
140°	Venezuela 1.6	Venezuela 1.4

However, as we mentioned before, literature is not unanimous: Mauro (1997) showed how corruption might be responsible of slow economic growth and lower quality of public services (rent-seeking); while others (Acemoglu and Verdier 1998; Acemoglu et al. 2000; Mo 2001; Musotto et al. 2017) showed that a certain level of corruption could improve public sector performance.

Moreover, it is interesting to note the outlier value of Venezuela that has the 140th position in ethics and corruption (with a score of 1.6) and the 140th position in government efficiency (with a score of 1.4). On the opposite way, it is relevant underline the first position for Singapore in both sides: 6.3 ethics and corruption and 5.8 government efficiency. The following table shows the podium of the top three and the worst three (Table 8.1).

These findings are supported by Yeo et al. (2015), which studied Singapore public sector organization showing that job satisfaction led to higher level of organizational citizenship behaviors. On the contrary, in Venezuela, corruption creates a negative spiral that leads to inefficiency in the public sector, which leads to further corruption and so forth (Weyland 1998).

8.5 Conclusion and Implications

Using a linear regression model, our results highlight a correlation between government efficiency and ethics: in particular, we have emphasized the cases of Singapore and Venezuela, which are the two extreme outliers.

These findings could be useful for policy makers: the main implication of this study is about ethical culture. Basically, our idea is to support the creation of a virtuous circle between ethics and government efficiency: higher government efficiency tends to be associated with higher per capita income.

In an environment characterized by high efficiency (which results in high levels of performance), corruption is a deviance element: in other words, creating an ethical culture is a driving force for government efficiency and improve its performance. On the contrary, as above mentioned for Venezuela, Weyland (1998) suggested that corruption in public sector generates a negative spiral that leads to government.

Shacklock et al. (2011) found a certain correlation between ethical climate in public environment and decision making. Instead, our conclusion is that there is also a positive correlation between ethics and government performance.

8.5.1 Limitations and Further Studies

From the theoretical point of view, the main limitation of this study is related to the selected variable. Indeed, this model could be extended consider other efficiency determinants such as: sociodemographic variables: education, natality, mortality etc. (Gupta and Verhoeven 2001; Afonso et al. 2005, 2010); security of property right, income level, competence of civil service (Afonso and Aubyn 2006); GDP and richness of the country (Hauner and Kyobe 2010).

This point could be the launching ramp for furthers researchers interested in studying other determinants of public sector performance: empowerment, commitment, allegiance to the flag, public spending, public debt, government investment and import/export balance also considering the Cultural Agency Theory (CAT) perspective (Yolles and Di Fatta 2017b) in order to add a predictive power to the research.

Another suggestion for further studies could be to repeat the analysis with the updated GCI data, which will be released in the next 2 years.[5] Thus, this paper is not a point of arrival, but a springboard for further studies.

Bibliography

Acemoglu, D., & Verdier, T. (1998). Property rights, corruption and the allocation of talent: A general equilibrium approach. *The Economic Journal, 108*(450), 1381–1403.

Acemoglu, D., Johnson, S., & Robinson, J. A. (2000). The colonial origins of comparative development: An empirical investigation (No. w7771). National bureau of economic research.

Afonso, A., & Aubyn, M. S. (2006). Cross-country efficiency of secondary education provision: A semi-parametric analysis with non-discretionary inputs. *Economic Modelling, 23*(3), 476–491.

Afonso, A., Schuknecht, L., & Tanzi, V. (2005). Public sector efficiency: An international comparison. *Public Choice, 123*(3–4), 321–347.

Afonso, A., Schuknecht, L., & Tanzi, V. (2010). Income distribution determinants and public spending efficiency. *The Journal of Economic Inequality, 8*(3), 367–389.

Alter, C., & Hage, J. (1993). *Organizations working together*. Newbury Park: Sage.

Balaguer-Coll, M. T., Prior, D., & Tortosa-Ausina, E. (2007). On the determinants of local government performance: A two-stage non parametric approach. *European Economic Review, 51*(2), 425–451.

Davidson, R., & MacKinnon, J. G. (1993). *Estimation and inference in econometrics*. New York: Oxford University Press.

Dawes, J. G. (2008). Do data characteristics change according to the number of scale points used? An experiment using 5 point, 7 point and 10 point scales. *International Journal of Market Research, 50*(1), 61–77.

Frederickson, H. G., & Rohr, J. A. (2015). *Ethics and public administration*. New York: Routledge.

Gould, D. J., & Amaro-Reyes, J. A. (1983). The effects of corruption on administrative performance. World Bank Staff Working Paper, 580, 2514.

Greene, W. H. (2011). *Econometric analysis* (7th ed.). Prentice Hall: New York University.

Gujarati, D. N. (2009). *Basic econometrics*. New York: Tata McGraw-Hill Education.

Gupta, S., & Verhoeven, M. (2001). The efficiency of government expenditure: Experiences from Africa. *Journal of Policy Modeling, 23*(4), 433–467.

Hauner, D., & Kyobe, A. (2010). Determinants of government efficiency. *World Development, 38*(11), 1527–1542.

Heidenheimer, A. J., Johnston, M., & LeVine, V. T. (1970). *Political corruption* (Vol. 24, pp. 26–27). New York: Holt, Rinehart & Winston.

Huhtala, M., Tolvanen, A., Mauno, S., & Feldt, T. (2015). The associations between ethical organizational culture, burnout, and engagement: A multilevel study. *Journal of Business and Psychology, 30*(2), 399–414.

Huxham, C., & Vangen, S. (2005). *Managing to Collaborate*. London: Routledge.

Jain, A. K. (2001). Corruption: A review. *Journal of Economic Surveys, 15*(1), 71–121.

Krugman, P. R. (1994). Competitiveness: A dangerous obsession. *Foreign Affairs, 73*(2), 28–44.

Lall, S. (2001). Competitiveness indices and developing countries: An economic evaluation of the global competitiveness report. *World Development, 29*(9), 1501–1525.

Mauro, P. (1995). Corruption and growth. *The Quarterly Journal of Economics, 110*(3), 681–712.

Mauro, P. (1997). *Why worry about corruption?* (Vol. 6). Washington DC: International Monetary Fund.

[5]As already said, our study used 2014–2015 GCI data.

Mo, P. H. (2001). Corruption and economic growth. *Journal of Comparative Economics, 29*(1), 66–79.

Montgomery, D. C., Peck, E. A., & Vining, G. G. (2015). *Introduction to linear regression analysis*. New York: John Wiley & Sons.

Musotto, R., Di Fatta, D., Morabito, G., D'Aleo, V., Bue, S. L., & Vesperi, W. (2017). Managing organized crime. In *Strategic human capital development and management in emerging economies* (pp. 41–58). Hershey: Pennsylvania (USA).

Nagelkerke, N. J. (1991). A note on a general definition of the coefficient of determination. *Biometrika, 78*(3), 691–692.

Olson, M., Sarna, N., & Swamy, A. V. (2000). Governance and growth: A simple hypothesis explaining cross-country differences in productivity growth. *Public Choice, 102*(3–4), 341–364.

Porter, M. E. (1990). The competitive advantage of nations. *Harvard business review, 68*(2), 73–93.

Provan, K. G., Fish, A., & Sydow, J. (2007). Interorganizational networks at the network level: A review of the empirical literature on whole networks. *Journal of Management, 33*, 479–516.

Rao, C. R. (2009). *Linear statistical inference and its applications* (Vol. 22). London: John Wiley & Sons.

Reinert, E. (1995). Competitiveness and its predecessors – a 500 year cross-national perspective. *Structural Change and Economics Dynamics, 6*(1), 23–42.

Sala-i-Martin, X., Blanke, J., Hanouz, M. D., Geiger, T., Mia, I., & Paua, F. (2007). The global competitiveness index: Measuring the productive potential of nations. The global competitiveness report, 2008, 3–50.

Schwab, K. (1979). *Report on the competitiveness of European industry 1979*. Geneva: European Management Forum.

Schwab, K., & Sala-i-Martin, X. (Eds.). (2011). *The global competitiveness report 2011–2012*. Geneva: World Economic Forum.

Sen, A. (1999). *On ethics and economics*. Cambridge: OUP Catalogue.

Shacklock, A., Manning, M., & Hort, L. (2011). Ethical climate type, self-efficacy, and capacity to deliver ethical outcomes in public sector human resource management. *Journal of New Business Ideas & Trends, 9*(2), 34–39.

Stock, J. H., & Watson, M. W. (2007). *Introduction to econometrics*. London: Pearson.

Weisberg, S. (2005). *Applied linear regression* (Vol. 528). London: John Wiley & Sons.

Weyland, K. G. (1998). The politics of corruption in Latin America. *Journal of Democracy, 9*(2), 108–121.

Yeo, M., Ananthram, S., Teo, S. T., & Pearson, C. A. (2015). Leader–member exchange and relational quality in a Singapore public sector organization. *Public Management Review, 17*(10), 1379–1402.

Yolles, M., & Di Fatta, D. (2017a). Antecedents of cultural agency theory: In the footsteps of Schwarz living systems. *Kybernetes, 46*(2), 210–222.

Yolles, M., & Di Fatta, D. (2017b). Modelling identity types through agency: Part 1 defragmenting identity theory. *Kybernetes, 46*(06), 1068–1084.

Chapter 9
Innovation in Cultural Districts: The Cases of Naples and Washington

Valentina Della Corte, Giovanna Del Gaudio, Fabiana Sepe, and Chiara D'Andrea

Abstract During the years, academics and practitioners have given great attention to the role played by cultural heritage and arts in revitalizing and regenerating central and peripheral areas of contemporary cities.

In the era of global markets and knowledge sharing, the production of culture represents an increasingly complex activity: on the one hand, culture should adapt to goods and services that are different for content and technology; on the other hand, it should try to satisfy a very heterogeneous demand. With these premises in mind, it seems to be clear that culture represents an essential resource to several geographical areas in order to re-launch themselves and to be competitive in the global arena.

The aim of the paper is to analyse evolved cultural districts in order to understand what is the role innovation plays both at the systemic and firm level; also, this research aims at capturing the way innovation can support cultural districts in their promotional activities, both at the organic phase and during the service provision.

In order to proceed with this analysis, the paper discusses the theme of innovation in cultural districts from a theoretical perspective to then present an empirical study that take into account two cultural districts, D.A.T.A.B.E.N.C. and the District of Washington, which successfully implemented innovation in their activities.

Keywords Cultural districts • Innovation • Collaboration

9.1 Introduction

The aim of the paper is to analyse evolved cultural districts in order to understand the role of innovation at different levels (systemic level and firm level) and phases (both organic – the phase of service provision and induced – the phase of promotion).

V.D. Corte (✉) • G. Del Gaudio • F. Sepe • C. D'Andrea
Department of Economics, Management, Institution of University of Naples Federico II, Via Cinthia, Naples (Napoli) 80126, Italy
e-mail: valentina.dellacorte@unina.it

G. Dominici et al. (eds.), *Governing Business Systems*, Springer Proceedings in Business and Economics, DOI 10.1007/978-3-319-66036-3_9

Nowadays, evolved cultural districts are forced to face with the creation, development, diffusion of innovation, the management of relationships between different stakeholders that have to generate/implement innovation as well as the valorization and promotion of the cultural district.

This complex perspective leads to a precise structure of the paper that develops the analysis in some main points. The first one regards the study of innovation in evolved cultural districts in order to understand its real meaning and how it is created and spread throughout the district. The second point deals with the investigation of interactions among stakeholders involved into an evolved cultural district, that can be defined as a "well-recognized, labeled, mixed-use area of a city in which a high concentration of cultural facilities serves as the anchor of attraction" (Frost-Kumpf 1998). It is a context in which it is possible to develop creative ideas, also through the support of high technology (van der Duim 2007). The third point refers to the analysis of districts' valorization and promotion according to an innovative lens. Hence, the bidding agent of the previous points is the study of innovation and its role as both keystone and transversal component in this precise configuration of district.

The current research deepens the literature on cultural districts related to innovation theories and the dynamic capabilities and relational view.

Given the above-mentioned reflections, the paper examines, through a comparative case study analysis, two districts: D.A.T.A.B.E.N.C. in Naples, Italy and the District of Washington, USA in order to understand how these districts innovate.

9.2 Theoretical Framework

Districts are expression of specific local vocation (Testa 2013) where it is possible to find a high territorial specialization either products or services, the so-called "flexible specialization" (Piore and Sabel 1984), depending on their relative nature. A district is a specific structure where "community and firms tend to merge" (Becattini 1990, p. 39). This definition supports the concept of "social embeddedness" that leads to the development of this issue according to different perspectives, either economic (Marshall 1925; Brusco 1982) or social (Bellandi and Sforzi 2001). The interplay between both economic and social mechanisms requires a solid entrepreneurial component from the start-up phase.

Before proceeding with the theoretical analysis, a clarification about the terms "district" and "cluster" is necessary.

Actually, some researchers (Sydow et al. 2011) use the terms "cluster" and "district" as synonymous even if many scholars (Bijaoui et al. 2011; Sciarelli 2007) agree that these concepts and the relative research streams are different.

According to Porter (1998), a cluster is a "geographic concentration of industries and specialized suppliers, complementary, independent, yet interdependent, that jointly carry out their activities and/or share research, human capital, technologies and infrastructures. They are both competitors and capable of a collaboration that increases productivity and competitiveness". Marshall (1919) sees a district as "a socio-economic entity formed by a set of companies, usually being part of the same productive sector, located in a circumscribed area, among which there is co-operation, but also competition". This belongs to what shapes the "economies of agglomeration" (Marshall 1919).

In spite of these definitions, the current paper is based on a concept of district as strategic network (Gulati et al. 2000; Jarillo 1988; Borch and Arthur 1995) of firms located in a specific geographic area. According to Gulati et al. (2000), strategic networks "encompass a firm's set of relationships, both horizontal and vertical, with other organizations" and "are composed of inter-organizational ties that are enduring, are of strategic significance for the firms entering them".

Some scholars analyzed districts' structural features (Rabellotti and Schmitz 1999), while others have discussed different themes such as the role of co-operation, the districts' competitiveness (Meneghetti and Chinese 2002), the importance of local culture, the role of institutional actors (Provasi 2002; Di Giacinto and Nuzzo 2006), etc.

The classic literature on districts (Piore and Sable 1984; Easton and Axelsson 1992; Hakansson and Johanson 1993) stresses the importance on the fact that "network supplies or can supply the firm with resources, which otherwise would not have been available to the firm, and the network offers flexibility when organizing production" (Havnes and Senneseth 2001).

Within this complexity, some firms consider the benefits of taking part to a network (i.e., access to resources or reduce risk costs (Kogut 2000), trying to overcome the classic resistances to cooperation.

The firms that activate or take part to the process of a district creation express their willingness to realize new ideas, to spread innovation or to create new job opportunities (Aldrich 1999), as districts act as incubators for canalizing already available resources and competences and create new sources of value.

The recall to entrepreneurship within district literature can be connected with the Schumpeterian view (1934) that conceives the entrepreneur as an innovator with the interpretation of new venture creation and able to generate opportunities in their broader meaning. In this direction, according to some scholars (Alvarez and Barney 2001), the creation/discovery of opportunities is related to entrepreneurial capabilities.

Trust, shared values and mutuality become evident only when collaboration is effectively spread among the members of the district. As regards co-operation within a district, some scholars argue that there is the necessity to balance co-operation and competition (You and Wilkinson 1994).

Such process seems to drive a coopetition context (Nalebuff et al. 1996; Dagnino and Padula 2002; Della Corte and Aria 2016) that can reveal itself to be very profitable since competition favours innovation and through collaboration it is possible to start strategic initiatives that increase the market power of the whole network.

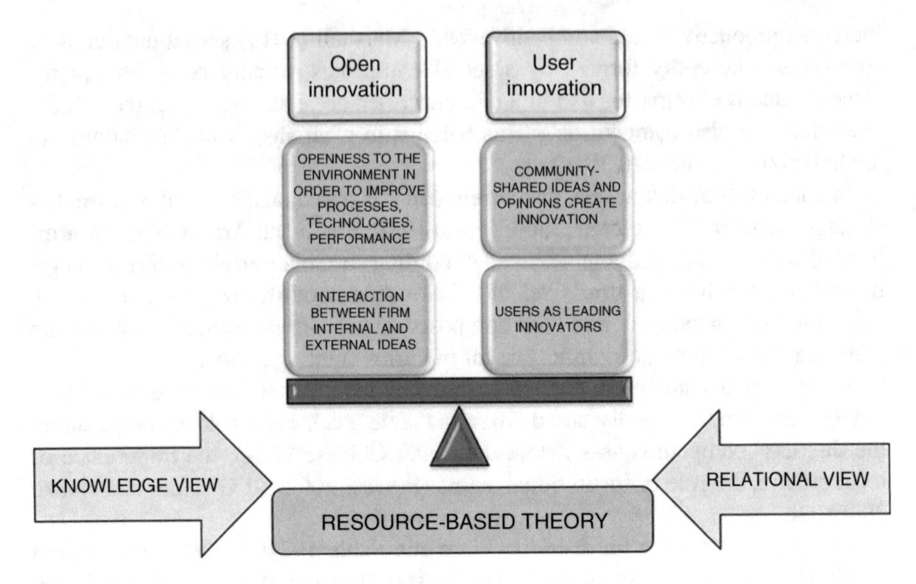

Fig. 9.1 The theoretical framework (Source: Our elaboration)

Starting from the analysis of the peculiar aspects that characterize the innovation in cultural districts, we have gone to research the links among the following frameworks:

- the Resource-Based Theory (RBT – Grant 1991; Barney 1996; Barney and Clark 2007);
- its most recent approaches, in terms of relational view (Hunt and Derozier 2004) and knowledge view (Grant 1991, 1996; Cabrera-Suárez et al. 2001);
- the theories that are at the basis of the innovation concept.

This connection allows us to define the assumptions of open and user innovation that are useful to the achievement of our research goal, which is the analysis of high technology cultural districts in order to understand the role of innovation at both systemic and firm level at the organic an induced levels.

As shown in Fig. 9.1, linking open and user innovation to RBT, it is possible to understand, with reference to the innovation dimension, what are the factors that can be considered sources of firm competitive advantage and to describe the different forms of involvement and interaction with the customer.

Taking into account the RBT foundations, the literature review confirms that one of the rarest and most inimitable resources is knowledge (Du Plessis 2007). This perspective suggests that the innovation dimension develops within the firm boundaries. On the other hand, the studies on Open Innovation state that most innovative firms are those able to combine new internal resources with the external ones in order to create innovation.

Moreover, studies on competitive advantage (Grant 1991; Barney 1996; Barney and Clark 2007; du Plessis 2007) consider the role of inter-firm relationships between the firm and its partners/stakeholders as strategic for the achievement of positive performance in the market. Hence, the major is the customer involvement in the firm's activities, the minor will be the effort that the firm itself has to bear in order to meet customer needs.

Users create innovation when they produce creative ideas that can be translated into radical or incremental products, processes or services improvements. These innovations create value for the consumers and for the entire firm. These concepts, linked to the innovation implemented within an evolved cultural district, stand out the necessity to create new products and services, starting from the ideas suggested from the external environment and implementing information that are potentially accessible for all.

The major is the users' engagement, the major is the possibility that consumers collaborate in order to swap and share information.

The competitive scenario imposes tourism and cultural firms, and more importantly districts, to search for new ideas that can come from the outside environment and assume new internal processes and technologies to improve their competitive position.

In line with these assumptions, the district logic underlines the presence of important social relationships with competitors in order to compete successfully.

Martín-de-Castro et al. (2011) argue that innovation process consists of a mix between current (recalling the definition of social capital these are "resources embedded within" and "available through") and new knowledge ("derived from" looking at social capital definition) implemented for commercial objectives.

This would explain the reason why in the current context – characterized by economic recession, uncertainty and dynamism – the district finds its raison d'être. The belonging to the district represents the main source able to adapt to market changes (Stieglitz and Heine 2007).

A set of privileged relationships can generate the creation/strengthening of innovation and improve the time-to-market (Rindfleisch and Moorman 2001). In sum, the willingness to commercialize their own products/services is what drives members to build relationships and to cooperate.

The presence of a wide number of firms and the mixture between public and private bodies can stiffen the process of innovation and slow down changes.

Actually, the concept of innovation perfectly joins the growth aspirations of entrepreneurs who decide to undertake the decision about the new venture within a district. Besides, although districts can favour innovation, the related process may be gradual rather than fast.

The locus of innovation may reside in networks but, sometimes, there could be limits to innovation due to insufficient internal capabilities (firm level) in supporting this process (Cohen and Levinthal 1990) or to the lack of knowledge transfer at network level.

9.3 An Outline of the Evolved Cultural District Model

Over the time great attention has been given to the role of cultural heritage and arts in revitalizing and regenerating central and peripheral areas of contemporary cities (Brooks and Kushner 2001; Ponzini 2009; Santagata 2002; Lorenzini 2011).

In the era of global markets and knowledge sharing, the production of culture represents an increasingly complex activity because, on the one hand, culture should adapt to goods and services that are different for content and technology; on the other hand, it should try to satisfy a very heterogeneous demand. With these premises, it seems to be clear that culture is a resource on which different areas should count on in order to re-launch themselves and to be competitive in the global arena. Since culture is becoming more and more a constitutive mechanism of the value creation process, the theories on industrial districts (Marshall 1919; Richardson 1972) pave the way to the study of the economic value of cultural districts. A cultural district is defined as a *territorially delimited system of relationships that integrates the valorisation process of both tangible and intangible cultural facilities with infrastructure and other productive sectors that are related to that process. The creation of a cultural district aims at making more efficient and effective the production process of "culture" and, optimizing, on local scale, its economic and social impacts* (Valentino 2001).

From this definition emerges that the cultural district is characterized by the presence of local firms, which show their willingness to valorise their resources and to take advantage of the products resulting from the enhancement and development of an area. In addition, the quality of these resources affects the quality of other factors such as infrastructure, or, more in general, the territory of reference.

There are four essential elements that characterize a district; it should be: complex (involving a large number of actors), relational (based, therefore, on a system of relationships), participated (able to engage and interconnect different actors) and planned (in the sense that comes from a top-down strategy and not from the historical and environmental characteristics of the area).

As emerges from Fig. 9.2, according to Valentino, the cultural district assumes a reticular form that is expressed in a system of relationships, which in turn can be divided into four homogeneous sub-systems (Valentino 2003):

- sub-system of territorial resources, for the valorisation of historical, cultural and environmental resources in the area;
- sub-system of human and social resources, in which there are elements such as 'human capital' (i.e. the workforce) and 'social capital' (i.e. education and institutions);
- sub-system of accessibility services, such as the transport service;
- sub-system of hospitality services, related to accommodation and entertainment;
- sub-system of enterprises belonging to different sectors, such as crafts, communication, restoration.

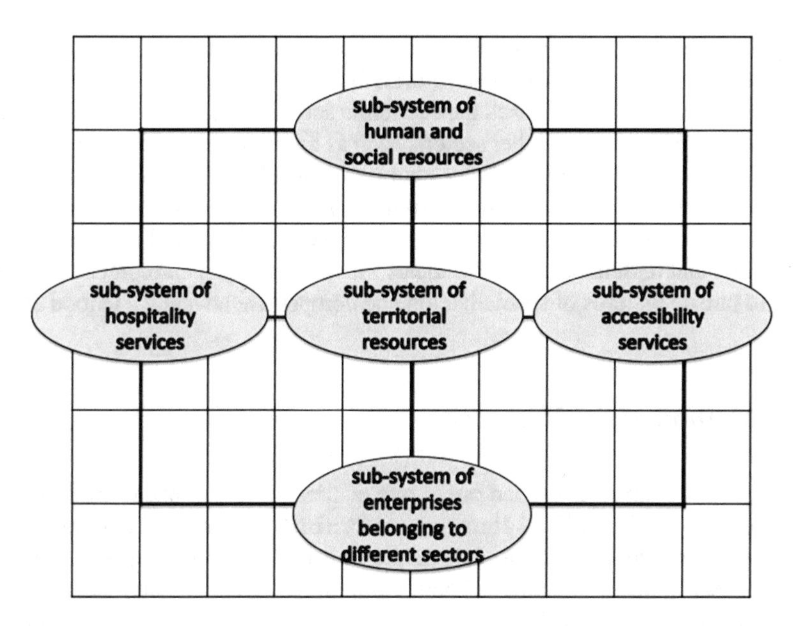

Fig. 9.2 Sub-systems of a cultural district (Source: our elaboration from Valentino 2003)

This classification highlights the idea of an "integrated valorisation process" theorized by Valentino, according to which the cultural district develops around the most valuable cultural assets of a territorial area, so that both the cultural sector, and the entire territory can generate a competitive advantage. This latter can be achieved only if there is a system of relationships, which aims at connecting the cultural and environmental, tangible and intangible resources towards a unique strategy shared by all actors there operating.

In order to promote cultural factors in a defined area, a central role is played by the systemic logics of the "evolved cultural district" (Sacco and Blessi 2006; Sacco 2010). Innovation, economy and culture are the pillars upon which this systemic district is based. The evolved cultural district is a "system of systems" made up of enterprises and cultural institutions that are homogeneous for specialization and belong to the same territory. These actors are able to establish vertical, horizontal and transversal relationships looking for internal and external integration (Usai 2016).

This systemic organization derives from a complex integration of a large number of actors, such as public administration, local entrepreneurs, universities, cultural operators and local communities.

All stakeholders aim at developing an area and a key role is played by local communities, which take actively part to the value generation process for the local system (Sacco 2006; Mizzau and Montanari 2008).

In this optic, there seems to be evident that the district is characterized by an eclectic combination of top-down and bottom-up elements; in other words, it is a kind of a *self-organization process*, where culture assumes the role of a "synergistic agent" for the development of the territorial factors.

In the evolved cultural district, the economic activities related to cultural heritage produce positive effects on other sectors, such as tourism and contribute to generate innovation, creativity and knowledge sharing for local production systems. In this conception, production and cultural fruition rather than to be intended as profit centers or direct factors of economic development, are conceived as elements able to generate and disseminate creative ideas. This is what local entrepreneurs need in order to pursue patterns of specialization and competitive advantage (Moon 2001).

9.4 Method of the Research

The empirical analysis is carried out in two districts. The first one is the District of High Technology for Cultural Heritage (DATABENC), an evolved cultural district, which was created in order to bridge the existing gaps in Campania Region's strategic management approach of both cultural and environmental heritage in its interconnections with tourism industry. Federico II University is the governing-promoting actor of this district, shaped by more than 60 members.

The second one is the District of Washington, in the United States of America. This district is analysed in the light of its tourism implications. The tourist soul of the district is expressed through the destination management organization that includes both private and public organizations.

The research methodology adopts a comparative case study analysis and analyzes the relative qualitative results. Furthermore, the case study methodology is in line with the exploratory nature of this paper since it is able to capture contextual richness and complexity of research issues (Yin 2003) and to understand the social structures (Riege 2003). According to Aarikka-Stenroos and Sandberg (2012, p. 201) two case studies "allow rich description and comparison" as well as to proceed with a cross-case comparisons (Eisenhardt 1989).

First, from the literature review, there is the necessity to study the role of the interactions among the members. Second, the literature review has emphasized key issues and, hence, the empirical part explores if the relations established within the district can be effectively considered as strategic.

In order to capture these reflections, in-depth interviews with the promoter actors and the other members were conducted following a predesigned protocol (Yin 2003). Indeed, the interviews used a snowball method that allows to catch information from both central actors and peripheral ones in order to obtain a more holistic view.

These interviews were semi-structured. Furthermore, the research group is still taking part to workshops and round tables as non-participant observer, studying the interactions among the internal members and between the latters and the entire referring ecosystem.

Data were collected from different sources such as semi-structured interviews, annual report, feasibility studies, other secondary sources and direct observations. Respondents were identified through the study of district composition.

9.5 Discussion

The District of high technology for Cultural Heritage (DATABENC) originates from the willingness of Federico II University of Naples. This governing actor, indeed, can be defined as accelerator in creating an advanced cultural district in order to bridge the existing gaps in Campania Region' strategic management approach of both cultural and environmental heritage in its interconnections with tourism industry.

This district is born within the National Operative Program (PON 2007–2013) called "Research and Competitivity" referring to the line of intervention n.2 "Districts of high technology and related networks" to whom the feasibility study of DATABENC is linked.

As regards the field of interest of this district, the entrepreneurial subject identified four thematic areas within archaeological areas, documentation and archiving and Smart historic centre (Fig. 9.2):

1. **Knowledge**: under this voice, it is included the knowledge about the cultural products within Databenc district in terms of their history, contents and technical characteristics such us used materials and techniques of construction.
2. **Preservation**: this mostly refers to the logic of preventive preservation rather than curative one. In this sense, the district activities contemplate a planned maintenance that is less invasive of the restoration. Both preservation and restoration are linked to the transversal activity of constant monitoring.
3. **Security and safety**: these concern the identification and realization of measures towards possible risks that cultural heritage could be subjected to. While the security refers to intentional causes, the safety concerns motivations that are not directly intentional (i.e., environmental risks, transportation of cultural products for exhibitions out of the museum, etc.).
4. **Valorisation, fruition and promotion**: these two terms, in entrepreneurial terms, are conceived as unique expression since the valorisation of cultural resources allows to give a unique fruition both for tourists and local community where the use of specific technologies helps intensifying the degree of involvement, offering a unique experience during the fruition phase.

The current configuration of this District of high technology for Cultural Heritage is the result of a collaborative process generating a network structure and shaping an integrated cultural heritage system. DATABENC is in fact a local operator of differentiated cultural offers, playing a pivotal role in the process of building brand identity.

The other opportunity can be referred to the fact that heritage and culture are still conceived and managed in a traditional, out of date approach, mainly focused on preservation rather than on valorization, promotion and fruition.

Furthermore, the district, as socio-territorial identity, characterized by an active pull of actors and firms needs capabilities able to form alliances even for its creation.

As regards the District of Washington, one of its main strength is the presence of Smithsonian. This latter is constituted by 19 Institutions (galleries, museums, National Zoological Park, etc.).

According to the managers of the district the current innovation activity is devoted to:

- Identify the type of leisure needs, linked to leisure, that the cultural district intends to cater for visitors/tourists with particular reference to the unmet needs;
- Identify the cultural experiences that can be targeted to the needs of specific tourists/visitors;
- Identify the additional experiences that are compatible with the mission and the cultural district's resources;
- Identify the ways through which potential users can be informed and attracted to the district experiences:
- Ensure that visitors tourists, both new repeaters, are completely satisfied with the experiences lived within the district and services and it connected;
- These described-above assets align perfectly with the strategic objective called "Audience" which aims to "attract a wider audience and engage him in deeper relationships and long-term."

An example is offered, for the innovation in this field, by the activation of summer camps for families with children by offering specific activities (meeting with experts of the artistic and cultural field, seminars and courses in the form of edutaiment on specific themes, musical program strongly customized, journey through history through imagination, etc.).

The collaboration with George Mason University is an example that allows understanding how a cultural district wants to attract the audience of university students. Students of the course "decorative arts" have, in fact, access to the museum spaces and private collections to be able to study on field the cultural, historical and artistic elements.

9.6 Main Implications and Findings

This paper outlines both theoretical and managerial implications. From a theoretical point of view, the paper stresses the attention on the role of cultural districts as expression of specific local vocation (Testa 2013) and strategic relationships among members. Secondly, the district configuration presumes the existence of relationships among competitors and, hence, the development of both competitive and cooperative attitudes (Nalebuff et al. 1996), that this paper deepens. Actors operating in cultural districts possess a high territorial either productive or service specialization.

From a managerial point of view, the paper shows the stakeholders involved into a cultural district and, particularly, the collaborative and competitive processes among actors, generating knowledge transfer and sharing, in a value co-creation perspective. Moreover, another managerial implication is connected with the opportunity of implementing efficient interactions within districts because the set of privileged relationships can generate the creation/strengthening of innovation and improve time-to-market (Rindfleisch and Moorman 2001; Arnaboldi and Spiller 2011). Although districts can favour innovation, this paper also explores if the related process may be gradual rather than fast.

Findings show that innovation plays a key role in high technology cultural districts innovation. The implementation of innovation process, consisting of a mix between current and new knowledge, is strategic for commercial objectives. The relationships among the stakeholders of the districts increase when members recognize the value of digital platforms in classifying and disseminating cultural heritage and its main peculiarities.

The districts' external scenario is increasingly dynamic and the interactions among the internal members are becoming complex to manage and may involve a large number of stakeholders. Therefore, firms have to implement creative strategies and innovative business models in order to increase fluidity related to the dynamic nature of the collaboration.

Theoretical findings show that, despite substantial research in this field, there remain gaps in the analysis of the stakeholder collaborations in developing creative and high technology tourism/cultural districts.

9.7 Conclusion

In conclusion, the previous considerations lead us to point out that the implementation of innovative policies in the cultural field allows contemporary cities to be proactive, offering exciting and qualifying opportunities for citizens.

Cultural development is a concept that links the past with the future: if on the one hand it is intended as an intelligent conservation of the existing heritage, on the other, it needs to innovate in order to generate social and economic benefits. This justifies the existence of the concept of evolved cultural district that is distinguished from earlier notions of cultural district and industrial district for its innovative component that allows to strategically define its resources and capabilities.

Evolved cultural districts can be compared to "learning" regions, which are places where the cognitive processes play a crucial role, combining know-how, interpretations, information with intellectual artefacts, allowing the exchange of experiences and cooperation.

References

Aarikka-Stenroos, L., & Sandberg, B. (2012). From new-product development to commercialization through networks. *Journal of Business Research, 65*(2), 198–206.

Aldrich, H. (1999). *Organizations evolving*. Los Angeles/London/New Delhi: Sage Publications.

Alvarez, S. A., & Barney, J. B. (2001). How entrepreneurial firms can benefit from alliances with large partners. *Academy of Management Executive, 15*(1), 139–148.

Arnaboldi, M., & Spiller, N. (2011). Actor-network theory and stakeholder collaboration: The case of cultural districts. *Tourism Management, 32*(3), 641–654.

Barney, J. B. (1996). The resource-based theory of the firm. *Organization Science, 7*(5), 469–469.

Barney, J. B., & Clark, D. N. (2007). *Resource-based theory: Creating and sustaining competitive advantage*. Oxford: Oxford University Press.

Becattini, G. (1990). The Marshallian industrial district as a socio-economic notion. In F. Pyke, G. Becattini, & W. Sengenberger (Eds.), *Industrial districts and inter-firm co-operation in Italy* (pp. 37–51). Geneva: International Institute for Labor Studies.

Bellandi, M., & Sforzi, F. (2001). La molteplicità dei sentieri di sviluppo locale. In G. Becattini, M. Bellandi, G. Dei Ottati, & F. Sforzi (Eds.), *Il caleidoscopio dello sviluppo locale. Trasformazioni economiche nell'Italia contemporanea*. Turin: Rosenberg and Sellier.

Bijaoui, I., Sultan, S., & Tarba, S. Y. (2011). The progressive model, an economic reconciliation process for regions in conflict. *Cross Cultural Management: An International Journal, 18*(3), 293–312.

Borch, O. J., & Arthur, M. B. (1995). Strategic networks among small firms: Implications for strategy research methodology. *Journal of Management Studies, 32*(4), 419–441.

Brooks, A. C., & Kushner, R. J. (2001). Cultural districts and urban development. *International Journal of Arts Management, 4*, 4–15.

Brusco, S. (1982). The Emilian model: Productive decentralisation and social integration. *Cambridge Journal of Economics, 6*(2), 167–184.

Cabrera-Suárez, K., De Saa-Perez, P., & García-Almeida, D. (2001). The succession process from a resource-and knowledge-based view of the family firm. *Family Business Review, 14*(1), 37–46.

Cohen, W. M., & Levinthal, D. A. (1990). Absorptive capacity: A new perspective on learning and innovation. *Administrative Science Quarterly, 35*, 128–152.

Dagnino, G. B., & Padula, G. (2002). Coopetition strategy: A new kind of interfirm dynamics for value creation. In *The European Academy of Management (EURAM) Second Annual Conference – Innovative Research in Management.*

Della Corte, V., & Aria, M. (2016). Coopetition and sustainable competitive advantage. *Tourism Management, 54*, 524–540.

Du Plessis, M. (2007). The role of knowledge management in innovation. *Journal of Knowledge Management, 11*(4), 20–29.

Easton, G., & Axelsson, B. (Eds.). (1992). *Industrial networks: A new view of reality*. Abingdon: Routledge.

Eisenhardt, K. M. (1989). Agency theory: An assessment and review. *Academy of Management Review, 14*(1), 57–74.

Frost-Kumpf, H. A. (1998). *Cultural districts: The arts as a strategy for revitalizing our cities*. New York: Americans for the Arts.

Giacinto, V. D., & Nuzzo, G. (2006). Explaining labour productivity differentials across Italian regions: The role of socio-economic structure and factor endowments. *Papers in Regional Science, 85*(2), 299–320.

Grant, R. M. (1991). The resource-based theory of competitive advantage: Implications for strategy formulation. *California Management Review, 33*(3), 114–135.

Grant, R. M. (1996). Toward a knowledge-based theory of the firm. *Strategic Management Journal, 17*(S2), 109–122.

Gulati, R., Nohria, N., & Zaheer, A. (2000). Guest editors' introduction to the special issue: Strategic networks. *Strategic Management Journal, 21*(3), 199–201.

Håkansson, H., & Johanson, J. (1993). *The network as a governance structure: Interfirm cooperation beyond markets and hierarchies*. London: Routledge.
Havnes, P. A., & Senneseth, K. (2001). A panel study of firm growth among SMEs in networks. *Small Business Economics, 16*(4), 293–302.
Hunt, S. D., & Derozier, C. (2004). The normative imperatives of business and marketing strategy: Grounding strategy in resource-advantage theory. *Journal of Business & Industrial Marketing, 19*(1), 5–22.
Jarillo, J. C. (1988). On strategic networks. *Strategic Management Journal, 9*(1), 31–41.
Kogut, B. (2000). The network as knowledge: Generative rules and the emergence of structure. *Strategic Management Journal, 21*(3), 405–425.
Lorenzini, E. (2011). The extra-urban cultural district: An emerging local production system: Three Italian case studies. *European Planning Studies, 19*(8), 1441–1457.
Marshall, A. (1919). *Industry and trade. A study of industrial technique*. London: Macmillan.
Marshall, A. (1925). The present position of economics. In A. C. Pigou (Ed.), *Memorials of Alfred Marshall* (pp. 152–174). London: Macmillan.
Martín-de-Castro, G., Delgado-Verde, M., López-Sáez, P., & Navas-López, J. E. (2011). Towards an intellectual capital-based view of the firm': Origins and nature. *Journal of Business Ethics, 98*(4), 649–662.
Meneghetti, A., & Chinese, D. (2002). Perspectives on facilities management for industrial districts. *Facilities, 20*(10), 337–348.
Mizzau, L., & Montanari, F. (2008). Cultural districts and the challenge of authenticity: The case of Piedmont, Italy. *Journal of Economic Geography, 8*(5), 651–673.
Moon, M. J. (2001). Cultural governance a comparative study of three cultural districts. *Administration & Society, 33*(4), 432–454.
Nalebuff, B., Brandenburger, A., & Maulana, A. (1996). *Co-opetition*. London: Harper Collins Business.
Piore, M., & Sabel, C. (1984). *The second industrial divide: Prospects for prosperity*. New York: Basic.
Ponzini, D. (2009). Urban implications of cultural policy networks: The case of the Mount Vernon cultural district in Baltimore. *Environment and Planning C: Government and Policy, 27*(3), 433–450.
Porter, M. E. (1998). Clusters and the new economics of competition. *Harvard Business Review, 76*(6), 77–90.
Provasi, G. (2002). *Le istituzioni dello sviluppo: i distretti industriali tra storia, sociologia ed economia*. Corigliano Calabro: Meridiana libri.
Rabellotti, R., & Schmitz, H. (1999). The internal heterogeneity of industrial districts in Italy, Brazil and Mexico. *Regional Studies, 33*(2), 97–108.
Richardson, G. (1972). The organization of industry. *Economic Journal, 82*, 883–896.
Riege, A. M. (2003). Validity and reliability tests in case study research: A literature review with "hands-on" applications for each research phase. *Qualitative Market Research: An International Journal, 6*(2), 75–86.
Rindfleisch, A., & Moorman, C. (2001). The acquisition and utilization of information in new product alliances: A strength-of-ties perspective. *Journal of Marketing, 65*(2), 1–18.
Sacco, P. L. (2006). *Il distretto culturale evoluto: competere per l'innovazione, la crescita e l'occupazione, in Nuove Dinamiche di sviluppo territoriale: I distretti culturali evoluti*. Forlì: AICCON.
Sacco, P. L. (2010). Cultura e sviluppo locale: il distertto culturale evoluto. *Sinergie, 82*, 115–119.
Sacco, P. L., & Blessi, G. T. (2006). *Verso un nuovo modello di sviluppo sostenibile: distretti culturali e aree urbane*. Venice: IUAV.
Santagata, W. (2002). Cultural districts, property rights and sustainable economic growth. *International Journal of Urban and Regional Research, 26*(1), 9–23.
Schumpeter, J. (1934). *Capitalism, socialism, and democracy*. New York: Harper & Row.
Sciarelli, S. (2007). *Il management dei sistemi turistici locali: strategie e strumenti per il governance*. Torino: Giappichelli.

Stieglitz, N., & Heine, K. (2007). Innovations and the role of complementarities in a strategic theory of the firm. *Strategic Management Journal, 28*(1), 1–15.

Sydow, J., Lerch, F., Huxham, C., & Hibbert, P. (2011). A silent cry for leadership: Organizing for leading (in) clusters. *The Leadership Quarterly, 22*(2), 328–343.

Testa, G. (2013). Knowledge transfer in vertical relationship: The case study of Val d'Agri oil district. *Journal of Knowledge Management, 17*(4), 617–636.

Usai, A. (2016). *Il distretto culturale evoluto. Beni culturali e pianificazione del territorio nella sfida future*. Florence: Altralinea Edizioni.

Valentino, P. A. (2001). *I distertti culturali. Nuove opportunità di sviluppo del territorio*. Rome: Associazione Civita

Valentino, P. A. (2003). *Le Trame del territorio. Politiche di sviluppo dei sistemi territoriali e distretti culturali*. Milan: Sperling and Kupfer Editori

Van der Duim, R. (2007). Tourismscapes an actor-network perspective. *Annals of Tourism Research, 34*(4), 961–976.

Yin, R. K. (2003). Case study research design and methods. (3rd ed.). *Applied social research methods series, 5*. Thousand Oaks, California: Sage Publications.

You, J. I., & Wilkinson, F. (1994). Competition and co-operation: Toward understanding industrial districts. *Review of Political Economy, 6*(3), 259–227.

Chapter 10
Only Pricing Policy Matters

Discount Is the Only Determinant of Conversion Rate on Apparel e-Commerce Websites

Davide Di Fatta and Ivan Nania

Abstract This paper aims to determine which factors affect e-commerce conversion rate, which is the relationship between website visitors and purchasers.

Focusing on apparel e-commerce websites, this paper uses a fixed effect estimator on a perfectly balanced panel, finding that pricing policy is the only relevant factor and, specifically, that discount has a positive effect on conversion rate.

This finding contributes to advancing the theory of conversion rate management, shedding light on its determinants and providing a better understanding of online consumer behavior. This research is also extremely relevant for practitioners, providing managerial implications for retailers addressing their e-commerce strategy.

Keywords E-commerce • Conversion rate • Pricing policy • Discounts • Fixed effect estimator

10.1 Introduction

Retailing is shifting and more and more towards retail firms focusing on digital distribution and sales channels, analyzing the online market and its customer needs (Kaufmann et al. 2012).

This paper focuses on the online apparel market. The total value of this industry is three trillion dollars, accounting for 2% of the world's gross domestic product (GDP). The online apparel market has grown from 16% to 33% of the overall

D. Di Fatta (✉)
SEAS Department, University of Palermo, Palermo, Italy
e-mail: difatta.davide@gmail.com

I. Nania
University of Messina, Messina, Italy
e-mail: ivan.nania@unime.it

G. Dominici et al. (eds.), *Governing Business Systems*, Springer Proceedings in Business and Economics, DOI 10.1007/978-3-319-66036-3_10

industry value in the last 5 years.[1] The growing importance of apparel market online sales since 2000 has led to academic interest from several authors, who have begun to study the phenomenon (Goldsmith and Goldsmith 2002; Young Kim and Kim 2004; Ha and Stoel 2012; Dominici et al. 2016).

Despite the increasing relevance of the online channel with respect to traditional channels, there is a very significant problem to be considered: 96% of e-commerce website visits do not end with a purchase (McDowell et al. 2016). The ratio of the number of visits ending in a purchase to the total number of website visits is called the conversion rate.

Generally speaking, the conversion rate on e-commerce websites is about 2–4% (Holzwarth et al. 2006; Sohrabi et al. 2012). This low value results from several reasons, such as the high price of products (Wolfinbarger and Gilly 2003; Grewal et al. 2004), price sensitivity—since competitors' websites are just one click away (Clarke 2001; Frost et al. 2010)—the risk of security breaches involving consumer personal information, credit cards or other payment methods (Koufaris and Hampton-Sosa 2004; Chen and Barnes 2007), and trust (McKnight and Cervany 2001; McKnight et al. 2002). In the fashion industry in particular, the conversion rate is often lower than 2% (Di Fatta et al. 2016).

This paper aims to focus on apparel e-commerce websites to determine which factor most affects the conversion rate once users have arrived on the website. This paper is not concerned with how users arrive at the website, focusing instead on purchase behavior on the site.

In this way, the paper contributes, on one hand, to advancing the theory of conversion-rate management and on the other hand to the practical implications, providing concrete guidelines for retailers wishing to decrease their cost-per-conversion by understanding online consumer behavior while browsing an e-commerce website.

The structure of the paper as follows: Sect. 10.2 provides a literature review on conversion rate management; Sect. 10.3 describes the data and methodology of the study; Sect. 10.4 presents the results, and the final section concludes with a discussion, the implications, and proposals for further study.

10.2 Literature Review

The main argument in the conversion-rate management literature is that a low conversion rate implies a high cost for the acquisition of each purchaser (McDowell et al. 2016). Unfortunately there is no magic formula to increase conversion rate, but this study aims to clarify the role of some of its determinants.

[1]Data Source: https://fashionunited.com/

With this in mind, taking conversion rate as a dependent variable, this paper examines the impact of pricing policy (e.g., discounts), logistics (e.g., free shipping and free returns) and webpage loading speed.

10.2.1 Logistics: Free Shipping and Free Returns

In order to satisfy e-commerce users' needs, a structural rethinking of the logistic function is often required to manage the delivery of goods purchased online (Simoni 2011; Ordanini 2011). Given this premise, online retailers have two strategic options (Lewis et al. 2006). In option (1), online retailers pay the full cost of delivery, providing a free shipping service to purchasers. In option (2), the online retailers pass delivery costs onto the purchaser.

Between these two extreme situations, there is a set of mixed strategies (Koukova et al. 2012), such as free shipping when the user reaches a certain order value (e.g., 100 euro) or free shipping for registered users (i.e., for those who have shared their personal information, such as an email address to receive newsletters, or a telephone number). Dominici and Di Fatta (2016), using the Kano Model for quality, argued the free shipping is an "attractive factor" for e-commerce website from the user point of view. From the retailers' point of view, it could be interesting to think about how to manage free shipping options.

This is only the first step of the delivery process. Once buyers have received the product or service, they may not like it (Petersen and Kumar 2015). In such cases, within a time period set by the law, the buyer can exercise their right of withdrawal. Depending on the retailer's return policy, users may find themselves in a difficult situation since, on one hand, they must properly organize the shipment, and on the other hand, they may be responsible for the costs of shipping. Given this, this paper asks the following questions:

RQ1a: Does free shipping affect e-commerce conversion rate?
RQ1b: Does free return affect e-commerce conversion rate?

10.2.2 Pricing Policy

The first study of online discounts in fashion e-commerce websites is that of Udo and Marquis (2002), who found that online customer satisfaction is positively related to promotional sales and discounted prices. Other scholars (Zhang et al. 2015) have also suggested that temporary discounts positively affect online user perception. Di Fatta et al. (2016) highlighted the factors that influence the user-perceived website quality of e-commerce (UPWQ) using a Pareto chart: the most significant factor was discount, the second was free shipping, and the third was ease of use; together, these three factors represent almost 70% of the UPWQ.

We aim to study how online retailers can use discounts as a lever to increase conversion rates. Therefore, we ask:

RQ2: Does pricing policy affect e-commerce conversion rate?

Discounts and promotions are often available at a particular time of year: in other words, this paper also considers the impact of seasonality on purchases. In the fashion sector in the northern hemisphere, as is well known, there are two seasons: the winter season from September to February, and summer season from March to August (Jackson 2007). In the last 2 months of each season, retailers tend to discount their products, in order to avoid large stocks of unsold merchandise, which will prove almost unsellable in the future.

10.2.3 Loading Speed

In the early 2000s, a steam of the literature studied how technical features such as loading speed, site navigability, and programming language affect the online user experience (Kim and Lee 2002; Kim and Stoel 2004). Focusing on e-commerce websites, Di Fatta et al. (2016) concluded that these technical aspects have a very low impact on customer perception: they are considered as a minimum functionality set which must reach a standard level (they are 'must be' requirements).

In practical terms, our research hypothesis is that when increasing the speed of navigation of the website over a particular "critical value", the conversion rate is not affected. However, if the speed falls below this critical value, the purchaser may be annoyed and therefore conversion rate will be negatively affected. We thus ask:

RQ3: Does loading speed affect e-commerce conversion rate?

10.3 Data and Methodology

This paper constructs a balanced data panel of 546 daily observations, covering three different e-commerce firms over 6 months.

The fundamental advantage of a panel of data is that it allows great flexibility in modeling differences in behavior across individuals. This paper uses a fixed-effect estimator, because the aim is to consider the impact of variables that vary over time within the same website, and this approach takes into consideration an individual-specific constant term in the regression model. It should be noted that the term "fixed" indicates that the term does not vary over time, and not that it is nonstochastic, which need not to be the case.

In order to build the research model, the following assumptions are made:

A1. Some time-invariant specific characteristics within an individual website may impact or bias the predictor or outcome variables, and this must be controlled for. The fixed-effect estimator removes these time-invariant characteristics, making it possible to determine the net effect of predictors on the outcome variable.
A2. The time-invariant characteristics of each website are uniqueness, and should not be correlated with other individual characteristics. Each website is different, and so each website's error term and this constant cannot be correlated with the others.

10.4 Empirical Analysis

In order to answer the research questions, this study implements a fixed effect estimator using the conversion rate as dependent variable and a set of independent variables:

$$\begin{aligned} Conversion_{it} = \alpha_{it} + \beta_1 speed_{it} + \beta_2 freeshipping_{it} + \beta_3 freereturns_{it} \\ + \beta_4 discount_{it} + \beta_5 day + \beta_6 month + \varepsilon_{it} \end{aligned}$$

Conversion is the ratio between the number of visits and the number of transactions registered by the *i*th website at time *t*; *speed* is the loading speed of images on the *i*th website at time *t*; *freeshipping* is a dummy variable that takes the value of 1 if the *i*th website offered free shipping at time *t*, and 0 otherwise; *freereturns* is a dummy variable that takes the value of 1 if the *i*th website offered free returns at time *t*, and 0 otherwise; *discount* is the discount rate of the *i*th website at time *t*; *day* and *month* are dummy variables for the days of the week and the months in the sample; these have been included in the model to check for seasonality and consumer time preferences for on-line shopping.

Table 10.1 summarizes the statistics of the variables included in the model for the entire sample.

Table 10.2 shows the correlation matrix between the variables in our model; as might be expected, the conversion rate is positively correlated with all the explanatory variables. In line with what we expected, the discount variable shows greater correlation with the dependent variable, while the correlation between the set of independent variables is quite low.

Table 10.1 Statistical summary

Variable	Obs	Mean	Std. Dev.	Min	Max
Conversion	546	7.021	0.844	4.4	10.562
Speed	546	63.3	0.979	60	66
Freeshipping	546	0.593	0.492	0	1
Freereturns	546	0.046	0.209	0	1
Discounts	546	0.114	0.175	0	0.7

Table 10.2 Correlation matrix

	Conver	Speed	Freesh	Freer	Discou
Conversion	1				
Speed	0.1879	1			
Freeshipping	0.1482	−0.2146	1		
Freereturns	0.0948	−0.0493	0.1813	1	
Discounts	0.6417	0.0684	0.5001	0.2582	1

Table 10.3 Estimations

	Coef.	Coef.
Speed	−0.067	−0.062
	[0.028]	[.035]
Freeshipping	0.162	0.173
	[0.187]	[.184]
Freereturns	−0.025	−0.026
	[0.203]	[.193]
Discounts	3.157**	3.197**
	[0.629]	[.671]
Day		0.004
		[.008]
Month		0.019
		[0.021]
R_sqrd	0.529	0.531
Wald	62.18	41.74
F	0.015	0.023

Standard errors in parentheses
*, **, *** indicate 1%, 5%, and 10% significance levels, respectively

Table 10.3 shows the results of the empirical analysis. Some surprising results emerged, which a weaker analysis would not capture. The signs of *Speed* and *Freereturns* are negative, contrary to expectations: loading speed and free returns are controversial variables (Dominici and Di Fatta 2016), as previous studies have argued they are respectively "must be" and "indifferent" requirements for website quality.[2] *Freeshipping* is, as expected, positive, but it is not statistically significant.

Only the *Discount* variable has the sign we expect and is statistically significant. Our results allow us to argue that only the discount rate that each website decides to apply each day is able to affect the conversion rate. Shifting the paradigm on

[2]In the Kano Model for quality (1984), indifferent requirements (such as free returns) imply that this feature does not affect customer satisfaction. On the other hand, must-be requirements (such as webpage loading speed) do not increase customer satisfaction by their presence, but their absence produces a negative effect on user perceptions.

the customer point of view, Di Fatta et al. (2016) argued that discount is the most important factor in User-Perceived Web Quality, representing 26% of the total e-commerce UPWQ.

There are two possible reasons for this: on one hand, we could affirm that only investing in greater discounts has a positive, significant impact on the conversion rate; on the other hand, we could affirm that once a website reaches a certain level of (say) loading speed, increasing this variable further does not affect the conversion rate. This finding is consistent with previous research showing that, the slower the webpage loads, the more significant were the observed user frustrations. Indeed, there are enormous differences occurring in loading time between 1–29 s and 31–59 s: in the latter case, most users quit the loading process before the page completely loaded.

The *Day* and *Month* variables were added to the model in the second equation in order to check for any effect of time on the conversion rate of the website. As shown in Table 10.3, neither of these variables is statistically significant and neither affects the value of the coefficients or the standard errors of the first equation.

It is thus possible to conclude that the days of the week (for example, weekdays versus weekend) do not play any role in the conversion rate. The same is true for the months of the year. Our model thus does not support any time effect.

10.5 Discussion and Conclusion

The research questions in the previous section rely on three different aspects of the e-commerce conversion rate: logistics (RQ1), pricing policy (RQ2), and webpage loading speed (RQ3). Of these three, the findings on RQ2 showed the greatest relevance, with the effect of discounts on the e-commerce conversion rate being both positive and statistically significant.

This finding does not mean that other variables have no influence at all on the conversion rate (Di Fatta and Musotto 2017); rather, the correct interpretation is that discount has a greater weight than with other variables in determining conversion rate.

10.5.1 Theoretical and Practical Implications

This reflection constitutes a step forward in the conversion-rate management field by highlighting the key role of pricing policy in e-commerce marketing strategies with direct impact on sales. Since the conversion rate is the number of purchases divided by the number of website visitors, increasing this ratio means increasing sales, given that the number of website visitors, an exogenous variable in our model, remains constant.

This theoretical argument is likely to be interpreted in terms of practical implications for managers and professionals in the apparel industry. Moreover, there is also an important managerial implication for decision makers of e-commerce websites: they should point to appropriate pricing policy management in order to increase conversion rate directly, and sales as a consequence.

10.5.2 Limitations and Further Studies

This research has not considered the impact of pricing policy and discount on the profitability of the firm. This limitation could became an interesting research opportunity for further study that aim to determine the break-even point between increasing sales (driven by discounts) and decreasing net profits.

Another very interesting topic for further study is the determinants of web visits. It may be worthwhile to split the sales process into two parts—the first involving attracting web-users to the e-commerce site, and the second involving the behavior of users once they have entered the site. This second part constitutes the main focus of the present research, but other scholars could deepen the first aspect and attempt to build a holistic framework.

Bibliography

Aladwani, A. M., & Palvia, P. C. (2002). Developing and validating an instrument for measuring userperceived web quality. *Information Management, 39*(2), 467–476.

Barrutia, J. M., & Gilsanz, A. (2009). E-service quality: Overview and research agenda. *International Journal of Quality and Service Sciences, 1*(1), 29–50.

Bendel, R. B., & Afifi, A. A. (1977). Comparison of stopping rules in forward "stepwise" regression. *Journal of the American Statistical Association, 72*(357), 46–53.

Bower, A. B., & Maxham, J. G., III. (2012). Return shipping policies of online retailers: Normative assumptions and the long-term consequences of fee and free returns. *Journal of Marketing, 76*(5), 110–124.

Brown, M., Pope, N., & Voges, K. (2003). Buying or browsing? An exploration of shopping orientations and online purchase intention. *European Journal of Marketing, 37*(11), 1666–1684.

Chen, Y. H., & Barnes, S. (2007). Initial trust and online buyer behaviour. *Industrial Management & Data Systems, 107*(1), 21–36.

Clarke, K. (2001). What price on loyalty when a brand switch is just a click away? *Qualitative Market Research: An International Journal, 4*(3), 160–168.

Di Fatta, D., Musotto, R., & Vesperi, W. (2016). Analyzing e-commerce websites: A quali-quantitative approach for the user perceived web quality (UPWQ). *International Journal of Marketing Studies, 8*(6), 33–44.

Di Fatta, D., & Musotto, R. (2017). Content and sentiment analysis on Online Social Networks (OSNs). In *Data analytics in digital humanities* (pp. 121–133). Cham: Springer International Publishing.

Dominici, G., & Di Fatta, D. (2016). Quali sono le determinanti della web-quality di un e-commerce? Applicazione del modello di Kano al caso Scalia Group. Proceeding of XXVIII Sinergie Annual Conference. Udine, Italy.

Dominici, G., Matić, M., Abbate, T., & Fatta, D. D. (2016). Consumer attitude toward using smart shopping carts: A comparative analysis of Italian and Croatian consumer attitudes. *International Journal of Electronic Marketing and Retailing, 7*(3), 229–244.

E-commerce in Italy. (2016). Aprile 13 Analisi dello studio "Casaleggio Associati" sullo stato dell'e-commerce in Italia. 13 April, Milan, Italy.

EMarketer. (2014). Retail sales worldwidewill top $22 trillion this year. Retrieved from: http://www.emarketer.com/Article/Retail-Sales-Worldwide-Will-Top-22-Trillion-This-year/1011765/. 23 December.

Frost, D., Goode, S., & Hart, D. (2010). Individualist and collectivist factors affecting online repurchase intentions. *Internet Research, 20*(1), 6–28.

Goldsmith, R. E., & Goldsmith, E. B. (2002). Buying apparel over the internet. *Journal of Product & Brand Management, 11*(2), 89–102.

Grewal, D., Gopalkrishnan, R. I., & Levy, M. (2004). Internet retailing: Enablers, limiters and marketing consequences. *Journal of Business Research, 57*(7), 703–713.

Ha, S., & Stoel, L. (2012). Online apparel retailing: Roles of e-shopping quality and experiential e-shopping motives. *Journal of Service Management, 23*(2), 197–215.

Holzwarth, M., Janiszewski, C., & Neumann, M. M. (2006). The influence of avatars on online consumer shopping behavior. *Journal of Marketing, 70*(4), 19–36.

Jackson, T. (2007). Chapter 9. The process of trend development leading to a fashion season. In *Fashion marketing: Contemporary issues* (pp. 168–187). Oxford, UK: Butterworth-Heinemann, imprint of Elsevier.

Jennrich, R. I., & Sampson, P. F. (1968). Application of stepwise regression to non-linear estimation. *Technometrics, 10*(1), 63–72.

Kaufmann, H. R., Loureiro, S. M. C., Basile, G., & Vrontis, G. (2012). The increasing dynamics between consumers, social groups and brands. *Qualitative Market Research: An International Journal, 15*(4), 404–419.

Kim, J., & Lee, J. (2002). Critical design factors for successful e-commerce systems. *Behaviour and Information Technology, 21*(3), 185–189.

Kim, M., & Stoel, L. (2004). Apparel retailers: Web site quality dimensions and satisfaction. *Journal of Retailing and Consumer Services, 11*(1), 109–117.

Koufaris, M., & Hampton-Sosa, W. (2004). The development of initial trust in an online company by new customers. *Information Management, 41*(3), 377–397.

Koukova, N. T., Srivastava, J., & Steul-Fischer, M. (2012). The effect of shipping fee structure on consumers' online evaluations and choice. *Journal of the Academy of Marketing Science, 40*(6), 759–770.

Laudon, K. C., & Traver, C. G. (2007). *E-commerce*. Boston: Pearson/Addison Wesley.

Le, T. (2015). Service quality in luxury e-commerce: Case Study in China. AaltoSchool of business, Thesis number: 14697. https://aaltodoc.aalto.fi/handle/123456789/21519

Lewis, M., Singh, V., & Fay, S. (2006). An empirical study of the impact of nonlinear shipping and handling fees on purchase incidence and expenditure decisions. *Marketing Science, 25*(1), 51–64.

Ling, K. C., Chai, L. T., & Piew, T. H. (2010). The effects of shopping orientations, online trust and prior online purchase experience toward customers' online purchase intention. *International Business Research, 3*(3), 63.

Longest, K. C., & Vaisey, S. (2008). Fuzzy: A program for performing qualitative comparative analyses (QCA) in Stata. *Stata Journal, 8*(1), 79.

McDowell, W. C., Wilson, R. C., & Kile, C. O. (2016). An examination of retail website design and conversion rate. *Journal of Business Research, 69*(11), 4837–4842.

McKnight, D. H., & Cervany, N. L. (2001). What trust means in e-commerce customer relationships: An interdisciplinary conceptual typology. *International Journal of Electronic Commerce, 6*(2), 35–59.

McKnight, D. H., Choudhury, V., & Kacmar, C. (2002). Developing and validating trust measures for e-commerce: An integrative typology. *Information Systems Research, 13*(3), 334–359.

Olšina, L., Godoy, D., Lafuente, G., & Rossi, G. (1999). Assessing the quality of academic websites: A case study. *New Review of Hypermedia and Multimedia, 5*(1), 81–103.
Ordanini, A. (2011). I servizi logistici nei digital marketplace e l'impatto sulle risorse strategiche d'impresa. *Sinergie Italian Journal of Management, 57*(2), 131–149.
Ostapenko, N. (2013). Online discount luxury: In search of guilty customers. *International Journal of Business and Social Research, 3*(2), 60–68.
Parasuraman, A., Zeithaml, V. A., & Malhotra, A. (2005). E-S-QUAL.: A multiple-item scale for assessing electronic service quality. *Journal of Service Research, 7*(3), 213–234.
Petersen, J. A., & Kumar, V. (2015). Perceived risk, product returns, and optimal resource allocation: Evidence from a field experiment. *Journal of Marketing Research, 52*(2), 268–285.
Schlosser, A. E., Barnett, T., & Lloyd, S. M. (2006). Converting web site visitors into buyers: How web site investment increases consumer trusting beliefs and online purchase intentions. *Journal of Marketing, 70*(2), 133–148.
Simoni, C. (2011). L'impatto del commercio elettronico business-to-consumer sulla logistica distributiva, con particolare riferimento alla logistica dell'ultimo miglio. *Sinergie Italian Journal of Management, 57*(2), 151–175.
Sohrabi, B., Mahmoudian, P., & Raessi, I. (2012). A framework for improving e-commerce websites' usability using a hybrid genetic algorithm and neural network system. *Neural Computing and Applications, 21*(5), 1017–1029.
Udo, G. J., & Marquis, G. P. (2002). Factors affecting e-commerce web site effectiveness. *The Journal of Computer Information Systems, 42*(2), 10–16.
Van der Heijden, H., Verhagen, T., & Creemers, M. (2003). Understanding online purchase intentions: Contributions from technology and trust perspectives. *European Journal of Information Systems, 12*(1), 41–48.
Wolfinbarger, M., & Gilly, M. C. (2003). eTailQ: Dimensionalizing, measuring and predicting etail quality. *Journal of Retailing, 79*(3), 183–198.
Woodside, A. G. (2014). Embrace perform model: Complexity theory, contrarian case analysis, and multiple realities. *Journal of Business Research, 67*(12), 2495–2503.
Young Kim, E., & Kim, Y. K. (2004). Predicting online purchase intentions for clothing products. *European Journal of Marketing, 38*(7), 883–897.
Zhang, X., Li Y., & Sun, P. (2015), Inventory optimization research on shampoo products of B2C e-commerce with temporary price discount, In *Logistics, Informatics and Service Sciences (LISS), 2015 International Conference on*, Barcelona, Spain, (pp. 1–6), IEEE.

Printed in the United States
By Bookmasters